MONEY MAP COACH

TRAINING COURSE TEXTBOOK

LARRY BURKETT

CROWN FINANCIAL MINISTRIES
True Financial Freedom

CROWN.ORG

ACKNOWLEDGMENTS

To Larry Burkett (1939-2003) for creating this material and putting it into practice during many years of coaching.

We want to express our deepest appreciation to the thousands of Crown coaches and coaching participants who have provided many of these insights into successful coaching techniques and also to Moody Press, publisher of *How to Manage Your Money, The Family Financial Workbook, Using Your Money Wisely,* and *The WORD on Finances.*

Special thanks to Steve Humphrey and Kathryn Gillespie for compiling this material, and Adeline Griffith for editing this course.

ISBN 1-56427-105-6

TABLE OF CONTENTS

WEEKLY ASSIGNMENTS

Week 1   Read and complete introduction and Chapters 1 and 2 from the *Family Financial Workbook*. Complete **God's Ownership/Our Stewardship** from *Money Map Coach Training Course*.

Week 2   Complete Chapter 3 from the *Family Financial Workbook*. Complete **Giving** from *Money Map Coach Training Course*.

Week 3   Complete Chapters 4 and 5 from the *Family Financial Workbook*. Complete **Debt** from *Money Map Coach Training Course*.

Week 4   Complete Chapter 6 from the *Family Financial Workbook*. Complete **Saving/Other Principles** from *Money Map Coach Training Course*.

Week 5   Complete Chapters 7, 8, 9, and 10 from the *Family Financial Workbook*. Complete **Family** from *Money Map Coach Training Course*.

Week 6   Complete the *Personality I.D.*® Complete *You Are Uniquely Made* on pages 93 to 96 on **Work** from *Money Map Coach Training Course*.

Week 7   Complete *Approach and Analyze* sections on **Peace and Contentment** from *Money Map Coach Training Course*.

Week 8   Review *SnapShot Gold.*® Review and complete Suggested Percentage Guidelines and Case Studies 1 and 2 from *Money Map Coach Training Course*.

Week 9   Complete Case Studies 3, 4, and 5 from *Money Map Coach Training Course*.

Week 10 Complete Case Studies 6, 7, 8, and 9 from *Money Map Coach Training Course*.

Week 11 Complete Case Studies 10, 11, and 12 and answer Review Questions on page 247 from *Money Map Coach Training Course*.

Week 12 Review *Journey to Financial Freedom* manual and CD and Appendix and Resources from *Money Map Coach Training Course*.

WELCOME AND INTRODUCTION

We are *very* grateful for your willingness to become a Crown Money Map Coach. It requires time and effort to serve others, but it is so rewarding to be involved with people as they take the road to true financial freedom.

This self-study course is designed to be completed in 12 weeks. It requires the average person about two hours to complete each weekly assignment. The most effective way to complete the course is to schedule and commit to a regular time of study. You may complete more than one lesson a week if you choose.

Please complete the lessons in order. When you finish a lesson, compare your answers to Crown's answers located at the end of each lesson. If you've answered a question incorrectly, review that portion of the lesson until you thoroughly understand it. Because your coaching participants will rely on your budgeting knowledge, invest sufficient time to learn the material well.

Another option for completing this course is to do it as a participant in a small group of other coaching students. The interaction, accountability, and fellowship of a small group can greatly enhance your study time. If you are interested in this format, you can gather a small group of students from your church or community, find a qualified facilitator, and use the facilitator's guide and syllabus in the Appendix in the back of this textbook.

After finishing the course, meet with your pastor to express your availability to serve others in the church as a Money Map Coach. Mail or fax Crown the Statement of Completion on page 328.

The objectives of the Money Map Coach training are

1. To teach coaches basic biblical financial principles and how to apply them practically.

2. To teach Crown's budget and start the coaching participants on the road to true financial freedom using the Money Map.

3. To teach proven methods of coaching.

4. To familiarize coaches with common financial terms, consumer laws, and techniques of Money Map coaching.

5. To provide an opportunity for those who successfully complete this course to join Crown's Money Map Referral Coach network and encourage their churches to become Crown Partner Churches.

Crown receives many requests for help in budgeting and managing debt. Crown refers these individuals to a network of Money Map Referral Coaches from around the nation. We would be very thankful if you would consider serving in this capacity.

It is important to understand that this training is designed to assist individuals who desire to serve as volunteers in the ministry of Money Map coaching. It is *not* intended for those who seek a professional career in debt or financial counseling.

The training kit you received contains

1. Several copies of *Crown Financial Ministries Money Map.*™
2. The *Money Map Coach Training Course* textbook, which contains God's financial principles, a description of the coaching process, and Case Studies.
3. The *Family Financial Workbook*, which will teach you how to use the Crown budget.
4. The *Journey to Financial Freedom* manual that every coaching participant will use.
5. The *Personality I.D.* booklet, which will help you understand your personality and how to relate to coaching participants most effectively.
6. A CD containing a debt repayment calculator, the book *Using Your Money Wisely*, and over 2,000 Bible verses dealing with money and possessions.

The *Crown Money Map*

We strongly encourage you to use the Crown Money Map in the first coaching session with each coaching participant and to give each participating person/couple a copy of the Money Map. Many people have no idea that there are financial goals beyond simply paying each month's bills. As you show them the destinations on the Money Map, you can give them hope and a vision for achieving long-term goals after their immediate financial dilemma is resolved.

The *Money Map Coach Training Course* textbook

This textbook contains 12 weekly lessons to equip you to become a Money Map Coach. The first six lessons concentrate on God's financial principles and start you on the Crown budget. The last six lessons focus on principles of Money Map coaching and practically applying these principles by completing a series of Case Studies.

Even if you have successfully completed the Crown small group study, we encourage you to complete the portion of this training that addresses God's financial principles in lessons 1-7. Approach these lessons from the viewpoint of a coach who needs to teach them to others.

Toward the end of the textbook is an Appendix that contains a glossary of commonly used financial terms, helpful resources, and the facilitator's guide and syllabus for completing this course as part of a small group training program.

Family Financial Workbook

Money Map Coach training begins with you, the coach, understanding how to live on a budget. There are many types of budgets. You will learn the method that has been used by Crown's coaches for more than 27 years.

For training purposes, we ask that you learn the budget in the *Family Financial Workbook.* If you already use a budget, we want you to use the Crown budget for at least three months, so you can experience what you will teach your coaching participants.

In Luke 6:40 we read, *"Everyone, after he has been fully trained will be like his teacher."* Another way of saying this is that we reproduce who we are. Because you can effectively teach only what you are doing, much of the training focuses on your personal application of the principles and your actually using the budget.

In Money Map coaching you will need to be flexible to adjust to the needs of the coaching participant. Crown provides a number of budget options. The budget in the *Family Financial Workbook* is best for the participants who have the necessary skills to develop a budget but need to be trained. The spreadsheet budget used in Crown's small group study is an option for the less skilled.

All coaching participants should use the *Journey to Financial Freedom* manual, which is provided in these materials. This will help teach them God's basic financial principles and guide them through the budgeting process.

Crown's Church Program

Crown Financial Ministries has developed a comprehensive program to teach people of all ages God's way of handling money. There are studies for children 7 and younger, ages 8 to 12, teenagers, college students, and adults.

There are four teaching methods in the adult portion of the program:

- Money Map Coach training.
- A remarkably effective small group study.
- An outstanding financial seminar, "The Journey to True Financial Freedom."
- The *Discovering God's Way of Handling Money Video Series.*

Crown's program is used in thousands of churches. Please contact Crown for more details on how to implement the program in your church.

Again, we appreciate your desire to be a Money Map Coach. We pray that the Lord will bless your efforts as you serve others in this much-needed area of ministry.

GOD OWNS EVERYTHING AND WE ARE STEWARDS

Principle to Memorize

God owns everything and we are stewards and managers of His possessions.

Scripture to Memorize

"Everything in the heavens and earth is yours, O Lord"
(1 Chronicles 29:11, TLB).

ASSIGNMENT: *Family Financial Workbook*

Whether you have been on a budget for years or have just begun, you will need to pay close attention to the steps and suggestions in the *Family Financial Workbook* and in the notes in Section One. Complete this section as if you were establishing a budget with a coaching participant. The goals are for you to begin a budget and to learn how to teach others the Crown budget. You also will complete a personal financial statement. You will use this form and others in your Money Map coaching sessions.

Remember a budget is an *Income Spending Plan* that is designed to help a person spend wisely.

Introduction

Read the Introduction in the *Family Financial Workbook*. You will face many of these questions and myths as you coach. To be able to respond to your coaching participants, it is important for you to know the answers to these questions.

Chapter One *If You Read Nothing Else . . . Read This!*

Review the quick reference of key points. This is a valuable checklist to use as you work with coaching participants. However, you will not use each point with every participant.

Chapter Two *Fail to Plan, Plan to Fail*

This chapter describes the need for a spending plan. This is foundational for coaching participants to understand. If they don't know why they should budget, then they are less likely to do it.

The *Family Financial Workbook* addresses the family. If you are working with a single person, substitute the word "personal" for "family" where appropriate. There are some questions relating to spiritual leadership that should be adjusted for the single person. If the participant is planning marriage, this is a good time to begin thinking about personal financial standards and convictions.

QUESTIONS TO ANSWER

1. **Read** *Isaiah 55:8-9.*

   Based on this passage, do you think God's financial principles will differ from how most people handle money?

   What do you think would be the greatest difference?

2. **Read** *Deuteronomy 10:14* **and** *Psalm 24:1.*

   What do these passages teach about the ownership of your possessions?

3. **Read** *Leviticus 25:23* **and** *Haggai 2:8.*

   What are some of the specific items that the Lord owns?

   Leviticus 25:23—

   Haggai 2:8—

   Prayerfully evaluate your attitude of ownership toward your possessions. Do you consistently recognize the true owner of those possessions? Write two practical ideas that will help you recognize God's ownership.

4. **Read** *1 Chronicles 29:11-12* **and** *Psalm 135:6.*

   What do these verses say about the Lord's control of circumstances?

5. **Read *Proverbs 21:1* and *Isaiah 40:21-24*.**

   What do these passages tell you about the Lord's control of people?

   Proverbs 21:1—

   Isaiah 40:21-24—

   Do you normally recognize the Lord's control of all events? If not, how can you become more consistent in recognizing His control?

6. **Read *Genesis 45:4-8* and *Romans 8:28*.**

   Why is it important to realize that God controls and uses even difficult circumstances for good in the life of a godly person?

   How does this perspective impact you today?

7. **Read *Psalm 34:9-10; Matthew 6:31-33*; and *Philippians 4:19*.**

   What has the Lord promised concerning meeting your needs.

   From the Bible, give an example of the Lord providing for someone's needs in a super-natural way.

8. **Read *Genesis 39:2-5; Exodus 36:1-2; and Psalm 75:6-7*.**

   What do each of these verses tell us about the Lord's involvement in our work?

   Genesis 39:2-5—

Exodus 36:1-2—

Psalm 75:6-7—

9. **Read *1 Corinthians 4:2*.**
   According to this verse, what is your requirement as a steward?

   How would you define a steward?

   Read *Luke 16:1-2*.
   Why did the master remove the steward from his position?

   Do you think this principle is applicable today? How?

   Read *Luke 16:10*.
   Describe the principle found in this verse.

   How does this apply in your situation?

   Read *Luke 16:12*.
   Are we required to be faithful with other people's possessions? What happens if we are not?

NOTES TO READ

It may surprise you to learn just how much the Bible says about finances. There are more than 2,350 verses on how to handle money and possessions. In fact, Jesus Christ said more about money than almost any other subject.

The Lord talked as much as He did about money because He knew that money would be a struggle for many of us. Because He loves us, God gave us His road map for handling money. Some of the topics the Bible covers are how to earn, spend, save, get out of debt, give, invest, budget, and train children to manage money.

The most important point to understand is the part God plays·in our finances.

THE LORD OWNS ALL OUR POSSESSIONS

"Behold, to the Lord your God belong . . . the earth and all that is in it" (Deuteronomy 10:14). *"The earth is the Lord's, and all it contains"* (Psalm 24:1). Scripture even reveals specific items God owns. Leviticus 25:23 identifies Him as the owner of all the land: *"The land, moreover, shall not be sold permanently, for the land is Mine."* Haggai 2:8 says that He owns the precious metals: *" 'The silver is Mine and the gold is Mine,' declares the Lord of hosts."*

The Bible reveals that the Lord is the Creator of all things, *"In the beginning God created the heavens and the earth"* (Genesis 1:1). And He has never transferred the ownership of His creation to people. When we acknowledge God's ownership, every spending decision becomes a spiritual decision. No longer do we ask, "Lord, what do You want me to do with *my* money?" The question is restated, "Lord, what do You want me to do with *Your* money?"

Consistently recognizing God's ownership is difficult. It is easy to believe intellectually that God owns all you have but still live as if this were not true.

THE LORD IS IN CONTROL

Besides being Creator and Owner, God is ultimately in control of every event that occurs on the earth. *"We adore you as being in control of every-*

thing" (1 Chronicles 29:11, TLB). *"Whatever the Lord pleases, He does, in heaven and in earth"* (Psalm 135:6).

It is important for the child of God to realize that His heavenly Father uses even seemingly devastating circumstances for ultimate good in the lives of the godly. *"We know that God causes all things to work together for good to those who love God, to those who are called according to His purpose"* (Romans 8:28).

THE LORD PROVIDES

The Lord promises to provide our needs. *"Seek first His kingdom and His righteousness, and all these things* [food and clothing] *will be added to you"* (Matthew 6:33). The same Lord who fed 5,000 with only five loaves and two fish has promised to provide our needs.

God is both predictable and unpredictable. He is absolutely predictable in His faithfulness to provide for our needs. What we cannot predict is *how* the Lord will provide. He uses various and often surprising means of meeting our needs—an increase in income or a gift. He may provide an opportunity to stretch our limited resources through money-saving purchases. Regardless of how He chooses to provide for our needs, He is completely reliable.

WE ARE STEWARDS

We are stewards or managers of the possessions the Lord has entrusted to us. And our only responsibility is to be faithful. *"It is required in stewards, that a man be found faithful"* (1 Corinthians 4:2, KJV). Before we can be faithful, we must know what we are required to do. Just as the purchaser of a complicated piece of machinery studies the manufacturer's manual to learn how to operate it, we need to examine the Creator's handbook—the Bible—to determine how He wants us to handle His possessions.

Two elements of our responsibility to be faithful are important to understand.

1. To be faithful with what we are given

The Lord requires us to be faithful regardless of how much He has entrusted to us. The parable of the talents illustrates this. *"It is just like a man about to go on a journey, who called his own slaves and entrusted his possessions to them. To one he gave five talents, to another, two, and to another, one, each according to his own ability"* (Matthew 25:14-15).

The Lord requires us to be faithful regardless of how much He has entrusted to us.

When the master returned, he held each slave accountable for faithfully managing his possessions. Read the master's commendation of the faithful slave who received the five talents: *"Well done, good and faithful slave. You were faithful with a few things, I will put in you in charge of many things; enter into the joy of your master"* (Matthew 25:21). Interestingly, the slave who had been given two talents received the identical reward as the slave who had been given the five talents (see Matthew 25:23). The Lord rewards faithfulness, regardless of the amount over which we are responsible.

We are required to be faithful whether we are given much or little. As someone once said, "It's not what I would do if $1 million were my lot; it's what I am doing with the $10 I've got."

2. To be faithful in every area

God requires us to be faithful in handling 100 percent of our money, not just 10 percent. Most Christians have been taught only how to handle 10 percent of their income—the area of giving. And although this area is crucial, by default we have allowed the body of Christ to learn how to handle the other 90 percent from the world's perspective, not from our Lord's perspective.

Ignorance of scriptural financial principles frequently causes money problems. Many Christians have wrong attitudes toward possessions, and this causes them to make incorrect financial decisions and suffer painful consequences. *"My people are destroyed for lack of knowledge"* (Hosea 4:6).

PRINCIPLES OF FAITHFULNESS

1. Faithfulness in little things

"He who is faithful in a very little thing is faithful also in much; and he who is unrighteous in a very little thing is unrighteous also in much" (Luke 16:10).

How do you know if your son is going to take good care of his first car? Observe how he cared for his bicycle. How do you know if a salesperson will do a competent job of serving a large client? Evaluate how he or she serves a small client. If we have the character to be faithful with small things, the Lord knows He can trust us with greater responsibilities. Small things are small things, but faithfulness with a small thing is a big thing.

2. Faithfulness with another's possessions

Faithfulness with another's possession will, in some measure, determine how much you are given. *"If you have not been faithful in the use of that which is another's, who will give you that which is your own?"* (Luke 16:12).

This is a principle that is often overlooked. Are you faithful with others' possessions? Are you careless with your employer's office supplies? When someone allows you to use something, are you careful to return it in good shape? Some people have not been entrusted with more because they have been unfaithful with the possessions of others.

COMPROMISE

Compared to some sins, compromises often do not seem so bad. If God was merely an accountant, weighing good against bad and one person against another, there would be no problem. However, God does not deal in comparisons, and each individual is responsible for his or her actions, regardless of what others do. Compromises of God's Word are external symptoms of internal spiritual problems.

As you work with some of your coaching participants, you will discover that of all the ways people compromise God's Word *money* is perhaps the most common. It may be the tendency to cheat on income taxes or to take bankruptcy in the face of uncomfortable debts. It may be a white lie to sell a product or to pad an expense account.

It is clear from God's Word that those who accept Christ as their Lord are to live by different standards than the rest of the world. We are to be lights in a dark world to lead others to God. What we say is not enough. God requires that we "show and tell." *"Prove yourselves to be blameless and innocent, children of God above reproach in the midst of a crooked and perverse generation, among whom you appear as lights in the world"* (Philippians 2:15).

Airlines practice what is called "preconditioned response." They have found that it is not wise to wait until inflight emergencies occur to acqaint pilots with emergency procedures. Therefore, they work to precondition their responses. The techniques for responding to every kind of emergency are practiced again and again.

Unfortunately, many Christians believe they can handle any temptation without the proper training of learning and applying God's Word. We should make decisions on the preconditioned response that God's way is not just the best way, it is the *only* way.

We are to be lights in a dark world to lead others to God.

The consequences of making decisions God's way might be less income or the loss of a job. However, the consequences of compromising God's way are lack of peace (James 4:4), less commitment to the Lord (James 4:17), a critical spirit (James 3:16), and less usefulness to God (Titus 1:16).

Encourage your coaching participants never to compromise the truths of Scripture.

DETERMINING GOD'S WILL

Have you ever witnessed someone who was doing something unwise but rationalizing it by saying, "God told me to do it."? For most of us, that's hard to debate, because you feel as if you're questioning God. Later, when disaster strikes, most wish that they had had the courage to speak up.

We should speak up when we see coaching participants doing something contrary to God's Word. Often, when confronted by a loving challenge, they will change direction. However, some simply refuse to believe they could be wrong and cloak themselves in spirituality by saying "God told me to do this."

Success does not necessarily constitute God's endorsement of our actions.

Open door philosophy

Others make decisions based solely on the open door philosophy. In other words, God would never let me do something wrong, and if the door is open I should go through it. This could be called the open-mine-shaft philosophy, because a lot of people stumble down open shafts, thinking God won't let them fall. Any course of action should conform to God's Word.

Confirmed by success

Success does not necessarily constitute God's endorsement of our actions. Every action must meet two criteria. First, it must be in accordance with God's written Word. Some decisions are objective enough to be eliminated, because they clearly contradict God's Word.

The second criterion that must be met is personal conviction. Paul wrote, *"The faith which you have, have as your own conviction before God. Happy is he who does not condemn himself in what he approves"* (Romans 14:22). The Christian life is not just a set of rules that must be obeyed. We are held to an even higher standard that requires us to be sensitive to the Holy Spirit's direction. It means that we are accountable if we do something we feel is wrong. How do we know? We know by a lack of inner peace and contentment.

Even with the best intention, coaching participants will do things that are out of God's will. Paul said that *"Now we see in a mirror dimly"* (1 Corinthians 13:12) and, therefore, our spiritual vision will be imperfect. Our attitude should be to thank God for showing us when we are headed in the wrong direction and then begin the task of discovering His direction for us. Only by regularly reading God's Word and seeking godly counsel can we avoid these traps.

If you find yourself outside of God's will and are experiencing a lack of peace, you must be willing to abandon everything and seek God's path again. *"I do not regard myself as having laid hold of it yet; but one thing I do: forgetting what lies behind and reaching forward to what lies ahead, I press on toward the goal for the prize of the upward call of God in Christ Jesus"* (Philippians 3:13-14).

THE JOURNEY TO PEACE AND CONTENTMENT

Part of the purpose of this training is to help you and your coaching participants learn to be content and to experience God's peace. Contentment is mentioned seven times in the Bible, and six of those refer to money. In Philippians 4:11-13 the apostle Paul wrote, *"I have learned to be content whatever the circumstances. I know what it is to be in need, and I know what it is to have plenty. I have learned the secret of being content in any and every situation. . . . I can do all things through him who gives me strength"* (NIV).

Examine these verses carefully. We are not born with the instinct for contentment; rather, it is learned. This Money Map Coach training is designed as a process for you and your coaching participants to learn how to be content.

APPLYING THE PRINCIPLES TO MONEY MAP COACHING

Communicate these principles to your coaching participants.

1. God loves you and wants what is best for you.

2. God is the owner of all that you have.

3. The Lord wants you to manage the possessions He entrusts to you His way.

4. The Bible says a lot about money. It contains the road map for how we should handle finances.

We are not born with the instinct for contentment; rather, it is learned.

5. We must be willing to allow God to be Lord of our financial matters.

6. We must be willing to change if we are not handling our resources God's way.

7. To be a good steward, you should use a budget to manage your spending well.

8 It is important to commit never to compromise the truths of God's Word.

HOW WOULD YOU RESPOND TO A COACHING PARTICIPANT?

The following questions and views are commonly expressed during coaching sessions. Describe how you would respond to each.

1. I worry about being able to pay my bills and provide for my family.

2. I'm having a tough time financially and feel the Lord just doesn't seem to care.

3. My parents didn't have much, but they never went without a meal. I don't understand how I get so behind in my bills.

4. I have ignored God's principles for so long that I believe He can never use me to glorify Himself.

Please review this section until you are thoroughly familiar with the practical and spiritual applications that you will use in coaching sessions.

ANSWERS TO THE QUESTIONS

1. **Read *Isaiah 55:8-9*.**

   Based on this passage, do you think God's financial principles will differ from how most people handle money?

   [Yes, the Lord's principles of money are contrary to the practices of our culture.]

   What do you think would be the greatest difference?

   [Most people leave God completely out of their finances, but Scripture reveals that He plays a central role.]

2. **Read *Deuteronomy 10:14* and *Psalm 24:1*.**

   What do these passages teach about the ownership of your possessions?

   [God owns everything in the world.]

3. **Read *Leviticus 25:23* and *Haggai 2:8*.**

   What are some of the specific items that the Lord owns?

   Leviticus 25:1—[God owns all the land.]

   Haggai 2:8—[The Lord owns all the gold and silver.]

   Write two practical ideas that will help you recognize God's ownership.

   - *[Alter your vocabulary by dropping the possessive pronouns ("my," "mine," and "ours" and substituting "His" instead.]*
   - *[For 30 days, each morning and night, meditate and prayerfully recite 1 Chronicles 29:11.]*

4. **Read *1 Chronicles 29:11-12* and *Psalm 135:6*.**

   What do these verses say about the Lord's control of circumstances?

   [The Lord is in control of all circumstances.]

5. **Read *Proverbs 21:1* and *Isaiah 40:21-24*.**

   What do these passages tell you about the Lord's control of people?

   Proverbs 21:1—[God controls the heart of each person.]

   Isaiah 40:21-24—[The Lord is in absolute control of all people.]

6. **Read *Genesis 45:4-8* and *Romans 8:28*.**

   Why is it important to realize that God controls and uses even difficult circumstances for good in the life of a godly person?

[God works every circumstance for good in the lives of those who love Him and are yielded to Him as Lord. Joseph suffered difficult circumstances, but God orchestrated those difficulties for ultimate good.]

7. **Read *Psalm 34:9-10; Matthew 6:31-33*; and *Philippians 4:19*.**

   What has the Lord promised concerning meeting your needs.

   [God has promised to provide our needs if we seek first the kingdom of God and His righteousness.]

   From the Bible, give an example of the Lord providing for someone's needs in a supernatural way.

   [Several examples of God's provision: Israel in the wilderness (Exodus 16:4-35), Jesus feeding the five thousand (Matthew 14:15-21) and the four thousand (Matthew 15:32-38), and the Lord sending ravens to feed Elijah (1 Kings 17:4-6).]

8. **Read *Genesis 39:2-5; Exodus 36:1-2*; and *Psalm 75:6-7*.**

   What do each of these verses tell us about the Lord's involvement in our work?

   Genesis 39:2-5—[The Lord gives us success.]

   Exodus 36:1-2—[God gives us our skills and abilities.]

   Psalm 75:6-7—[The Lord controls promotions.]

9. **Read *1 Corinthians 4-2*.**

   According to this verse, what is your requirement as a steward?

   [We are responsible to be faithful as stewards.]

   How would you define a steward?

   [A steward is a manager of another's property.]

   Read *Luke 16:1-2*.
   Why did the master remove the steward from his position?

   [The steward was removed because he squandered the master's possessions.]

   Do you think this principle is applicable today?

   [Yes, this principle is applicable today.]

   Read *Luke 16:10*.
   Describe the principle found in this verse.

   [If a person is unfaithful in a little matter, he or she will be unfaithful in much, and vice versa.]

Read *Luke 16:12.*

Are we required to be faithful with other people's possessions? What happens if we are not?

[Yes, if we are unfaithful with what is another's, the Lord will not entrust us with possessions of our own.]

ANSWERS TO: HOW WOULD YOU RESPOND TO A COACHING PARTICIPANT?

1. I worry about being able to pay my bills and provide for my family.

   [God plays a role and we have certain responsibilities in the handling of money. Our part is to be faithful in working hard and applying God's other financial principles. God has promised to meet our needs. He is trustworthy and we can be worry free because of His promises.]

2. I'm having a tough time financially and feel the Lord just doesn't seem to care.

   [The Lord loves you more than you can possibly realize. He has promised never to leave you or forsake you (Hebrews 13:5).]

3. My parents didn't have much, but they never went without a meal. I don't understand how I get so behind in my bills.

   [Learn and apply God's financial principles. Establish your budget and spending priorities and be faithful.]

4. I have ignored God's principles for so long that I believe He can never use me to glorify Himself.

   [Nothing could be further from the truth. Carefully study 1 John 1:9, "If we confess our sins, He is faithful and righteous to forgive us our sins and to cleanse us from all unrighteousness." The Lord delights in us when we seek to obey Him and will often use our past mistakes to teach others.]

GIVE GENEROUSLY

Principle to Memorize

Giving generously should be a priority.

Scripture to Memorize

"Remember the words of the Lord Jesus, that He Himself said, 'It is more blessed to give than to receive' " (Acts 20:35).

ASSIGNMENT: *Family Financial Workbook*

Chapter Three *Everybody Needs a Budget*

This chapter deals with decisions and motivations in spending. Defining needs, wants, and desires is difficult for most people. Understanding the distinction between them is essential for good spending decisions. Evaluate your own attitude toward needs, wants, and desires. How does it compare to the principles found in this chapter?

QUESTIONS TO ANSWER

1. **Read *1 Corinthians 13:3* and *2 Corinthians 9:7*.**

   What do these passages communicate about the importance of the proper attitude in giving?

   1 Corinthians 13:3—

   2 Corinthians 9:7—

   How can a person develop the proper attitude in giving?

After prayerfully evaluating your attitude in giving, how would you describe it?

2. **Read *Acts 20:35*.**
   How does this principle from God's economy differ from the way most people view giving?

   List the benefits for the giver, which are found in each of the following passages.

   Proverbs 11:24-25—

   Matthew 6:20—

   Luke 12:34—

   1 Timothy 6:18-19—

3. **Read *2 Corinthians 8:1-5*.**
   Identify three principles from this passage that should influence how much you give.

   1.

   2.

   3.

Prayerfully (with your spouse if you are married) seek the Lord's guidance to determine how much you should give.

4. **Read *Numbers 18:8-10,24; Galatians 6:6;* and *1 Timothy 5:17-18.***
   What do these verses tell you about financially supporting your church and those who teach the Scriptures?

   Numbers 18:8-10,24—

   Galatians 6:6—

   1 Timothy 5:17-18—

5. **Read *Isaiah 58:6-11.***
   What do these verses say about giving to the needy?

   Study *Matthew 25:35-45.*
   How does Jesus Christ identify with the poor?

   Are you currently giving to the poor? If not, what is hindering you?

NOTES TO READ

One of the most common principles that your coaching participants will violate is that of giving generously. It requires faith to give if a person is in financial difficulty. If you understand God's perspective of giving and do it, giving becomes a blessing. We will examine the proper attitudes in giving, the advantages of giving, and the several practical principles of giving.

Because God loved, He gave. Because God is love, He is also a giver.

ATTITUDES IN GIVING

God evaluates our giving on the basis of our attitude. God's attitude in giving is best summed up in John 3:16: *"For God so loved the world, that He gave His only begotten Son."* Because God loved, He gave. Because God is love, He is also a giver. He set the example of giving motivated by love.

An attitude of love in giving is crucial: *"If I give all my possessions to feed the poor . . . but do not have love, it profits me nothing"* (1 Corinthians 13:3). It is hard to imagine anything more commendable than giving everything to the poor. But if it is done with the wrong attitude, without love, it is no benefit to the giver whatsoever.

In God's economy the attitude is more important than the amount. Jesus emphasized this in Matthew 23:23: *"Woe to you, scribes and Pharisees, hypocrites! For you tithe mint and dill and cummin, and have neglected the weightier provisions of the law: justice and mercy and faithfulness; but these are the things you should have done without neglecting the others."*

The Pharisees had been careful to give precisely the correct amount—down to the last mint leaf in their gardens. But because of their wrong attitudes, Christ rebuked them. He looks past the amount of the gift to the heart of the giver.

The only way you can give out of a heart filled with love is to recognize that your gifts are actually given to the Lord Himself. An example of this perspective is found in Numbers 18:24: *"The tithe of the sons of Israel, which they offer as an offering to the Lord, I have given to the Levites for an inheritance."* If giving is merely to a church, a ministry, or a needy person, it is only charity. But if it is to the Lord, it becomes an act of worship. Because God is our creator, our Savior, and our faithful provider, we can express our gratefulness and love by giving our gifts to Him.

For example, when the offering plate is being passed at church, we should consciously remind ourselves that we are giving our gifts to the Lord Himself.

In addition to giving out of a heart filled with love, we are to give cheefully. *"Each one must do just as he has purposed in his heart, not grudgingly or under compulsion, for God loves a cheerful giver"* (2 Corinthians 9:7).

How do we develop this joy in giving? Consider the early churches of Macedonia. *"Now, brethren, we wish to make known to you the grace of God which has been given in the churches of Macedonia, that in a great ordeal of affliction their abundance of joy and their deep poverty overflowed in the wealth of their liberality"* (2 Corinthians 8:1-2).

How did the Macedonians, who were in terrible circumstances still manage to give with an *"abundance of joy?"* The answer is in verse 5: *"They first gave themselves to the Lord and to us by the will of God."* The key to cheerful giving is to submit yourself to Christ and ask Him to direct how much He wants you to give. Only then are we in a position to give with the proper attitude and reap the advantages.

Stop and examine yourself. What is your attitude toward giving?

ADVANTAGES OF GIVING

Obviously a gift benefits the recipient. The local church continues its ministry, the hungry are fed, the naked are clothed, and missionaries are sent. But, according to God's economy, if a gift is given with the proper attitude, the giver benefits more than the receiver. *"Remember the words of the Lord Jesus, that He Himself said, 'It is more blessed to give than to receive' "* (Acts 20:35). As we examine Scripture, we find that the giver benefits in three areas.

1. Increase in intimacy

Above all else, giving directs our attention and heart to Christ. Matthew 6:21 tells us, *"Where your treasure is, there will your heart be also."* This is why it is so necessary to go through the process of consciously giving each gift to the person of Jesus Christ. When you give your gift to Him, your heart will automatically be drawn to the Lord. And nothing in life can compare to entering into His joy and knowing Christ more intimately.

2. Increase in heaven

Matthew 6:20 reads, *"Store up for yourselves treasures in heaven, where neither moth nor rust destroys, and where thieves do not break in or steal."* The

In addition to giving out of a heart filled with love, we are to give cheerfully.

Lord tells us that there really is something akin to the "First National Bank of Heaven." And He wants us to know that we can invest for eternity.

Paul wrote, *"Not that I seek the gift itself, but I seek for the profit which increases to your account"* (Philippians 4:17). There is an account for each of us in heaven that we will be privileged to enjoy for eternity. And although it is true that we "can't take it with us," Scripture teaches that we can make deposits to our heavenly account before we die.

3. Increase on Earth

Many people do not believe that giving results in material blessings flowing to the giver—only spiritual blessings. However, in Proverbs 11:24-25 we read, *"There is one who scatters, yet increases all the more, and there is one who withholds what is justly due, and yet it results only in want. The generous man will be prosperous, and he who waters will himself be watered."*

Examine 2 Corinthians 9:6-11: *"He who sows sparingly will also reap sparingly, and he who sows bountifully shall also reap bountifully . . . God is able to make all grace abound to you, that always having all sufficiency in everything, you may have an abundance for every good deed; as it is written, 'He scattered abroad, He gave to the poor, His righteousness endures forever.' Now He who supplies seed to the sower and bread for food will supply and multiply your seed for sowing and increase the harvest of your righteousness; you will be enriched in everything for all liberality."*

These verses clearly teach that giving results in a material increase: *"shall also reap bountifully . . . always having all sufficiency in everything . . . may have an abundance . . . will supply and multiply your seed . . . you will be enriched in everything."*

But note carefully *why* the Lord is returning an increase materially: *"Always having all sufficiency in everything, you may have an abundance for every good deed . . . will supply and multiply your seed for sowing . . . you will be enriched in everything for all liberality."* The Lord produces a material increase so that we may give more and have our needs met at the same time.

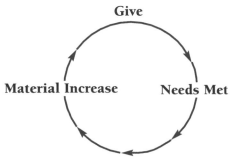

Give

Material Increase   Needs Met

"Honor the Lord from your wealth and from the first of all your produce" (Proverbs 3:9).

One reason the Lord reveals that a gift will result in material increase is because He wants us to recognize that He is behind the multiplication of our seed. God has chosen to be invisible, but He wants us to experience His reality.

When we give, we should do so with a sense of expectancy—anticipating the Lord to provide a material increase but not knowing when or how the Lord may choose to provide this increase. And He can be very creative! Remember, the giver can reap the advantages of giving only when he gives cheerfully out of a heart filled with love. And this precludes the motive of just giving to get.

PRACTICAL PRINCIPLES OF GIVING

Priority of giving

"Honor the Lord from your wealth and from the first of all your produce" (Proverbs 3:9). As soon as we receive any income, we should set aside the amount we are going to give. This habit helps us remember to put Christ first in all we do, and it defeats the temptation to spend on ourselves the portion we have decided to give.

Places for giving

We are told to give to two areas.

1. The local church, Christian workers, and ministries

Throughout its pages the Bible focuses on funding ministry. The Old Testament priesthood was to receive support: *"To the sons of Levi, behold, I have given all the tithe in Israel . . . in return for their service which they perform, the service of the tent of meeting"* (Numbers 18:21). And the New Testament teaching on funding God's work is just as strong.

We believe that we should give a minimum of 10 percent of our income through our churches because this is a tangible expression of our commitment to the local church. But we also give to others who are directly impacting us. *"The one who is taught the word is to share all good things with the one who teaches"* (Galatians 6:6).

2. The needy

In Matthew 25:34-45 we are confronted with one of the most exciting and yet sobering truths in Scripture. Read this passage carefully: *"Then the King will say . . . 'for I was hungry, and you gave Me something to eat; I was thirsty, and you gave Me something to drink' . . . Then the righteous will answer Him, saying, 'Lord, when did we see You hungry, and feed You, or thirsty, and give You something to drink? . . . The King will answer and say to them, 'Truly I say to you, to the extent that you did it to one of these brothers of Mine, even the least of them, you did it to Me.' Then He will say to those on His left, 'Depart from me, accursed ones, into the eternal fire . . . for I was hungry, and you gave Me nothing to eat; I was thirsty, and you gave Me nothing to drink . . . to the extent that you did not do it to one of the least of these, you did not do it to Me.' "*

In some mysterious way we cannot fully comprehend, Jesus, the Creator of all things, personally identifies Himself with the poor. When we share with the needy we are actually sharing with Jesus Himself. And when we do not give to the poor, we leave Jesus hungry and thirsty.

When we share with the needy we are actually sharing with Jesus Himself.

APPLYING THE PRINCIPLES TO MONEY MAP COACHING

Communicate these principles to your coaching participants.

1. It is important to give with the proper attitude—cheerfully and out of a heart of love.

2. The Lord wants us to give generously.

3. A generous giver receives wonderful blessings: closer fellowship with the Lord, eternal rewards, and a material increase on earth.

4. Giving should be a priority to help us put Christ first in our lives.

5. We should give first to our church, then to other ministries and to the needy.

6. If God prompts us to give to a person or specific organization, we should meet those needs.

HOW WOULD YOU RESPOND TO A COACHING PARTICIPANT?

The following questions and views are commonly expressed during Money Map coaching sessions. Describe how you would respond to each.

1. I'm deeply in debt and have a hard time paying all my bills. Should I tithe (give 10 percent)?

2. We believe it's important for our children to attend a Christian school. We don't have the money to send them, unless we cut back on our giving.

3. Just because I make a good living, I don't see why I should always be asked to help others.

4. My gift is giving to others, but I never have as much as I want to give.

5. When I calculate my tithe, should it be on my net or my gross income?

6. Should I give if I am in debt?

7. Is it okay to take my tithe money and put it toward Bible college tuition?

8. Should I give money to support secular organizations?

9. Wouldn't you be exempt from tithing if you were on a fixed income (Social Security, pension, annuity) and barely making ends meet?

10. Should I give from my alimony or child suport from my ex-husband?

Please review this section until you are thoroughly familiar with the practical and spiritual applications that you will use in Money Map coaching sessions. More information on giving and tithing can be found on the CD included in this course.

ANSWERS TO THE QUESTIONS

1. **Read *1 Corinthians 13:3* and *2 Corinthians 9:7*.**

   What do these passages communicate about the importance of the proper attitude in giving?

   > *1 Corinthians 13:3—[Giving without a heart of love is of no value to the giver.]*

   > *2 Corinthians 9:7—[Do not give grudgingly or under compulsion but rather give cheerfully. The proper attitude is crucial.]*

   How can a person develop the proper attitude in giving?

   [The proper attitude is the key issue in the area of giving. The only way to give out of a heart of love is consciously to give each gift to Jesus Christ Himself as an act of worship.]

2. **Read *Acts 20:35*.**

   How does this principle from God's economy differ from the way most people view giving?

   [In the Lord's economic system it is more blessed to give than to receive. Most people believe the opposite.]

   List the benefits for the giver, which are found in each of the following passages.

   > *Proverbs 11:24-25—[There is a material increase—in the Lord's time and way—to the giver.]*

   > *Matthew 6:20—[We can lay up treasures in heaven, which we will be able to enjoy throughout all eternity.]*

   > *Luke 12:34—[The heart of the giver is drawn to Christ as treasures are given to Him.]*

   > *1 Timothy 6:18-19—[We can store treasures in heaven and "take hold of that which is life indeed."]*

3. **Read *2 Corinthians 8:1-5*.**

   Identify three principles from this passage that should influence how much you give.

   1. *[They first gave themselves to the Lord, asking Him to direct their giving. In the same way we need to submit ourselves to the Lord when determining how much to give.]*

   2. *[They were so yielded to the Lord that despite difficult circumstances they begged to give.]*

   3. *[They experienced tremendous joy as a result of their sacrificial giving.]*

4. **Read *Numbers 18:8-10,24; Galatians 6:6*; and *1 Timothy 5:17-18*.**

What do these verses tell you about financially supporting your church and those who teach the Scriptures?

Numbers 18:8-10,24—[Godly people have always been required to participate in the maintenance of the ministry. The Old Testament believer was required to care for the place of worship and the Levites who served in the ministry.]

Galatians 6:6—[Those who are taught the Scriptures should financially support their teachers.]

1 Timothy 5:17-18—[God's New Testament instrument is the church, and we are to adequately support those who serve as pastors and teachers.]

5. **Read *Isaiah 58:6-11*.**

What does this verse say about giving to the needy?

[When we give to the poor, the Lord will protect us, answer our prayers, and bless us with His joy.]

Study *Matthew 25:35-45*.

How does Jesus Christ identify with the poor?

[Jesus identifies personally with the poor. When we give to the poor, we are giving to Christ Himself. When we do not give to the poor, we are not giving to Christ, and He is left hungry and naked.]

ANSWERS TO: HOW WOULD YOU RESPOND TO A COACHING PARTICIPANT?

1. I'm deeply in debt and have a hard time paying all my bills. Should I tithe (give 10 percent)?

[Yes, giving should be a priority for all of us. When we are in financially difficult times, it requires an act of faith to give and trust the Lord to provide as He has promised.]

2. We believe it's important for our children to attend a Christian school. We don't have the money to send them, unless we cut back on our giving.

[This is a very challenging issue, but it is clear that we should be generous in our giving. You may need to be creative in earning additional income or deciding to spend less in some other areas.]

3. Just because I make a good living, I don't see why I should always be asked to help others.

[Giving is a privilege. One of the reasons the Lord allows us to earn a good income is so that we will have the resources to share with others.]

4. My gift is giving to others, but I never have as much as I want to give.

   [Scripture tells us, "If the readiness is present, it is acceptable according to what a person has, not according to what he does not have" (2 Corinthians 8:12). Your responsibility is to be ready to give, God's responsibility is to provide the resources for you to give.]

5. When I calculate my tithe, should it be on my net or my gross income?

   [Proverbs 3:9-10 says that God has asked for our firstfruits, which is the first and best of all that we receive. That means we should tithe from our total income before taxes (gross).]

6. Should I give if I am in debt?

   [Yes. If there is anybody in the world who needs God's wisdom in the area of finances, it is a person who is already in debt.]

7. Is it okay to take my tithe money and put it toward Bible college tuition.

   [Malachi 3 says we are actually stealing from God if we don't pay an honest tithe, as well as give liberal offerings as we are able. It's wise to save for a Christian education. You should not use the tithe for it.]

8. Should I give money to support secular organizations?

   [In our opinion, we should focus our giving on the work of Christ unless the Lord clearly directs otherwise.]

9. Wouldn't you be exempt from tithing if you were on a fixed income (Social Security, pension, annuity) and barely making ends meet?

   [God doesn't "need" our money. His desire is to bless His children, and it is for our good that he has instituted the principle of tithing in His Word.]

   [Remember the widow who put two "mites" into the treasury? Jesus knew her situation and commended her by saying, "This poor widow put in more than all the contributors to the treasury; for they all put in out of their surplus, but she, out of her poverty, put in all she owned, all she had to live on" (Mark 12:43-44).]

10. Should I give from my alimony or child support from my ex-husband?

    [Alimony is part of your income from which you should give, but child support belongs to the children and isn't part of your personal "increase."]

BECOMING DEBT FREE

Principle to Memorize

Scripture encourages us to become free of debt.

Scripture to Memorize

"Just as the rich rule the poor, so the borrower is servant to the lender" (Proverbs 22:7, TLB).

ASSIGNMENT: *Family Financial Workbook*

Chapter Four *Where Are You Now?*

You are beginning the budgeting process in this chapter. Tracking spending and compiling a list of debts are fundamental to developing an accurate budget. Review how this chapter suggests these items be collected and tracked. Every method does not meet the needs for all people. Adjustments may have to be made.

Chapter Five *Setting Your Budget*

This chapter offers a method of establishing a spending plan, based on the information collected in Chapter Four. Anytime the word "guideline" is used it refers to a suggested standard, not an inflexible one.

QUESTIONS TO ANSWER

1. **Read *Deuteronomy 28:1,2,12* and *Deuteronomy 28:15,43-45.***
   According to these passages, how was debt viewed in the Old Testament?

   What was the cause of someone getting in debt (becoming a borrower) or getting out of debt (becoming a lender)?

2. **Read *Romans 13:8; Proverbs 22:7*; and *1 Corinthians 7:23*.**
   Is debt encouraged in Scripture? Why?

   Romans 13:8—

   Proverbs 22:7—

   1 Corinthians 7:23—

   How does this apply to you personally and to your business?

   Do you have a strategy to get out of debt? If you have a plan, please describe it.

3. **Read *Psalm 37:21* and *Proverbs 3:27-28*.**
   What do these verses say about debt repayment?

   Psalm 37:21—

   Proverbs 3:27-28—

   How will you implement this?

4. **Read *Proverbs 22:26-27* and *Proverbs 17:18*.**

   What does the Bible say about cosigning (striking hands, surety)?

   Proverbs 22:26-27—

   Proverbs 17:18—

   Then read *Proverbs 6:1-5*. If someone has cosigned, what should he or she attempt to do?

   How do these principles of cosigning apply to you?

Notes to Read

The dictionary defines debt as: "Money that one person is obligated to pay to another."

Without a doubt, the most common challenge facing your coaching participants will be their debt. We have so much personal debt in our nation that the average person has been described as someone driving on a bond-financed highway, in a bank-financed car, fueled by charge card-financed gasoline, going to purchase furniture on an installment plan to put in a mortgaged home!

We are drowning in a sea of debt. Each year more than one million individuals in our country file bankruptcy. And more sobering, a Gallup Poll found that a majority of all those who had gone through a divorce indicated that financial tension at home was a major factor in the breakups.

Such financial tension was created largely by believing the "gospel" according to Madison Avenue: Buy now and pay later with those easy monthly payments. We all know that nothing about those monthly payments is easy. Advertisers fail to tell us the whole truth. They leave out one little word: *debt*.

WHAT IS DEBT?

The dictionary defines debt as "Money that one person is obligated to pay to another." Debt includes money owed to credit card companies, bank loans, money borrowed from relatives, the home mortgage, and past due medical bills. Bills that come due, such as the monthly electrical bill, are not considered debt if they are paid on time.

WHAT DOES DEBT REALLY COST?

We need to understand the real cost of debt. Debt imposes both a fiscal and physical cost. For example, examine the true cost of credit card debt.

Assume you have $5,560 in credit card debt at an 18 percent interest rate and there are no tax consequences on the interest earned or spent. This would cost you $1,000 in interest annually. Study the chart on the next page.

You can see what lenders have known for a long time: the incredible impact of compounding interest. The lender will accumulate more

Credit Card Debt of $5,560 at 18 Percent Interest

1. Amount of interest you paid

Year 5	Year 10	Year 20	Year 30	Year 40
$5,000	$10,000	$20,000	$30,000	$40,000

2. What you would accumulate on $1,000 invested annually earning 12 percent

Year 5	Year 10	Year 20	Year 30	Year 40
6,353	17,549	72,052	241,333	767,091

3. How much the lender earns from your interest payment at 18 percent interest

Year 5	Year 10	Year 20	Year 30	Year 40
7,154	23,521	146,628	790,948	4,163,213

than $4 million if you pay $1,000 a year for 40 years, and the lender earns 18 percent on your payment! Is there any wonder credit card companies are eager for you to become one of their borrowers?

Now compare the $40,000 you paid in interest over 40 years with the $767,091 you could have accumulated, earning 12 percent on $1,000 each year. The monthly income on $767,091 is $7,671 if it's earning 12 percent, without ever touching the principal.

Stop to consider this: When a person assumes debt of $5,560 and pays $1,000 a year in interest, if 12 percent is earned, it actually costs him or her $767,091 over 40 years. Debt has a much higher cost than many realize. Next time you are tempted to purchase something with debt, ask yourself if the long-term benefits of staying out of debt outweigh the short-term benefits of the purchase.

The physical cost of debt

Debt also extracts a physical toll. It often increases stress, which contributes to mental, physical, and emotional fatigue. It can harm relationships. Many people raise their lifestyles through debt, only to discover that the burden of debt then controls their lifestyles. The car bumper sticker "I owe, I owe, it's off to work I go" is an unfortunate reality for too many people.

WHAT DOES SCRIPTURE SAY ABOUT DEBT?

The Bible does not say that it is sin to be in debt, but it does discourage indebtedness. Read the first portion of Romans 13:8 from several different Bible translations: *"Owe no man any thing"* (KJV). *"Let no debt remain outstanding"* (NIV). *"Pay all your debts"* (TLB). *"Owe nothing to anyone"* (NASB). *"Keep out of debt and owe no man anything"* (Amplified).

Debt is considered slavery

In Proverbs 22:7 we learn why our Lord discourages debt: *"Just as the rich rule the poor, so the borrower is servant to the lender"* (TLB). When we are in debt, we are in a position of servitude to the lender. The deeper we are in debt, the more like servants we become. We do not have the full freedom to decide where to spend our incomes. We legally have obligated ourselves to meet these debts.

Debt may deny God an opportunity

Ron Blue, an outstanding financial author, tells of a young man who wanted to go to seminary to become a missionary. The young man had no money and thought the only way he could afford seminary was to secure a student loan. However, this would have encumbered him with $40,000 of debt by the time he graduated, which would have been impossible to pay back on a missionary's salary.

After a great deal of prayer, he decided to enroll without the help of a student loan and to trust the Lord to meet his needs. He graduated without borrowing anything and grew in his appreciation for how God could creatively provide his needs. This was the most valuable lesson learned in seminary as he prepared for life on the mission field. Borrowing may deny God an opportunity to demonstrate His reality.

HOW TO GET OUT OF DEBT

There are six steps for getting out of debt. The steps are easy, but following them requires hard work. The goal is D-Day—Debtless Day—when you become absolutely free of debt.

1. Pray.

In 2 Kings 4:1-7 a widow was threatened with losing her children to her creditor, and she appealed to the prophet Elisha for help. Elisha instructed the widow to borrow many empty jars from her neighbors. The Lord supernaturally multiplied her only possession—a small amount of oil—and all the jars were filled. She sold the oil and paid her debts to free her children.

"Just as the rich rule the poor, so the borrower is servant to the lender" (Proverbs 22:7, TLB).

The same God who provided for the widow is interested in your becoming free from debt. The most important step is to pray. Seek the Lord's help and guidance in your journey toward Debtless Day. He can either act immediately, as in the case of the widow, or slowly and over time. In either case, prayer is essential.

2. Establish a budget.

In our experience, few people in debt have been using a budget. They may have had one—neatly filed away in a drawer or loaded on their computer—but they have not been using it. A budget helps you plan ahead, analyze your spending patterns, and control the biggest budget buster of them all: impulse spending. Crown has developed *Money Matters* software, which is an outstanding budgeting program.

3. List your assets—everything you own.

Evaluate your assets to determine if there is anything you do not need that might be sold to help you to get out of debt more quickly. What about the clothes you no longer wear? That set of golf clubs gathering dust in the garage? Is there anything you can sell to enable you to get out of debt?

4. List your liabilities—everything you owe.

Many people, particularly if they owe a lot of money, do not know exactly what they owe. It must be human nature: If I avoid unpleasant things, perhaps they will go away. However, you must list your debts to determine your current financial situation. You also need to list the interest rate your creditors are charging for each debt.

5. Establish a debt repayment plan for each creditor.

We suggest you decide which debts to pay off first, based on two factors.

- Focus on paying off smaller debts first. You will be encouraged as they are eliminated, and this will free cash to apply against other debts. After you pay off the first debt, apply its payment toward the next debt you wish to retire. After the second debt is paid off, take what you were paying on the first and second debts and pay that toward the next debt you wish to eliminate, and so forth.

- Determine what rate of interest you are being charged on each debt, and try to pay off first those that charge the highest rate of interest.

6. Do not give up!

The last step is most difficult in getting out of debt. It is hard work get-

Seek the Lord's help and guidance in your journey toward Debtless Day.

ting out of debt. But the freedom of becoming debt free is worth the struggle.

AUTOMOBILE DEBT

Automobile debt is one of the leading causes of consumer indebtedness. Sixty percent of all the automobiles in our nation are financed. There's a way to live free of car debt. First, decide in advance to keep your car for at least three years longer than your existing automobile debt. Second, pay off your automobile loan. Third, continue paying the monthly car payment, but pay it to yourself into a special account for your next car. Then, when you are ready to replace your car, the saved cash plus the trade-in should be sufficient to buy your car without credit. It may not be a new car, but you should be able to purchase a reliable used car without any debt.

Investment debt

Automobile debt is one of the leading causes of consumer indebtedness

Should you borrow money to make an investment? In our opinion, it is permissible to borrow for an investment, but only if you are not required to personally guarantee repayment of the debt. The Bible calls this surety. The investment for which you borrow (and any money invested) should be the only collateral for the debt.

For instance, if you wanted to purchase land for $10,000 but could only put up $1,000, you would finance the remaining $9,000, with the land pledged as total security. Therefore, if ever you couldn't continue to pay the note, the land would be surrendered and the debt canceled. Would it be ethical to give the collateral in lieu of payment? Certainly, if that's what you agreed to with the lender. This would allow you to avoid surety.

It is painful to lose your investment, but it is much more serious to jeopardize meeting your family's needs by risking all your assets on investment debt.

Business debt

We also want to encourage you to pray about becoming debt free in your business if you have one. Paying off all business-related debts provides wonderful financial stability in a business.

Debt repayment responsibilities

Many delay payments to use the creditor's money as long as possible, but this is not biblical. *"Do not withhold good from those to whom it is due, when it is in your power to do it. Do not say to your neighbor, 'Go and come back, and tomorrow I will give it,' when you have it with you"* (Proverbs 3:27-28).

Godly people pay their debts and bills as promptly as they can.

Bankruptcy

In bankruptcy, a court of law declares a person unable to pay his or her debts. Depending on the type of bankruptcy, the court will either allow the debtor to develop a plan to repay his or her creditors or the court will distribute the property among the creditors as payment for the debts.

Bankruptcy is sweeping our country. Should a godly person declare bankruptcy? The answer is generally no. Psalm 37:21 tell us, *"The wicked borrows and does not pay back, but the righteous is gracious and gives."*

However, Crown's view is that bankruptcy is permissible under two circumstances: (1) if a creditor forces a person into bankruptcy, or (2) if a counselor believes the debtor's emotional health is at stake because of inability to cope with the pressure of unreasonable creditors. For example, a husband may desert his wife and children, leaving her with business and family bills and debts for which she is responsible. She may not have the resources to meet those obligations. The emotional trauma of an unwanted divorce, coupled with harassment from unsympathetic creditors, may be too much for her to bear.

After a person goes through bankruptcy, he or she should make every effort to repay the debt. For a large debt, this may be a long-term goal that is largely dependent on the Lord's supernaturally providing resources. Seek the counsel of an attorney before beginning to repay this debt.

Cosigning

Cosigning relates to debt. Anytime you cosign, you become legally responsible for the debt of another. It is just as if you went to the bank, borrowed the money, and gave it to your friend or relative who is asking you to cosign.

A Federal Trade Commission study found that 75 percent of those who cosigned for finance company loans ended up making the payments! Unfortunately, few cosigners plan for default. The casualty rate is so high because the professional lender has analyzed the loan and said "I won't touch this loan unless I can get someone who is financially responsible to guarantee this loan."

Godly people should pay their debts and bills as promptly as they can.

Fortunately, Scripture speaks very clearly about cosigning. In Proverbs 17:18 we read, *"It is poor judgment to countersign [cosign] another's note, to become responsible for his debts"* (TLB). The words poor judgment are better translated "destitute of mind!"

Parents often cosign for their son's or daughter's first automobile. Consider modeling for your children the importance of not cosigning, and discourage them from using debt. Instead, train them to plan ahead and save for the cash purchase of their first cars.

Please use sound judgment and never cosign a note or become surety for any debt. If you have already cosigned for a loan, the Scripture gives you counsel: *"Son, if you endorse a note for someone you hardly know, guaranteeing his debt, you are in serious trouble. You may have trapped yourself by your agreement. Quick! Get out of it if you possibly can! Swallow your pride; don't let embarassment stand in the way. Go and beg to have your name erased. Don't put it off . . . If you can get out of this trap you have saved yourself like a deer that escapes from a hunter, or a bird from the net"* (Proverbs 6:1-5, TLB).

LENDING TO OTHERS

There's an old cliché: "The definition of a distant friend is a close friend who owes you money." That is not always true, but it has enough truth in it to cause us to evaluate lending as a biblical principle. Let's first evaluate lending from a human viewpoint.

Why would anyone want to lend another person money? There are three reasons. (1) *To make a profit.* When you place money in an interest bearing account, you have *loaned* the money. The interest represents a profit on the loan you made. (2) *Because someone has a need.* You may know someone who is short of funds for a business or a personal need and want to help but don't feel you can give the money. (3) *Because someone asks you.* Many lend money to close friends or to family because they were asked and don't feel they should say no.

The Bible doesn't say that you must be a lender, but it also doesn't say you cannot be a lender. It is interesting that *lending* is one of the blessings promised by God for being obedient to His ways. *"You shall lend to many nations, but you shall not borrow"* (Deuteronomy 28:12). Clearly, lending is not prohibited.

Charging interest

Scripture seems to be very clear: Don't charge interest to other

Christians. *"You shall not charge interest to your countrymen: interest on money, food, or anything that may be loaned at interest"* (Deuteronomy 23:19). A loan can be made to anyone, but loans to those within God's family are to be a demonstration that God can provide without charging interest to one another.

In regard to lending to others, God's Word says, *"You may charge interest to a foreigner, but to your countryman you shall not charge interest, so that the Lord your God may bless you in all that you undertake in the land which you are about to enter to possess"* (Deuteronomy 23:20). Thus we *can* charge interest on loans to nonbelievers. This doesn't mean that we *have to* charge interest. God may well lead someone to extend a loan at no interest as a means of sharing the message of Christ.

Lending versus giving

There are conditions under which God would have us give rather than lend. This is particularly true when basic necessities are involved. This principle of lending without any consideration for whether the money can be repaid is shown in Luke 6:34: *"If you lend to those from whom you expect to receive, what credit is that to you? Even sinners lend to sinners in order to receive back the same amount."* The obvious meaning is to give to those who have needs and might never have the ability to repay.

Collecting

If you're going to lend, you're going to be faced with decisions about what to do if someone doesn't pay the debt. If you're not willing to confront borrowers who refuse to pay what is due, it's better never to lend.

God's principles of lending and collecting do not require a Christian to sit by passively if someone refuses to pay what is due; however, there are boundaries within which we are to operate that are much narrower than those of the world.

Assuming a Christian is owed a debt, what are the boundaries for collecting? Christians are clearly admonished *never* to take another Christian before the secular court. *"Does any one of you, when he has a case against his neighbor, dare to go to law before the unrighteous and not before the saints?"* (1 Corinthians 6:1). We are told that it is better to be defrauded than to lose our witness by suing one another (1 Corinthians 6:7). According to Matthew 18:15-17, we are to confront the issue: sin. Christian Peacemakers Conciliation Service is a ministry that provides Christians with an organized method to settle disputes. Using

Christians are clearly admonished never to take another Christian before the secular court.

Everything we do must be measured against eternal values and not short-term profit or loss.

non-biased lay volunteers, they act as a Christian "court" to settle disputes between believers.

Collecting from non-Christians

Many Christians assume that, since Paul said not to sue other Christians, it must be okay to sue non-Christians to collect debts. Just because there is a direct reference not to sue a Christian, that does not mean we *should* sue non-Christians.

To understand the principle of suing non-Christians to collect personal debts, it is necessary to look at our purpose. Our purpose as Christians is to represent our Lord Jesus Christ. In Luke 6:30-31, the Lord said, *"Give to everyone who asks of you, and whoever takes away what is yours, do not demand it back. Treat others the same way you want them to treat you."* This does not absolutely state that a Christian should never sue to collect a debt. But it certainly does imply that God desires a much higher standard of behavior from believers than is expected of others. Everything we do must be measured against eternal values and not short-term profit or loss.

Business loans

One of the most difficult areas associated with lending is that of business loans. Usually, this is credit extended for services or products. Obviously, the lender has incurred expenses for time or products, and when the loan is not repaid additional hardships are experienced. It is easy for the lender to feel resentful. Therefore, we must be especially careful not to be vengeful but to deal in love with those who don't pay.

APPLYING THE PRINCIPLES TO MONEY MAP COACHING

Communicate these principles to your coaching participants.

1. The Scriptures encourage us to become debt free.

2. When we are in debt, we are in a position of servitude to the lender.

3. Establish a workable plan to get out of debt.

4. Debt really costs more than most people realize.

5. Make every effort to be faithful in paying all your obligations on time.

6. Do not cosign unless you are willing to lose the total amount for which you have cosigned.

HOW WOULD YOU RESPOND TO A COACHING PARTICIPANT?

The following questions and views are commonly expressed during Money Map coaching sessions. Describe how you would respond to each.

1. I haven't been able to work due to poor health. I'll have to borrow money to make ends meet.

2. I don't have the money to send my son to college. I'm going to get a second mortgage on my house to pay his way.

3. I need a realiable car to drive to work. I'm going to apply for a five-year loan so I can afford the payments for a good car.

4. This is a good opportunity to make extra money. It will only take a few hours each week, but it costs $15,000 to start. Should I borrow this money from my retirement account?

5. I'm going to declare bankruptcy. I can't stand the pressure and just want to get it behind me.

Please review this section until you are thoroughly familiar with the principles that you will use in Money Map coaching sessions.

ANSWERS TO THE QUESTIONS

1. **Read *Deuteronomy 28:1,2,12* and *Deuteronomy 28:15,43-45.***

   According to these passages, how was debt viewed in the Old Testament.

   [Debt was considered a curse. Being free from debt (being a lender) was a blessing.]

   What was the cause of someone getting in debt (becoming a borrower) or getting out of debt (becoming a lender)?

   [Disobedience led to debt and obedience led to getting out of debt (being a lender).]

2. **Read *Romans 13:8*; *Proverbs 22:7*; and *1 Corinthians 7:23.***

   Is debt encouraged in Scripture? Why?

   Romans 13:8—[We are encouraged to stay out of debt.]

   Proverbs 22:7—[The debtor is servant to the lender.]

   1 Corinthians 7:23—[We are instructed not to be slaves of people. Therefore, make every effort to get out and stay out of debt. To summarize: the Bible does not say that debt is sin, but it discourages indebtedness.]

3. **Read *Psalm 37:21* and *Proverbs 3:27-28.***

   What do these verses say about debt repayment?

   Psalm 37:21—[A person who borrows but does not repay debts is called "wicked."]

   Proverbs 3:27-28—[Pay debts promptly if you have the resources. Many are taught to delay repayment to use other people's money as long as possible, but this is not biblical.]

4. **Read *Proverbs 22:26-27* and *Proverbs 17:18.***

   What does the Bible say about cosigning (striking hands, surety)?

   Proverbs 22:26-27—[Do not cosign. It may cause you to lose assets you need.]

   Proverbs 17:18—[It is poor judgment to cosign.]

   Then read *Proverbs 6:1-5.* If someone has cosigned, what should he or she attempt to do?

   [If we have cosigned, we are to humbly and diligently seek the release of our obligation.]

ANSWERS TO: HOW WOULD YOU RESPOND TO A COACHING PARTICIPANT?

1. I haven't been able to work due to poor health. I'll have to borrow money to make ends meet.

   [God has promised to meet our needs. Ask the Lord to show you what you truly need. Then do

all you can do to meet your needs and trust the Lord with the outcome. It pleases the Lord when we place our faith in Him to provide our needs.]

2. I don't have the money to send my son to college. I'm going to get a second mortgage on my house to pay his way.

   [Instead of assuming more debt, pray for the Lord's guidance and provision. Seek counsel from others and consider college education options that are less expensive.]

3. I need a reliable car to drive to work. I'm going to apply for a five-year loan so I can afford the payments for a good car.

   [God can provide reliable transportation without your taking on excessive debt. Pray for the Lord to lead you to just the right car. Ask your friends at church to join you in prayer as you look for reasonably priced transportation.]

4. This is a good opportunity to make extra money. It will only take a few hours each week, but it costs $15,000 to start. Should I borrow this money from my retirement account?

   [Very seldom is it wise to remove funds from a retirement plan. Carefully weigh the risks, rate of return, and legitimacy of the investment. Pray for the Lord's direction.]

5. I'm going to declare bankruptcy. I can't stand the pressure and just want to get it behind me.

   [In our opinion, bankruptcy is permissible only if a creditor forces a person into bankruptcy or if the debtor's emotional health is at stake because of inability to cope with the pressure of unreasonable creditors or if a creditor has garnished wages, causing unfair treatment of other creditors. A Chapter 13 bankruptcy will enable the court to force all creditors to be treated fairly. Chapter 7 bankruptcy should be used only as a last resort (i.e. if the court will not allow Chapter 13). Review the bankruptcy section found on the CD included in this course.]

Principle to Memorize

We should consistently save.

Scripture to Memorize

"The wise man saves for the future, but the foolish man spends whatever he gets" (Proverbs 21:20, TLB).

ASSIGNMENT: *Family Financial Workbook*

Chapter Six *Making Your Budget Work*

Whether the coaching participant chooses to use personal finance software, the cash envelope system, the forms found in the *Family Financial Workbook,* or the spreadsheet method used in Crown's Small Group Study, the result should be the same: a balanced budget.

The categories are defined. Be sure you thoroughly understand what each category contains. Not all of the categories will be used in every situation.

Under the Tax Category, it is preferable to reduce any excess deduction from the paycheck now and use this additional income for debt reduction. When a participant is self-employed, it is best to keep a separate checking account just for business income.

QUESTIONS TO ANSWER

1. **Read *Genesis 41:34-36*; *Proverbs 21:20*; and *Proverbs 30:24-25*.**

   What do these passages say to you about savings?

   Genesis 41:34-36—

   Proverbs 21:20—

   Proverbs 30:24-25—

2. **Read *Proverbs 21:5; Proverbs 24:27; Proverbs 27:23-24*; and *Ecclesiastes 11:2*.**
   What investment principle(s) can you identify from each of these verses, and how will you apply each principle to your life?

   Proverbs 21:5—

   Proverbs 24:27—

   Proverbs 27:23-24—

   Ecclesiastes 11:2—

3. **Read *Matthew 22:15-22* and *Romans 13:1-7*.**
   Does the Lord require us to pay taxes to the government? Why?

   Do you think it is biblically permissible to reduce your taxes by using legal tax deductions? Why?

4. Gambling is defined as playing games of chance for money and betting. Some of today's most common forms of gambling are casino wagering, betting on sporting events, horse races, dog races, and state-run lotteries. What are some of the motivations that cause people to gamble?

Do these motives please the Lord? Why?

Read *Proverbs 28:20* **and** *Proverbs 28:22*.
According to these passages, why do you think a godly person should not gamble (play lotteries, bet on sporting events)?

How does gambing contradict the scriptural principles of working diligently and being a faithful steward of the Lord's possessions?

5. **Read** *Leviticus 19:11-13* **and** *Ephesians 4:25*.
What do these verses communicate to you about God's demand for honesty?

Leviticus 19:11-13—

Ephesians 4:25—

Are you consistently honest in even the smallest details? If not, how do you propose to change?

Unfortunately, most people are not consistent savers. The average person in our country is three weeks away from bankruptcy, with little or no money saved and significant monthly credit obligations. Many are totally dependent on next week's paycheck to keep the budget afloat.

Scripture encourages us to save. *"The wise man saves for the future, but the foolish man spends whatever he gets"* (Proverbs 21:20, TLB). The ant is commended for saving for a future need. *"Four things on earth are small, yet they are extremely wise: ants are creatures of little strength, yet they store up their food in the summer"* (Proverbs 30:24-25, NIV). Saving is the opposite of being in debt. Saving is making *provision* for tomorrow, but debt is *presumption* upon tomorrow.

We call saving the "Joseph principle," because saving requires self-denial. Joseph saved during seven years of plenty in order to survive seven years of famine. That is what saving is: denying an expenditure today so that you will have something to spend in the future. One of the major reasons most people are poor savers is that our culture does not practice self-denial. When we want something, we want it now!

How to save and how much to save

The most effective way to save is to immediately save a portion of your income each time you are paid. When you receive income, the first check you write should be for the Lord's work and the second check for your savings. An automatic payroll deduction can ensure that a portion of your income is saved regularly. Some commit income from tax refunds or bonuses for savings.

The Bible does not teach an amount or percentage to be saved. Try saving 10 percent of your income. This may not be possible initially, but you should begin the habit of saving—even if only a small amount. Financial experts recommend that people save the equivalent of three to six months of their income for emergencies. For most, this is a goal that will take time to accomplish.

INVESTING

People place some of their savings in investments with the expectation

> *"The wise man saves for the future, but the foolish man spends whatever he gets"* (Proverbs 21:20, TLB).

of receiving an income or growth in value. ***The purpose and intention of Crown Financial Ministries is not to recommend any specific investments. No one is authorized to use affiliation with Crown Financial Ministries to promote the sale of any investments or financial services.*** Our objective is to draw attention to the scriptural framework for savings and investing. Visit Crown's Web site at www.crown.org for more detailed information on investing.

Steady plodding

"Steady plodding brings prosperity, hasty speculation brings poverty" (Proverbs 21:5, TLB). The original Hebrew words for *steady plodding* picture a person filling a large barrel one handful at a time. Little by little the barrel is filled to overflowing. **The fundamental principle you need to practice to become a successful investor is to spend less than you earn. Then save and invest the difference over a long period of time.**

Examine various investments. Almost all of them are well suited for "steady plodding." Your home mortgage is paid off after years of steady payments. Savings grow because of compounding interest, and your business can increase steadily in value through the years as you develop its potential.

Understanding compound interest

A wealthy businessman was once asked if he had seen the seven wonders of the world. He responded, "No, but I do know the advantages of the eighth wonder of the world: compound interest." Understanding compounding is important. There are three variables in compounding: the amount, the percentage rate you earn on your savings, and the length of time you save.

1. The amount

The amount you save will be dictated by your level of income, how much you give, your living expenses, how much debt you have, and how faithfully you budget.

2. Rate of return

The second variable is the rate you earn on an investment. The following table demonstrates how an investment of $1,000 a year grows at various rates.

The fundamental principle you need to practice to become a successful investor is to spend less than you earn.

		Investment of $1,000 a year			
Rate Earned	Year 5	Year 10	Year 20	Year 30	Year 40
6%	$5,975	$13,972	$38,993	$83,802	$164,048
8%	6,336	15,645	49,423	122,346	279,781
10%	6,716	17,531	63,003	180,943	486,851
12%	7,115	19,655	80,699	270,293	859,142

As you can see, the increase in the rate of return has a remarkable effect on the amount accumulated. A 2 percent increase almost doubles the amount over 40 years. However, be careful not to invest in too risky an investment in order to achieve a high return. Usually, the higher the rate, the higher the risk.

3. Time

Time is an element we cannot control. However, we can start saving now. Answer this question: Who do you think would accumulate more by age 65, a person who started to save $1,000 a year at age 21, saved for eight years, and then completely stopped, or a person who saved $1,000 a year for 37 years who started at age 29? Both earned 10 percent on their savings. Is it the person who saved a total of $8,000 or the one who saved $37,000? Study the following chart.

	INDIVIDUAL A			INDIVIDUAL B	
Age	Contribution	Year-End Value	Age	Contribution	Year-End Value
21	$1,000	$1,100	21	$0	$0
22	1,000	2,310	22	0	0
23	1,000	3,641	23	0	0
24	1,000	5,105	24	0	0
25	1,000	6,716	25	0	0
26	1,000	8,487	26	0	0
27	1,000	10,436	27	0	0
28	1,000	12,579	28	0	0
29	0	13,837	29	1,000	1,100
30	0	15,221	30	1,000	2,310
31	0	16,743	31	1,000	3,641
32	0	18,417	32	1,000	5,105
33	0	20,259	33	1,000	6,716
34	0	22,284	34	1,000	8,487
35	0	24,513	35	1,000	10,436
36	0	26,964	36	1,000	12,579
37	0	29,661	37	1,000	14,937
38	0	32,627	38	1,000	17,531
39	0	35,889	39	1,000	20,384
40	0	39,478	40	1,000	23,523
41	0	43,426	41	1,000	26,975
42	0	47,769	42	1,000	30,772
43	0	52,546	43	1,000	34,950
44	0	57,800	44	1,000	39,545
45	0	63,580	45	1,000	44,599
46	0	69,938	46	1,000	50,159
47	0	76,932	47	1,000	56,275
48	0	84,625	48	1,000	63,003
49	0	93,088	49	1,000	70,403
50	0	103,397	50	1,000	78,543
51	0	112,636	51	1,000	87,497
52	0	123,898	52	1,000	97,347
53	0	136,290	53	1,000	108,182
54	0	149,919	54	1,000	120,100
55	0	164,911	55	1,000	133,210
56	0	181,402	56	1,000	147,631
57	0	199,542	57	1,000	163,494
58	0	219,496	58	1,000	180,943
59	0	241,446	59	1,000	200,138
60	0	265,590	60	1,000	221,252
61	0	292,149	61	1,000	244,477
62	0	321,364	62	1,000	270,024
63	0	353,501	63	1,000	298,127
64	0	388,851	64	1,000	329,039
65	0	$427,736	65	1,000	$363,043

Total Investment $8,000   Total Investment $37,000

Incredibly, the person who saved only $8,000 accumulated more because saving started earlier. So start saving now.

Avoid risky investments

"There is another serious problem I have seen everywhere—savings are put into risky investments that turn sour, and soon there is nothing left to pass on to one's son. The man who speculates is soon back to where he began—with nothing" (Ecclesiastes 5:13-15, TLB).

Scripture clearly warns of avoiding risky investments, yet each year thousands of people lose money in highly speculative and sometimes fraudulent investments. How many times have you heard of people losing their life's savings on some get-rich-quick scheme? Sadly, it seems that Christians are particularly vulnerable to such schemes because they trust others who appear to live by the same values they have. To help you identify a potentially risky investment, we have listed three characteristics that often appear.

1. The prospect of an unusually high profit or interest rate that is "practically guaranteed."

2. The decision to invest must be made quickly. There will be no opportunity to investigate the investment or promoter who is selling the investment. The promoter often will be doing you a "favor" by allowing you to invest.

3. Little will be said about the risks of losing money, and the investment will usually require no effort on your part. Sometimes a portion of the profits will be "dedicated to the Lord's work."

Before participating in any investment, please be patient and do your homework.

Diversify

"Divide your portion to seven, or even to eight, for you do not know what misfortune may occur on the earth" (Ecclesiastes 11:2). No investment on this earth is guaranteed. Money can be lost on any investment. The government can make gold illegal. The value of real estate can decrease. Money can be inflated until it is valueless. The stock market can perform well or suffer loss.

The perfect investment does not exist. You need to diversify. Consider the following steps as you diversify. It is recommended that you not skip any of the steps. Begin with one step, and then take each step at a time.

"Divide your portion to seven, or even to eight, for you do not know what misfortune may occur on the earth" (Ecclesiastes 11:2).

"Develop your business first before building your house" (Proverbs 24:27, TLB).

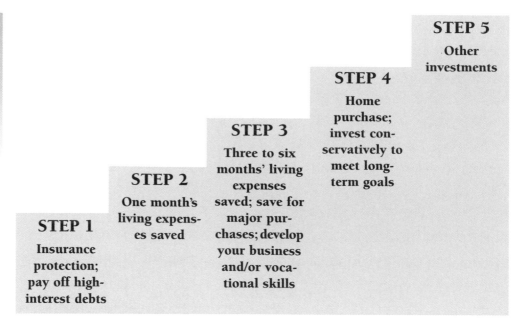

STEP 1
Insurance protection; pay off high-interest debts

STEP 2
One month's living expenses saved

STEP 3
Three to six months' living expenses saved; save for major purchases; develop your business and/or vocational skills

STEP 4
Home purchase; invest conservatively to meet long-term goals

STEP 5
Other investments

Counting the cost

With every investment there are costs: financial, time commitments, efforts required, and even emotional stress. For example, the purchase of a rental house will require time and effort to lease and maintain. If the tenant is irresponsible, you may have to try to collect rent from someone who does not want to pay—talk about emotions flaring! Before you decide on any investment, carefully consider all the costs.

Build business before building your house

A principle in Scripture is to invest in your vocation or business, which will be productive, then build your house: *"Develop your business first before building your house"* (Proverbs 24:27, TLB). Many people today reverse this order. The large house, purchased too early in life, tends to require so much money that investing in a vocation or business is seriously hampered.

GAMBLING AND LOTTERIES

Government-sanctioned lotteries and gambling of all types are sweeping our country. The Bible does not specifically prohibit gambling. However, many who gamble do so in an attempt to *get rich quick*. This is a violation of Scripture.

Sadly, hundreds of thousands of compulsive gamblers regularly deplete their family income. Their stories are heart breaking. We should not expose ourselves to the risk of becoming compulsive gamblers; nor should we support an industry that enslaves so many.

TAXES

What is the biblical perspective on paying taxes? That is the same question that was asked of Jesus. *"Is it lawful for us to pay taxes to Caesar or not? . . . [Jesus] said to them, 'Show Me a denarius [Roman coin]. Whose likeness and inscription does it have?' They said, 'Caesar's.' And He said to them. 'Then give to Caesar the things that are Caesar's' "* (Luke 20:22-25). This is an example of the contrast between the practices of our society and the teaching of Scripture. Avoid paying taxes at any cost, people rationalize. After all, the government squanders much of what it collects.

However, we are responsible to pay our taxes. *"Every person is to be in subjection to the governing authorities. For there is no authority except from God, and those which exist are established by God . . . Because of this you also pay taxes, for rulers are servants of God, devoting themselves to this very thing. Render to all what is due them: tax to whom tax is due"* (Romans 13:1,6-7). It is permissible to reduce your taxes by using legal tax deductions, but Christians should be careful not to make unwise decisions simply to avoid paying taxes.

INSURANCE

Two questions are often asked: "Is insurance scriptural?" and "Does owning insurance reflect a lack of faith?" The answer is both yes and no. Insurance is not referred to in Scripture; however, the principle of future provision is. Owning insurance does not necessarily reflect a lack of faith in God.

"Give to Caesar the things that are Caesar's" (Luke 20:25).

Unfortunately, some have developed an insurance ethic that rationalizes cheating insurance companies. People are willing to use insurance funds to do things they would never consider doing with their own money.

A coaching participant shared what he called God's "answer to prayer." His car had been damaged in an airport parking lot, and the perpetrator didn't leave a note. He didn't carry collision insurance that would cover the damage because of the cost; so, he drove the car as it was for several weeks. Then he was hit from the rear in a multiple-car collision. Although the damage from the collision was slight, in getting an estimate for damages he neglected to mention the previous damage done at the airport. Consequently, his entire car was repaired by the insurance of the car that struck him from the rear. "What an answer from the Lord!" he exclaimed.

Why is it people are tempted to cheat and then rationalize it? Insurance companies are perceived to be wealthy and impersonal. Also, since they don't actually know anyone at the insurance company, they believe it's not like cheating a person. Cheating an insurance company is wrong!

Types of insurance

There are many types of insurance. Some of the most common are homeowner's, automobile, liability, life, health, disability, and business.

The amount and type of insurance you carry will be dictated by your needs and your budget. Many cannot afford to purchase all the insurance they may need. If you are in this situation, prayerfully determine what insurance you can afford and which type you should purchase initially.

Because insurance can be complex and difficult to understand, seek experienced counsel when making your insurance decisions.

▪ Health insurance

Health insurance pays for the doctor, hospital, and other related expenses. The cost of health care, particularly if there is a major illness, can be very expensive. It's important to have health insurance if at all possible.

We must use health insurance as carefully as we would our own money. Never sign a bill without thoroughly reviewing it. Require documentation for every expenditure. Ask for a reasonable estimate before committing to any health care plan or hospital stay. If you are an employer, check into higher deductible plans that may cost less but provide better catastrophe care.

▪ Life insurance

The purpose of life insurance is to provide for the survivors' living expenses and lump-sum needs, if the bread winner dies. A lump-sum need is any debt, educational expense, or other obligation that would not be a normal recurring expense that you would like to fund or pay off. We recommend that you carry adequate, but not excessive, life insurance.

HONESTY

All of us have to make daily decisions about whether to handle money honestly. Do you tell the cashier at the store when you receive too much change? Have you ever tried to sell something and been tempted not to tell the whole truth because you might have lost the sale?

These decisions are made more difficult because everyone around us

Because insurance can be complex and difficult to understand, seek experienced counsel when making your insurance decisions.

seems to be acting dishonestly. This is in sharp contrast to the standard we find in Scripture. God demands absolute honesty. *"The Lord loathes all cheating and dishonesty"* (Proverbs 20:23, TLB). And Proverbs 12:22 states, *"Lying lips are an abomination to the Lord."* And in Proverbs 6:16-17 we read, *"The Lord hates . . . a lying tongue."*

The God of truth

Truthfulness is one of God's attributes. He is repeatedly identified as the God of truth. *"I am . . . the truth"* (John 14:6). Moreover, the Lord commands us to reflect His honest and holy character: *"Be holy yourselves also in all your behavior; because it is written, 'You shall be holy, for I am holy' "* (1 Peter 1:15-16).

Absolute honesty

God has imposed the standard of absolute honesty for Christians, because we cannot disobey by practicing dishonesty and still love God. When being dishonest, we are acting as if the living God doesn't even exist! We believe that God is not able to provide exactly what we need, even though He has promised to do so (Matthew 6:33). We decide to take things into our own hands and do it in our own dishonest way. We are also acting as if God is incapable of discovering our dishonesty and is powerless to discipline us. If we really believe God will discipline us, then we will not consider acting dishonestly.

Honest behavior is an issue of faith. An honest decision may look foolish in light of the circumstances we can observe. But the godly person has mastered the art of considering another fact which is valid, even though invisible: the person of Jesus Christ. Every honest decision affirms and strengthens our faith in the living God and helps us grow into a closer relationship with Christ. However, if we choose to be dishonest, we essentially deny our Lord. It is impossible to love God with all our hearts, if at the same time we are dishonest and act as if He does not exist.

God requires us to be *absolutely honest,* because even the smallest act of dishonesty is sin. And even the smallest sin interrupts our fellowship with the Lord and harms our maturity in Christ. The smallest white lie will harden our hearts, making our consciences increasingly insensitive to sin and deafening our ears to the still small voice of the Lord. This single cancer cell of small dishonesty multiplies and spreads to greater dishonesty. *"Whoever is dishonest with very little will also be dishonest with much"* (Luke 16:10, NIV).

Every honest decision affirms and strengthens our faith in the living God and helps us grow into a closer relationship with Christ.

The people of God must be honest in even the smallest, seemingly inconsequential matters.

An event in Abraham's life will challenge us to be honest in small matters. In Genesis 14 the king of Sodom offered Abraham all the goods Abraham recovered when he returned from successfully rescuing the people of Sodom. But Abraham responded to the king, *"I have sworn to the Lord God Most High, possessor of heaven and earth, that I will not take a thread or a sandal thong or anything that is yours"* (Genesis 14:22-23).

Just as Abraham was unwilling to take so much as a thread or a sandal thong, we challenge you to make a similar commitment in this area of honesty. Covenant not to steal a stamp or a photocopy or a paper clip or a long distance telephone call or a penny from your employer, the government, or anyone else. The people of God must be honest in even the smallest, seemingly inconsequential matters.

APPLYING THE PRINCIPLES TO MONEY MAP COACHING

Communicate these principles to your coaching participants.

1. The Scriptures encourage us to save regularly.

2. Work to save three to six months of income for emergencies.

3. Investing is biblically permissible.

4. Invest within the framework of God's financial principles.

5. Never gamble, even for entertainment.

6. Pay the taxes you owe the government.

7. Carry adequate insurance for your needs.

8. Be absolutely honest in all financial matters.

HOW WOULD YOU RESPOND TO A COACHING PARTICIPANT?

The following questions and views are commonly expressed during Money Map coaching sessions. Describe how you would respond to each.

1. I don't have enough income to be able to save anything. What should I do?

2. I enjoy playing golf. I know it's expensive, but it is the only way I can relax.

3. I have a good retirement fund set aside, but I believe that I need to increase my savings before I lose my health or am unable to work.

4. We believe that a vacation home is a good investment.

5. Since this investment is so good, I have no choice but to borrow money to take advantage of this opportunity.

   Please review this section until you are thoroughly familiar with the principles you will use in Money Map coaching sessions.

ANSWERS TO THE QUESTIONS

1. **Read *Genesis 41:34-36; Proverbs 21:20;* and *Proverbs 30:24-25.***
   What do these passages communicate to you about savings?

   Genesis 41:34-36—[Joseph saved during a time of plenty to prepare for a coming famine.]

   Proverbs 21:20—[Those who are wise save, but the foolish only consume.]

   Proverbs 30:24-25—[Ants are commended as wise because they save.]

2. **Read *Proverbs 21:5; Proverbs 24:27; Proverbs 27:23-24;* and *Ecclesiastes 11:2.***
   What investment principle(s) can you identify from each of these verses, and how will you apply each principle to your life?

   Proverbs 21:5—[Be a diligent, steady plodder and not hasty in investing.]

   Proverbs 24:27—[Develop your means of producing an income before securing a house.]

   Proverbs 27:23-24—[Know the status of your assets at all times.]

   Ecclesiastes 11:2—[Diversify your investments.]

3. **Read *Matthew 5:25-26* and *Romans 13:1-7.***
   Does the Lord require us to pay taxes to the government? Why?

   [The Lord requires us to pay taxes because He has instituted the government to serve people. The consequence of tax evasion is punishment.]

   Do you think it is biblically permissible to reduce your taxes by using legal tax deductions? Why?

   [The government has authorized the use of legal tax deductions to reduce taxes and as an incentive for certain actions.]

4. Gambling is defined as playing games of chance for money and betting. Some of today's most common forms of gambling are casino wagering, betting on sporting events, horse races, dog races, and state-run lotteries. What are some of the motivations that cause people to gamble?

   [People are motivated to gamble by the desire to get rich quick, greed, and by the prospect of getting something for nothing. Many want to become wealthy so they can quit working.]

   Do these motives please the Lord? Why?

   [The motives do not please the Lord because they are contrary to His principles found in the Bible.]

   Read *Proverbs 28:20* and *Proverbs 28:22.*
   According to these passages, why do you think a godly person should not gamble (play lotteries, bet on sporting events)?

[A person who hastens after wealth is identified as evil and will experience poverty. Never bet one penny. State lotteries are particularly enticing because they have been legalized by the government and glamorized by the media.]

How does gambing contradict the scriptural principles of working diligently and being a faithful steward of the Lord's possessions?

[Gambling is in direct opposition to the scriptural principles of diligent work and faithful stewardship. No productive work is required in gambling; thus, a person's character is not properly developed. The odds of winning are absurdly low, and a gambler is wasting the possessions the Lord has entrusted to him.]

5. **Read *Leviticus 19:11-13* and *Ephesians 4:25*.**

   What do these verses communicate to you about God's demand for honesty?

   > *Leviticus 19:11-13—[The Lord commands us to be honest.]*

   > *Ephesians 4:25—[We are not to lie to one another.]*

ANSWERS TO: HOW WOULD YOU RESPOND TO A COACHING PARTICIPANT?

1. I don't have enough income to be able to save anything. What should I do?

   [Even if it is a very small amount, begin the habit of saving. The Luke 16:10 principle of faithfulness in a small thing gives the Lord the freedom to entrust you with larger responsibilities.]

2. I enjoy playing golf. I know it's expensive, but it is the only way I can relax.

   [It is acceptable to play golf if it's within your budget. If you cannot afford it, you may need to play less frequently or at a less expensive course. If your budget is very tight, discontinue it all together.]

3. I have a good retirement fund set aside, but I believe that I need to increase my savings before I lose my health or am unable to work.

   [Planning for the future is wise and is strongly suggested in Scripture. But we balance planning for the future with trust in God's provision.]

4. We believe that a vacation home is a good investment.

   [Research the resale market for the vacation home you want to buy and the long-term prospect for the vacation area. Then determine if you can afford this investment and if it fits your personality. A vacation home typically requires time and effort to maintain. Be sure not to sign surety, especially for a non-necessity.]

5. Since this investment is so good, I have no choice but to borrow money to take advantage of this opportunity.

   [Never borrow to invest unless the investment is the sole security for the debt.]

FAMILY

Principle to Memorize

*We should serve our families and help them grow
in their relationship with Christ.*

Scripture to Memorize

*"Train up a child in the way he should go, even when he
is old he will not depart from it"* (Proverbs 22:6).

ASSIGNMENT: *Family Financial Workbook*

Chapter Seven *Budget Challenges*

This chapter deals with budgeting challenges. Until coaching participants are able to build up a reserve, borrowing from one category to supplement another will happen. This should not become a habit, or the reason for using a budget will be defeated. Be sure to examine the guideline percentage levels for Housing, Food, and Automobiles. If all of these categories are excessive, a balanced budget will be difficult to maintain. Carefully review the section on budgeting on a variable income.

Chapters Eight and Nine provide very helpful resources and suggestions.

Chapter Ten contains the forms. Familiarize yourself with these forms.

QUESTIONS TO ANSWER

1. **Read** *Matthew 15:4-6* **and** *1 Timothy 5:8*.
    Does the Bible require us to take care of our family members?

    How does this apply in your situation?

2. **Read** *Proverbs 1:8-9*.
    Who should be among your counselors?

In your opinion, who should be the number one human counselor of a husband? Of a wife? Why?

If you are married, on a scale of 1 to 10 (10 being the best) how would you rate your communication with your spouse concerning money? What will you do to improve this communcation?

3. **Read *Deuteronomy 6:6-7*; *Deuteronomy 11:18-19*; *Proverbs 22:6*; and *Ephesians 6:4*.** According to these passages, who is responsible for teaching children how to handle money from a biblical perspective?

    Stop and reflect for a few minutes: Describe how well were you prepared to manage money when you first left home as a young person?

4. **Describe how you are going to teach children to:**

    Give generously—

    Spend wisely—

    Keep out of debt—

    Save—

    Invest—

5. **Read *Genesis 24:35-36; Proverbs 13:22;* and *2 Corinthians 12:14.***
   Should parents attempt to leave a material inheritance to their children?

   How are you going to implement this principle?

   Then read *Proverbs 20:21* and *Galatians 4:1-2.* What caution should a parent exercise?

   Proverbs 20:21—

   Galatians 4:1-2—

NOTES TO READ

In our culture we are experiencing a tragic breakdown in the area of taking care of our family. Husbands have failed to provide for their wives; parents have neglected their children; and grown sons and daughters have forsaken their elderly parents. Such neglect is solemnly condemned. *"If anyone does not provide for his own, and especially for those of his household, he has denied the faith and is worse than an unbeliever"* (1 Timothy 5:8). Meeting the needs of your family and relatives is a priority and one in which there should be no compromise.

HUSBAND AND WIFE COMMUNICATION

In marriage, God's Word says that two people become one. *"For this reason a man shall leave his father and his mother, and be joined to his wife; and they shall become one flesh"* (Genesis 2:24). Marriage has been compared to the left and right hands of the same person. They are perfectly matched but totally opposite. One hand working alone will not accomplish half as much as two. Many tasks are impossible without two hands working together.

It is amazing to observe how opposite husbands and wives usually are. One gets up early; the other stays in bed. One has a good sense of direction; the other gets lost. One is punctual; the other is late. There is an old cliché that says, "If husband and wife are identical, one of them is unnecessary."

Unfortunately, in many marriages one personality overwhelms the other and communication is damaged. If a couple knows how to communicate, this will keep them out of most financial difficulties. For example, many women dislike being in debt, and if they find themselves in financial trouble they will quickly seek help and do what is necessary to correct the situation. Not so with many men whose pride or indifference keep them from seeking help.

Turning it around

The first step is to recognize that being different is not being inferior. God intentionally placed different gifts and abilities in the marriage, and it takes two people working as one to succeed. Honesty between partners is an absolute necessity. Almost anyone can handle a situation if he

"For this reason a man shall leave his father and his mother, and be joined to his wife; and they shall become one flesh" (Genesis 2:24).

or she knows the facts and is a part of the planning and solution. Trust is destroyed if one deceives the other and this is discovered.

If the problems and the communication gap are intense, most couples will need outside help. Seeking counsel for marriage or financial problems should be as accepted as seeking medical counsel.

Set goals

In order to establish good communication about finances in the home, husband and wife together must establish specific goals. Plan a weekend alone together when every aspect of the finances can be discussed and some specific goals set. Remember that financial planning involves two people, seeking mutually compatible goals, under the umbrella of God's plan for their lives.

Quite often a "reasonable compromise" will be necessary when establishing goals. One may be more committed to giving than the other. A home may be more important to one. A bass boat may seem like a basic necessity to the other. One helpful method is for both spouses to write down the areas they can agree on first, before moving on to more controversial areas. When an impasse is reached over an area, such as clothing or education, each should list possible solutions. Together they should pray for the Lord's direction and then seek to discover what they can agree on.

Financial problems

If serious problems exist, the husband must assume the burden of interfacing with the creditors. He is to act as a buffer for his wife. One of the greatest causes of stress in many women is creditor pressure. The wife's responsibility is assisting and implementing the necessary financial controls, not worrying about them.

Bookkeeping

Assuming that there are no major financial problems, the task of record-keeping should fall to the one best equipped to do it. Often the wife is a better bookkeeper. If so, and both agree, she should maintain the records after a workable budget has been agreed on. They should regularly review the budget and discuss any problems.

Seeking counsel of spouse

If you are married, the first person you need to consult is your spouse. Regardless of your spouse's business background or financial aptitude, you should cultivate and seek your spouse's counsel. Women tend to be

In order to establish good communication about finances in the home, husband and wife together must establish specific goals.

gifted with a wonderfully sensitive and intuitive nature that is usually very accurate. Men tend to focus objectively on the facts. The husband and wife need each other to achieve the proper balance for a correct decision. The Lord honors the wife's "office" or "position" as helpmate to her husand. Many times the Lord communicates most clearly to the husband through his wife.

The husband and wife should agree on major decisions, because they both will exierence the consequences. Even if their choice proves to be disastrous, their relationship remains intact. There are no grounds for an "I told you so" response.

TRAINING CHILDREN

Each generation is responsible for passing on the Gospel and the truths of Scripture, including God's financial principles, to its children. Proverbs 22:6 reads, *"Train up a child in the way he should go, even when he is old he will not depart from it."*

Answer this question: When you left home, how well prepared were you to make financial decisions? Parents and teachers spend years preparing youth for occupations but generally less than a few hours teaching children the value and use of the money they will earn during their careers. To teach biblical principles of handling money, parents should use these three methods: verbal communication, modeling, and practical experience.

Verbal communication

The Lord charged the Israelites, *"These words, which I am commanding you today, shall be on your heart; and you shall teach them diligently to your sons and shall talk of them when you sit in your house and when you walk by the way and when you lie down and when you rise up"* (Deuteronomy 6:6-7). We must verbally instruct our children in the ways of the Lord, but children need more than mere verbal instruction; they also need a good example.

Modeling

Children soak up parental attitudes toward money like a sponge soaks up water. Parents need to be models of how to handle money faithfully. Paul recognized the importance of example when he said, *"Be imitators of me, just as I also am of Christ"* (1 Corinthians 11:1).

Luke 6:40 is a challenging passage for parents. It reads, *"Everyone, after he has been fully trained, will be like his teacher."* Another way of say-

> *Women tend to be gifted with a wonderfully sensitive and intuitive nature that is usually very accurate.*

ing this is that we can teach what we believe, but we only reproduce who we are. We must be good models. When parents encounter challenges, the way they respond in front of their children will demonstrate whether Christ is really Lord in their lives.

Practical experiences

Children then need to be given opportunities to apply what they have heard and seen. Learning to handle money should be part of a child's education. This is a part that the parents must direct themselves and not delegate to teachers, because spending experiences are found outside the classroom. Consider five areas where this is possible.

1. Income

As soon as a child is ready for school, he or she should begin to receive an income to manage. The amount of the income will vary according to such factors as the child's age, his or her ability to earn, and the financial circumstances of the family. However, the amount of the income is not as important as the responsibility of handling money. At first it is a new experience, and the child will make many mistakes. Do not hesitate to let the "law of natural consequences" run its course. You are going to be tempted to help your child when he or she spends all the income the first day on an unwise purchase. *But do not bail the child out!* Mistakes will be the best teacher.

Parents should establish boundaries and offer advice on how to spend money, but your child must have freedom of choice within those boundaries. Excessive restrictions will only reduce his or her opportunities to learn by experience. The first few pennies and nickels will make a lasting impression.

2. Budgeting

When children start to receive an income, teach them how to budget.

Begin with a simple bank consisting of three categories, each labeled separately—GIVE, SAVE, and SPEND. The child distributes a portion of the income into each section. Thus a simple budget is established by using visual control. Even a six-year-old can understand this method, because when there is no more money to spend the spending section is empty!

During the budget training, teach your child to become a wise con-

Learning to handle money should be part of a child's education.

sumer. Teach shopping skills, the ability to distinguish needs from wants, and the fine art of waiting on the Lord to provide. Warn about the powerful influence of advertising and the danger of impulse spending.

3. Saving and investing

The habit of saving should be established as soon as a child receives an income. It is helpful to open a savings account in the child's name at this time. As children mature, they also should be exposed to various types of investments: stocks, bonds, real estate. Teach your children the benefits of compounding interest. If they grasp this concept and become faithful savers, they will enjoy financial stability as adults.

4. Debt

It is also important to teach the cost of money and how difficult it is to get out of debt. A father loaned his son and daughter the money to buy bicycles. He drew up a credit agreement with a schedule for repayment of the loan, including the interest charged. After they went through the long, difficult process of paying off the loan, the family celebrated with a "mortgage burning" ceremony at a family picnic. The father said that his children appreciated those bikes more than any of their possessions and vowed to avoid debt in the future.

5. Giving

The best time to establish the personal habit of giving is when you are young. It is helpful for children to give a portion of their gifts to a tangible need they can visualize. For example, children understand the impact of their gifts when their contributions are helping to build the church they can see under construction or buying food for a needy family they know.

Richard Halverson, U.S. Senate chaplain, gave his son Chris this rich heritage as a child. Chris gave money to support Kim, an orphan who had lost his sight during the Korean War. Chris was taught to feel that Kim was like an adopted brother. One Christmas, Chris bought Kim a harmonica. He cherished this gift from Chris and learned to play it well. Today, Kim is an evangelist and his presentation of the Gospel includes playing the harmonica. By being trained to give as a youth, Chris experienced firsthand the value of meeting people's needs; and, as a result of faithful giving, he saw God change lives.

The habit of saving should be established as soon as a child receives an income.

We recommend a family time each week for dedicating that week's gifts to the Lord. It is important for children to participate in this time. The more involvement children can have with their parents in the proper handling of money, the better habits they will have as adults.

Any track coach will tell you that relay races are won or lost in the passing of the baton from one runner to another. Seldom is the baton dropped, once it is firmly in the grasp of a sprinting runner. If it is going to be dropped, it is in the exchange between the runners. As parents we have the responsibility to pass the baton of practical biblical truths to our children. At times during the training, it seems as if there is little progress. But be *consistent* and *persistent!*

INHERITANCE

Parents should attempt to leave a material inheritance to their children. *"A good man leaves an inheritance to his children's children"* (Proverbs 13:22). The inheritance should not be dispensed until the child has been thoroughly trained to be a wise steward. *"An inheritance gained hurriedly at the beginning will not be blessed in the end"* (Proverbs 20:21). You should make provision in your will for distributing an inheritance over several years or until the heir is mature enough to handle the responsibility of money. Select those you trust to supervise the youth until he is a capable steward. *"Now I say, as long as the heir is a child, he does not differ at all from a slave although he is owner of everything, but he is under guardians and managers until the date set by the father"* (Galatians 4:1-2).

Wills

As Isaiah told Hezekiah, *"Thus says the Lord, 'Set your house in order, for you shall die' "* (2 Kings 20:1). Some day, unless the Lord returns first, you will die. One of the greatest gifts you can leave your loved ones for that emotional time will be an organized estate and a properly prepared will or trust. If you do not have a current will or trust, please make an appointment with an attorney this week to prepare one.

APPLYING THE PRINCIPLES TO MONEY MAP COACHING
Communicate these principles to your coaching participants.

1. We have the responsibility to care for our family members.

2. The husband and wife are one. Our spouses should be our number one counselors.

3. Parents are responsible to train their children how to handle money

We recommend a family time each week for dedicating that week's gifts to the Lord.

God's way. They should effectively model these principles to their children.

4. If we allow our children to live financially undisciplined lifestyles, we do them a great disservice. When they become adults, they will struggle financially.

5. Parents should attempt to leave a financial inheritance to their children.

6. Every adult should have a will.

HOW WOULD YOU RESPOND TO A COACHING PARTICIPANT?

The following questions and views are commonly expressed during Money Map coaching sessions. Describe how you would respond to each.

1. I want my children to enjoy life. They can learn the hard facts of life when they get older.

2. I am going to work as much as I can so my children won't have to struggle like I had to.

3. It seems that all our friends have their children in Christian schools. We want to send our kids there, but we don't have enough money and don't want to borrow.

4. I want to leave my children and grandchildren a good inheritance, but I also want to spend as much time with them as I can while they are small.

5. My husband and I should work together to make financial decisions, but we get into a lot of arguments because I just don't understand financial matters.

6. Should we let our children know what we are giving and tithing?

7. We need to enlarge our house to take care of our parents when they are elderly. We can borrow on the equity in our house to cover the costs.

8. My children are teased when they don't wear the latest styles.

Please review this section until you are thoroughly familiar with the principles that you will use in Money Map coaching sessions.

ANSWERS TO THE QUESTIONS

1. **Read *Matthew 15:4-6* and *1 Timothy 5:8*.**

   Does the Bible require us to take care of our family members?

   [Yes, we are required to take care of our families.]

2. **Read *Proverbs 1:8-9*.**

   Who should be among your counselors?

   [Our parents.]

   In your opinion, who should be the number one human counselor of a husband? Of a wife? Why?

   [Our spouses should be our number one human counselors. They know us well and will experience the consequences of our financial decisions. Because the husband and wife are one, God will often communicate His will through the spouse.]

3. **Read *Deuteronomy 6:6-7*; *Deuteronomy 11:18-19*; *Proverbs 22:6*; and *Ephesians 6:4*.**

   According to these passages, who is responsible for teaching children how to handle money from a biblical perspective?

   [It is the responsibility of the parents. It is wise to establish a strategy for independence—the goal of having each child independently managing his or her finances (with the exception of food and housing) by the senior year in high school.]

   Stop and reflect for a few minutes: Describe how well were you prepared to manage money when you first left home as a young person?

   [Most children leave home ill-equipped to manage money.]

5. **Read *Genesis 24:35-36*; *Proverbs 13:22*; and *2 Corinthians 12:14*.**

   Should parents attempt to leave a material inheritance to their children?

   [Yes, parents should try to leave a material inheritance to their children.]

   Then read *Proverbs 20:21* and *Galatians 4:1-2*. What caution should a parent exercise?

   Proverbs 20:21—*[An inheritance should not be given into a child's care until the child is mature enough to manage the inheritance faithfully.]*

   Galatians 4:1-2—*[The appointment of a guardian through a will or trust helps ensure a child's maturity before receiving an inheritance.]*

ANSWERS TO: HOW WOULD YOU RESPOND TO A COACHING PARTICIPANT?

1. I want my children to enjoy life. They can learn the hard facts of life when they get older.

   [Parents are to love and train their children in the ways of the Lord. There is a balance in this training. Children need to learn to handle responsibility and work hard. Yet they should also be given the opportunity to enjoy the Lord, their family, and life.]

2. I am going to work as much as I can so my children won't have to struggle like I had to.

   [God established work as an important part of our lives. But we must balance work with spending time with our children. We must provide for their material needs and train them to live godly lives. This requires a regular investment of time with them.]

3. It seems as if all our friends have their children in Christian schools. We want to send our kids there, but we don't have enough money and don't want to borrow.

   [If it is God's will for them to be in a Christian school, He will provide the necessary funds without using debt.]

4. I want to leave my children and grandchildren a good inheritance, but I also want to spend as much time with them as I can while they are small.

   [Leaving a godly inheritance means more than leaving money. Spending time and teaching children while they are small will give them the foundation they need for living a productive and satisfied life.]

5. My husband and I should work together to make financial decisions, but we get into a lot of arguments because I just don't understand financial matters.

   [It is important for the spouse who understands financial matters to help the other. Teaching is a process and it takes time to learn.]

6. Should we let our children know what we are giving and tithing?

   [Yes, whenever possible the parents should model handling money God's way.]

7. We need to enlarge our house to take care of our parents when they are elderly. We can borrow on the equity in our house to cover the costs.

   [If this is not an immediate need, do not place additional debt on your house. Build the addition as God provides the resources.]

8. My children are teased when they don't wear the latest styles.

   [You can use this as an opportunity to teach your children to be thankful for what the Lord has provided, to take care of what they have (Luke 16:10), and to be kind to those less fortunate.]

WORK
YOU ARE UNIQUELY MADE

Principle to Memorize

The Lord wants us to work hard for His glory.
God has made each of us uniquely for His purpose.

Scripture to Memorize

"Whatever you do, do your work heartily, as for
the Lord rather than for men. . . . It is the Lord Christ
whom you serve" (Colossians 3:23-24).

ASSIGNMENT

1. Complete the *Personality I.D.*
2. Complete *You Are Uniquely Made* on pages 93 to 96.

QUESTIONS TO ANSWER

1. **Read *Genesis 2:15*.**

   Did the Lord first institute work prior to sin entering the world? Why is this important to recognize?

2. **Read *Genesis 3:17-19*.**

   What was the consequence of sin on work?

3. **Read *Genesis 39:2-5*; *Exodus 36:1-2*; and *Psalm 75:6-7*.**

   What do each of these verses tell us about the Lord's involvement in our work?

Genesis 39:2-5—

Exodus 36:1-2—

Psalm 75:6-7—

How will this perspective impact your work?

4. **Read *Exodus 20:9* and *2 Thessalonians 3:10-12*.**
   What do these passages communicate to you about work?

   Exodus 20:9—

   2 Thessalonians 3:10-12—

5. **Read *Proverbs 6:6-11*; *Proverbs 18:9*; and *2 Thessalonians 3:7-9*.**
   What is God's perspective on working hard?

   Proverbs 6:6-11—

   Proverbs 18:9—

   2 Thessalonians 3:7-9—

Do you work hard? If not, describe what steps you will take to improve your work habits.

6. **Read *Colossians 3:23-24.***

For whom do you really work?

In light of this, should we attempt to be excellent in our work? Are you? If not, what will you do to become excellent?

7. **Read *Exodus 34:21.***

What does this verse communicate to you about rest?

Do you get sufficient rest?

How do you guard against overwork?

8. **Read *2 Corinthians 6:14-18.***

How does this concept of "yoking," of "being bound together," apply to partnerships in business and work?

How does this apply to your current situation?

9. **Read** *Ephesians 2:10.*
   Has the Lord created and equipped you for specific good works?

   How do you think you can identify the good works He intends for you to do?

NOTES TO READ

Over a lifetime, the average person spends 100,000 hours working. Most of an adult's life is involved in work, but often with the job comes some degree of dissatisfaction. Boredom, lack of fulfillment, inadequate wages, overwork, and countless other pressures have contributed to this high level of discontent. To find satisfaction in our work and to place ourselves in a position in which the Lord can prosper us, we need to understand what Scripture teaches.

BIBLICAL PERSPECTIVE OF WORK

Even before sin entered the human race, God instituted work. *"The Lord God took the man and put him into the garden of Eden to cultivate it and keep it"* (Genesis 2:15). The very first thing the Lord did with Adam was to put him to work. Despite what many have come to think, work was initiated for our benefit in the sinless environment of the garden of Eden. Work is not a result of the curse!

After the fall, work became more difficult. *"Cursed is the ground because of you; in toil you will eat of it all the days of your life. Both thorns and thistles it shall grow for you; and you will eat the plants of the field; by the sweat of your face you will eat bread"* (Genesis 3:17-19).

Work is so important that in Exodus 34:21 God gives this command: *"You shall work six days."* The Old Testament believer was required to work six days. In the New Testament we discover that Paul is just as direct when he says, *"If anyone is not willing to work, then he is not to eat either"* (2 Thessalonians 3:10). Examine the verse carefully. It says, *"If anyone is not willing to work."* It does not say, "If anyone *cannot* work." This principle does not apply to those who are physically or mentally unable to work. It is for those who are able but choose not to work.

One of the primary purposes of work is to develop the character of the worker. While the carpenter is building a house, the house is also building the carpenter. His skill, diligence, manual dexterity, and judgment are refined. A job is not merely a task designed to earn money; it's also intended to produce godly character in the life of a worker.

The Lord in our work

Scripture also reveals that the Lord has three responsibilities in our work.

> *"The Lord God took the man and put him into the garden of Eden to cultivate it and keep it"* (Genesis 2:15).

1. God gives job skills

Exodus 36:1 illustrates this truth: *"Every skillful person in whom the Lord has put skill and understanding to know how to perform all the work."* God has given each of us unique skills. People have a wide variety of abilities, manual skills, and intellectual capacities. It is not a matter of one person being better than another; it is simply a matter of having received different abilities.

2. God gives success

The life of Joseph is a perfect example of God helping a person to succeed. *"The Lord was with Joseph, so he became a successful man . . . Now his master saw that the Lord was with him and how the Lord caused all that he did to prosper in his hand"* (Genesis 39:2-3). We have certain job responsibilities, but we need to recognize that it is ultimately God who gives us success.

3. God controls promotion

In Psalm 75:6-7 we read, *"Promotion and power come from nowhere on earth, but only from God"* (TLB). As surprising as it may be, our bosses are not who control whether we will be promoted. Understanding this should have a tremendous impact on the way we perform as employees. Most people find this hard to believe. Our culture leaves God out of work. People believe they alone control their successes and promotions and are solely responsible for their job skills. However, those with a biblical understanding will approach work with an entirely different frame of reference.

One of the major reasons people experience stress and frustration in their jobs is because they don't understand God's part in work. Stop reading for a few minutes and think about this: God gives us our skills and controls success and promotions. How should this perspective impact us and our jobs?

All honest professions are equally honorable

Scripture does not elevate any honest profession above another. A wide variety of vocations are represented in the Bible. David was a shepherd and a king. Luke was a doctor. Lydia was a retailer who sold purple fabric. Daniel was a government worker. Paul was a tentmaker. Amos was a fig-picker. If God can use a fig-picker, he can certainly use us in our jobs! And, finally, the Lord Jesus was a carpenter.

In God's economy there is equal dignity in the labor of the automobile mechanic and the president of General Motors, as the pastor of a church and as a church secretary.

We work for the Lord

Scripture reveals that in our work we actually are serving the Lord and not people. *"Whatever you do, do your work heartily, as for the Lord rather than for men. . . . It is the Lord Christ whom you serve"* (Colossians 3:23-24). Recognizing that we are actually working for the Lord has profound implications.

Consider your attitude toward work. If you could see the person of Jesus Christ as your boss, would you try to be more faithful in your job? The most important question you need to answer every day as you begin your work is this: For whom do I work? You work for Christ.

Work hard

"Whatever your hand finds to do, do it with all your might" (Ecclesiastes 9:10). *"The precious possession of a man is diligence"* (Proverbs 12:27). In Scripture hard work and diligence are encouraged while laziness is repeatedly condemned: *"He also who is slack in his work is brother to him who destroys"* (Proverbs 18:9).

Paul's life was an example of hard work. *"With labor and hardship we kept working night and day so that we would not be a burden to any of you . . . in order to offer ourselves as a model for you, so that you would follow our example"* (2 Thessalonians 3:8-9).

But do not overwork!

Hard work, however, must be balanced by the other priorities of life. Clearly our first priority is our relationship with the Lord. *"But seek first His kingdom and His righteousness"* (Matthew 6:33).

The second priority is the family. If your job demands so much of your time and energy that you neglect your relationship with Christ or your family, you are working too hard. You should determine whether the job is too demanding, or if your work habits need changing. If you tend to be a workaholic, take extra precautions to guard against forsaking the other priorities of life.

Exodus 34:21 reads, *"You shall work six days, but on the seventh day you shall rest; even during plowing time and harvest you shall rest."* This Old Testament principle of resting one day out of seven still has application for us today. This is difficult, particularly during *"plowing time or harvest,"*

> *"Whatever your hand finds to do, do it with all your might"* (Ecclesiastes 9:10).

when a project deadline is approaching or we are under unusual financial pressure.

Rest can become an issue of faith. Is the Lord able to make our six days of work more productive than seven days? Yes! The Lord instituted this weekly rest for our physical, mental, and spiritual health.

Being excellent in a mediocre world

"Do you see a man skilled in his work? He will stand before kings; he will not stand before obscure men" (Proverbs 22:29).

Many people in financial difficulty do not work hard in their jobs to be excellent. Therefore, their employers or customers are unwilling to compensate them well for average or slothful work.

God tells us in no uncertain terms *"Whatever you do, do your work heartily, as for the Lord rather than for men"* (Colossians 3:23). God demands that, no matter what others are doing, we serve Him through every action we take.

Many people do no more than is necessary to meet the minimum requirements of their jobs. Solomon described them well. *"Poor is he who works with a negligent hand, but the hand of the diligent makes rich"* (Proverbs 10:4).

Our work should be at such a level that people will never equate laziness and mediocrity with God. It means adopting a steward's attitude about everything we do. If the job is sweeping the floors, it should be done with such excellence that God is honored. *"Whether, then, you eat or drink or whatever you do, do all to the glory of God"* (1 Corinthians 10:31). To accept less dishonors God and does not properly reflect the Lord to those around us.

RETIREMENT

The goal of retirement is deeply ingrained in our culture. Many people retire at an arbitrary age and cease all labor in the pursuit of a life filled with leisure.

Scripture gives no examples of people retiring and gives only one reference to retirement, which is found in Numbers 8:24-26. The instruction here applied exclusively to the Levites who worked on the tabernacle. As long as one is physically and mentally capable, there is no scriptural basis for a person to retire and become unproductive. The concept of putting an older but able person "out to pasture" is unbibli-

"Do you see a man skilled in his work? He will stand before kings; he will not stand before obscure men" (Proverbs 22:29).

cal. Age is no obstacle in finishing the work the Lord has for you to accomplish. He will provide you with the necessary vigor and stamina. For example, Moses was 80 years old when he began his 40 years of leading the children of Israel.

In Scripture we do have the sense that the type or the intensity of work may change as we grow older—a shifting of the gears to a less demanding pace and becoming more of an elder seated at the gate (see Joshua 20:4). In this season of life we can actively employ the experience and wisdom gained during a lifetime. If we have sufficient income to meet our needs apart from our jobs, we may choose to leave our jobs to invest more time in serving others in whatever capacity the Lord directs.

As long as one is physically and mentaly capable, there is no scriptural basis for a person to retire and become unproductive.

PARTNERSHIPS

What does the Bible tell us about partnerships? Second Corinthians 6:14-17 reads, *"Do not be bound together* [unequally yoked] *with unbelievers; for what partnership have righteousness and lawlessness, or what fellowship has light with darkness? Or what harmony has Christ with Belial, or what has a believer in common with an unbeliever? Or what agreement has the temple of God with idols? For we are the temple of the living God; just as God said, 'I will dwell in them and walk among them; and I will be their God, and they shall be My people, therefore, come out from their midst and be separate,' says the Lord."* Scripture clearly discourages business partnerships with those who do not know Christ. Many have violated this principle and have suffered financially.

We should also be careful before entering into a partnership with another Christian. We should consider only a few people as potential partners. These are people you should know well. *Do not rush into a partnership!* Prayerfully evaluate what it may entail.

Before forming a partnership, transfer your understandings and agreements into written form. Develop this agreement with your future partner, and be sure to include a way to dissolve the partnership. If you are not able to agree in writing, do not become partners.

APPLYING THE PRINCIPLES TO MONEY MAP COACHING
Communicate these principles to your coaching participants.
1. We actually work for the Lord. We should attempt to be excellent in our work to glorify the Lord and reflect His excellence to those around us.

2. Everyone who is physically and mentally able should work hard. Some people who are in financial difficulty do not work hard enough.

3. Hard work should be balanced by the other priorities of life.

4. Retirement as it is practiced by many in our culture—living a life filled only by leisure—is not biblical. We should be productive as long as we are able.

5. Scripture discourages Christians from entering into partnerships with those who do not know Christ.

6. The Lord created each of us for particular purposes and equipped us with the skills and personalities to fulfill our calling.

7. It is important for the coach to understand his or her personality type and that of the coaching participant. It provides insight as to how the individual will react and view life.

8. Having a certain personality type does not excuse you from applying God's financial principles.

HOW WOULD YOU RESPOND TO A COACHING PARTICIPANT?

The following questions and views are commonly expressed during Money Map coaching sessions. Describe how you would respond to each.

1. What I do is not that important. It really doesn't matter if I am faithful to the Lord or with my money.

2. It seems that I spend all my time at work, but I never seem to get ahead.

3. I cannot understand why my coworker reacts that way!

4. I am in a position at work in which people look up to me and I need to maintain a certain lifestyle and image, even if I can't really afford it.

5. I have health problems so I need a job with a good medical insurance plan.

6. My husband is always looking for a way to make a lot of money. He won't get a regular job to provide for our family.

7. I like to be in charge of everything in which I am involved.

Please review this section until you are thoroughly familiar with the principles that you will use in Money Map coaching sessions.

ANSWERS TO THE QUESTIONS

1. **Read *Genesis 2:15*.**

   Did the Lord first institute work prior to sin entering the world? Why is this important to recognize?

   [Yes, work was instituted prior to sin entering the world. In the perfect, sinless environment of the garden of Eden, God created work for our benefit. Work is not a result of sin and the curse.]

2. **Read *Genesis 3:17-19*.**

   What was the consequence of sin on work?

   [Work became difficult as a result of sin.]

3. **Read *Genesis 39:2-5*; *Exodus 36:1-2*; and *Psalm 75:6-7*.**

   What do each of these verses tell us about the Lord's involvement in our work?

   Genesis 39:2-5—[The Lord gives us success.]

   Exodus 36:1-2—[God gives us our skills and abilities.]

   Psalm 75:6-7—[The Lord controls promotions.]

4. **Read *Exodus 20:9* and *2 Thessalonians 3:10-12*.**

   What do these passages communicate to you about work?

   Exodus 20:9—[Old Testament believers were required to work six days each week.]

   2 Thessalonians 3:10-12—[In the New Testament work is also required. This verse does not recommend hunger for those who cannot work because of physical or mental limitations— only those who are capable of working but choose not to work.]

5. **Read *Proverbs 6:6-11*; *Proverbs 18:9*; and *2 Thessalonians 3:7-9*.**

   What is God's perspective on working hard?

   Proverbs 6:6-11—[The ant is commended for its diligence and a lazy person will experience poverty.]

   Proverbs 18:9—[A lazy person is compared to one who destroys.]

   2 Thessalonians 3:7-9—[Paul was a model of hard work.]

6. **Read *Colossians 3:23-24*.**

   For whom do you really work?

   [We work for Jesus Christ.]

In light of this, should we attempt to be excellent in our work? Are you? If not, what will you do to become excellent?

[Yes, we should make every effort to be excellent in our work in order to glorify the Lord and reflect His excellence.]

7. **Read *Exodus 34:21*.**

   What does this verse communicate to you about rest?

   [Hard work should be balanced with adequate rest and tempered by other biblical priorities—even during busy times, one day of rest each week was required.]

8. **Read *2 Corinthians 6:14-18*.**

   How does this concept of "yoking" or "being bound together" apply to partnerships in business and work?

   [The principle of yoking applies to business partnerships. It is permissible for an employee to work for an employer who does not know Christ, but partnership with an unbeliever is discouraged.]

9. **Read *Ephesians 2:10*.**

   Has the Lord created and equipped you for specific good works?

   [Yes, the Lord has given us our unique abilities to fulfill His calling for us.]

   How do you think you can identify the good works He intends for you to do?

   [There are a number of steps you can take to discover your calling: (1) Pray for the Lord to make you aware of your purpose, (2) Seek the counsel of those who know you well, (3) Identify your spiritual gifts, (4) Take Crown's Career Direct testing.]

ANSWERS TO: HOW WOULD YOU RESPOND TO A COACHING PARTICIPANT?

1. What I do is not that important. It really doesn't matter if I am faithful to the Lord or with my money.

   [According to 1 Corinthians 12:13-18, as members of the body of Christ, we are all important for the building of God's kingdom.]

2. It seems that I spend all my time at work, but I never seem to get ahead.

   [We are to balance hard work with the other priorities in life. We have the responsibility to work hard and with excellence, and the Lord has the responsibility to promote us if He chooses.]

3. I cannot understand why my coworker reacts that way!

   [God made each of us with different personalities. As we interact with others, it is important to understand that people think differently and are motivated in different ways.]

4. I am in a position at work in which people look up to me and I need to maintain a certain lifestyle and image, even if I can't really afford it.

   [Scripture tells us that people look at the outside, but God looks at the heart. What is highly esteemed among people is detestable in God's sight. In our jobs we should humbly focus on serving the Lord and others. Beware of pride when the Lord elevates you to a position of influence.]

5. I have health problems, so I need a job with a good medical insurance plan.

   [This may be wise thinking. Medical costs are expensive, and providing for this can be a blessing to a family. Encourage the coaching participant to pray specifically for God's direction during the job search.]

6. My husband is always looking for a way to make a lot of money. He won't get a regular job to provide for our family.

   [Some people try to get rich quick and others are simply lazy. Both violate Scripture. These people need to have jobs that meet the needs of their families. Once this is accomplished, they may investigate ways to earn additional income.]

7. I like to be in charge of everything in which I am involved.

   [This may be the way the Lord made you. Although we are all different, no personality type is superior to another. If we ignore the way God made us, then our effectiveness will be limited.]

You Are Uniquely Made

Complete the *Personality I.D.*® booklet. Take time to read the information provided in the booklet and the information that follows. You will find that although everyone has personality traits that fit within certain categories, everyone is unique.

The Money Map Coach's personality has a significant impact on how he or she conducts Money Map coaching. For example, do you attend to detail or do you look at the big picture? The coach's personality is covered here.

HOW YOUR PERSONALITY IMPACTS MONEY MAP COACHING

Adaptive

It is difficult for *Adaptive* coaches to confront coaching participants. They want to be cooperative when the participants need the coaches to address difficult issues. They may not have the courage to challenge the participants to make the necessary changes in their spending and lifestyle.

Directing

It is hard for *Directing* coaches to do anything but be in total charge and make decisions the coaching participants should make. They are inclined to move quickly without carefully considering the impact. They tend to be bold. Many participants shy away from this personality, unless the coaches have learned to communicate with gentleness and kindness.

Reserved

The *Reserved* coaches will sometimes appear to be distant and detached from the situation. They will almost seem uncaring. The Reserved coaches need to demonstrate warmth and a caring spirit.

Interacting

The *Interacting* coaches love to talk and may take most of the first session just getting to know the coaching participants. Even though this friendly approach can be encouraging to the participants, the Interacting coaches must remember to focus and address the issues of Money Map coaching.

Objective

The *Objective* coaches have no trouble logically getting to the bottom of the problem. They will quickly identify a problem, suggest a solution, and move on to the next challenge. Conflict is not a problem. The Objective coaches need to make sure that they take sufficient time to teach God's financial principles to the coaching participants instead of suggesting the solution prematurely. Objective coaches need to evaluate if change is really needed or if they are suggesting change only for change's sake.

Supportive

The *Supportive* coaches should be careful not to compromise God's principles. They will tend to trust the coaching participants too much and not ask the difficult questions. The Supportive coaches need to establish a reasonable time frame for the participants to accomplish tasks and not be overly patient. They will avoid conflict at all costs.

Unconventional

Unconventional coaches will be inclined to ignore the forms, homework, and procedures that have proved effective in thousands of Crown coaching sessions. Instead, they will invent their own process. This spontaneity often proves ineffective and damages the budgeting efforts. An Unconventional coach needs to be careful not to compromise the basic coaching principles of this training.

Conscientious

Conscientious coaches will follow the rules to a fault. The percentage guidelines will turn into a rigid set of rules that cannot be deviated from even one percentage point. The unorganized coaching participants will be very frustrating to a Conscientious coach and the coach's body language will communicate this frustration. The Conscientious coach will not meet with a participant until every form and the homework is completely finished. The Conscientious coach needs to nurture balance and flexibility.

Summary

Each personality has its tendencies and challenges. Your strengths will become apparent to you as you counsel. Remember that God has created you. He has given you what you need to be an effective Money Map Coach. Remember that no one fits only into one personality category. Being aware of the tendencies of your personality will help you avoid your weaknesses.

PERSONALITY FACTORS AND THE COACHING PARTICIPANT

We have considered how the personality of coaches impacts the coaching process; now we need to address how personality traits may affect the actions and responses of coaching participants. It's important to recognize that prayer and the Lord's intervention can overrule our natural personality tendencies.

There are three factors that will impact the coaching participant's actions and responses. The first factor is the severity of the financial situation. If the participant is in a survival mode, his or her dominant personality trait will rapidly become evident. Another factor is the personality blend of the participant. (Which personality trait will dominate?) The last factor applies to married couples. How do the personality traits of each spouse combine within the marriage relationship? Are they at opposite extremes or is there a common ground on which to work?

Whether you are working with a single coaching participant or with a married couple, understanding what to expect from a participant will help you react appropriately and experience less frustration.

There are some key indicators that you will observe in the coaching participant that will give you direction. Do you see a drive to achieve in the participant or does he or she need frequent, personal reinforcement? Is the participant creative or dependent on rigid order and organization? Is there evidence of respect for authority or a rebellion against authority? Is the participant a loner or is there a definite need for fellowship and personal interaction? Is there an ability to deal with stress or does the participant avoid dealing with stress?

Obviously, there is a balance of the extremes listed above. However, as you gain experience you will be able to discern tendencies that will help you become more effective. You will want to affirm the strengths of the coaching participants and begin ministering to their weaknesses through God's Word. *The WORD on Finances* will help you find specific verses for the challenges you face.

Adaptive

You will find that the coaching participant who is Adaptive is cooperative and mild mannered. The challenge for this personality type is that they are oversensitive and will lack confidence in their abilities. Emphasize that we can do all things through Christ. He is the one who enables us to accomplish things (Philippians 4:13).

Directing

This may be the easiest personality trait to detect. These coaching participants will be confident (even when wrong), assertive, and independent. You will find that they will not pay attention to you, they will skip over details, and they will be impulsive. They will try to control you and the coaching situation. Emphasize that you are there to help them as they make decisions based on God's Word. Use Scripture as your authority to reach the participants with a Directing personality.

Reserved

The Reserved coaching participants prefer to work alone. They will be focused as you work with them and will exhibit a realistic approach to their situations. Nevertheless, they tend to be pessimistic and abrupt. Your challenge will be to help them to become optimistic about their financial future and what can be accomplished through this effort. Proverbs 3:9-10 is encouraging Scripture for those who lack enthusiasm.

Interacting

Interacting coaching participants will do their best to make great first impressions. They may even inspire you! As you dig deeper you will find that they are poor money managers and are very disorganized. They seem to be too optimistic and in some cases are very emotional. Filling out the Monthly Income and Expense form may help bring them back to reality.

Objective

Objective coaching participants will react. They are impatient and in some cases critical; however, you can work with them because they are flexible and action-oriented. You will need to impress the importance of completing the tasks assigned, because they enthusiastically begin but rarely finish the tasks. Point out Hebrews 12:1-2 when they are distracted or negligent.

Supportive

You will find Supportive coaching participants steady and loyal. Initially, you will notice the desire to be considerate and understanding. Your challenge will be that they will not like change and in some cases will be wary of committing themselves. Change will come slowly. Calm their hearts and encourage them by reminding them of Philippians 4:6-9.

Unconventional

Unconventional types are rather free-spirited. They are skilled in impromptu situations and will have an independence that will try your patience. They will overlook details and be rather disorganized. You will find it challenging to get any documented evidence of their financial situation. First Corinthians 10:31 and Colossians 3:23 can help direct these coaching participants.

Conscientious

Most Conscientious coaching participants are probably having financial challenges because of circumstances beyond their control. They will be too hard on themselves and inflexible in their expectations. Using the Monthly Income and Expense form will help them become realistic. Remind them of Psalm 50:14-15.

Summary

Remember that God made everyone different and for His purpose. Romans 12:6-8 reminds us. *"Since we have gifts that differ according to the grace given to us, each of us is to exercise them accordingly: if prophecy, according to the proportion of faith; if service, in his servings; or he who teaches, in his teaching; or he who exhorts, in his exhortation; he who gives, with liberality; he who leads, with diligence; he who shows mercy, with cheerfulness."*

WEEK

PEACE AND CONTENTMENT

Principle to Memorize

The Lord invites us to experience contentment and His peace.

Scripture to Memorize

"I have learned to be content in whatever circumstances I am. I know how to get along with humble means, and I also know how to live in prosperity. . . . I can do all things through Him who strengthens me" (Philippians 4:11-13).

ASSIGNMENT

Complete the *Approach* and *Analyze* sections of the Budgeting Process. The *Approach* section is on pages 117 to 130. The *Analyze* section is on pages 131 to 134.

QUESTIONS TO ANSWER

1. **Read *Luke 3:14*; *Philippians 4:11-13*; and *1 Timothy 6:6-8*.**

   What do each of these passages communicate to you about contentment?

   Luke 3:14—

   Philippians 4:11-13—

   1 Timothy 6:6-8—

   How does our culture discourage contentment?

How do you propose to practice contentment?

2. **Read *Luke 12:15; Ephesians 5:3,5;* and *Colossians 3:5.***
   What do each of these passages say about coveting and greed?

   Luke 12:15—

   Ephesians 5:3,5—

   Colossians 3:5—

   Define coveting:

   Define greed:

   Do you personally struggle with coveting or greed? How do you propose to conquer these sins?

3. **Read *Deuteronomy 30:15-16; Joshua 1:8;* and *Hebrews 11:36-40.***
   What do each of these passages communicate to you about financial prosperity for the believer?

   Deuteronomy 30:15-16—

   Joshua 1:8—

Hebrews 11:36-40—

Reflect on the lives of Job, Joseph, and Paul. Did these men ever experience periods of financial abundance and at other times a lack of financial prosperity? Was their lack of financial prosperity a result of sin and lack of faith?

Should all Christians always prosper financially? Why?

4. **Read *Mark 8:36-37; Acts 4:32-37;* and *1 Thessalonians 4:11-12.***
   What do these passages communicate to you about lifestyle?

   Mark 8:36-37—

   Acts 4:32-37—

   1 Thessalonians 4:11-12—

   How do the following factors influence your present spending and lifestyle?

   1. Comparing your lifestyle with that of friends and other people—

   2. Television, magazines, catalogs, and other advertisements—

   3. Your study of the Bible—

4. Your commitment to Christ and to things that are important to Him—

Do you sense that the Lord would have you alter any part of your standard of living? If so, what?

5. **Read *John 3:16*.**
Is it possible for an individual to know Jesus Christ as his or her personal Savior and have eternal life?

How does a person enter into this relationship with Jesus Christ?

Do you know Christ as your personal Savior?

NOTES TO READ

Many of your participants will be in financial difficulty and need to understand how to experience God's peace and contentment.

CONTENTMENT

First Timothy 6:8 issues this challenging statement: *"If we have food and covering, with these we shall be content."* Study this passage carefully. It declares that if you have food and covering (clothes and shelter), you should be content. Our culture has restated this verse to read something like this, "If you can afford the finest food to eat, wear the latest fashions, drive the newest luxury automobile, and live in a beautiful home, then you can be happy." Our culture has been described as a consumption-oriented society that operates on the assumption that more is always better and happiness is based on acquiring possessions.

As we studied before, the word "contentment" is mentioned seven times in Scripture, and six times it has to do with money. Paul wrote, *"I have learned to be content in whatever circumstances I am. I know how to get along with humble means, and I also know how to live in prosperity; in any and every circumstance I have learned the secret of being filled and going hungry, both of having abundance and suffering need. I can do all things through Him who strengthens me"* (Philippians 4:11-13). Review this passage. Paul "learned" to be content. We are not born intuitively content; rather, we learn contentment.

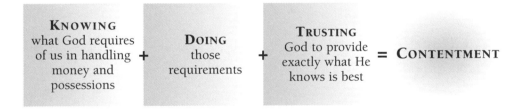

Note carefully that it is not just knowing these things that brings contentment; it is doing them. As Francis Schaeffer said, "These two words, know and do, occur throughout Scripture and always in that order. We cannot do until we know, but we can know without doing. The house built on the rock is the house of the man who knows and does. The house built on the sand is the house of the man who knows but does not do."

"The steadfast of mind You will keep in perfect peace, because he trusts in You" (Isaiah 26:3).

Once we have been faithful in the doing, we can be content in knowing that our loving heavenly Father will entrust the precise quantity of possessions He knows will be best for us at any particular time—whether much or little. Because we serve the living and dynamic God, Christians should always be improving. Contentment does not exclude properly motivated ambition. We have already discovered that God wants us to work hard. In fact, we should have a desire to be increasingly faithful stewards of the talents and possessions He has entrusted to us. Biblical contentment is not to be equated with laziness or complacency.

Biblical contentment is an inner peace that accepts what God has chosen for our present vocation and financial state. Hebrews 13:5 emphasizes this: *"Make sure that your character is free from the love of money, being content with what you have; for He Himself has said, 'I will never desert you, nor will I ever forsake you.'"*

God's peace

The basis for experiencing God's peace is knowing the Lord and understanding how much He loves you. Read these verses slowly, allowing the Lord to express His care for you.

"The steadfast of mind You will keep in perfect peace, because he trusts in You" (Isaiah 26:3).

"What then shall we say to these things? If God is for us, who is against us?" (Romans 8:31).

"Be anxious for nothing, but in everything by prayer and supplication with thanksgiving let your requests be made known to God. And the peace of God, which surpasses all comprehension, will guard your hearts and your minds in Christ Jesus" (Philippians 4:6-7).

"Peace I leave with you; My peace I give to you; not as the world gives do I give to you. Do not let your heart be troubled, nor let it be fearful" (John 14:27).

"These things have I [Jesus] spoken to you, so that in Me you may have peace. In the world you have tribulation, but take courage; I have overcome the world" (John 16:33).

DISCONTENTMENT

There are a number of factors that contribute to a sense of discontentment.

1. Do not determine your lifestyle by comparing it to others

Some use comparison to justify spending more than they should. Many have suffered financially because they tried but could not afford to "keep up with the Joneses." Someone once said, "You can never keep up with the Joneses. Just about the time you've caught them, they go deeper in debt to buy more things!"

2. Learn to avoid coveting

Coveting means to crave another person's property. Coveting is expressly prohibited throughout Scripture. The last of the Ten Commandments reads, *"You shall not covet your neighbor's house; you shall not covet your neighbor's wife or his male servant or his female servant or his ox or his donkey or anything that belongs to your neighbor"* (Exodus 20:17). Note that the Lord ended the tenth commandment prohibiting coveting with an infinitely broad application: *"or anything that belongs to your neighbor."* In other words, we are commanded not to covet anything that belongs to anyone!

Greed is similar to coveting. *"Immorality or any impurity or greed must not even be named among you . . . For this you know with certainty, that no immoral or impure person or covetous man, who is an idolater, has an inheritance in the kingdom of Christ and God"* (Ephesians 5:3,5).

A greedy or covetous person is an idolater. Coveting and greed have been called the universal, silent sins. Rarely are they addressed or confronted. Ask the Lord to show you if you are guilty of coveting what is another's. If so, ask the Lord to change your heart.

3. Make an effort to live more simply

Every possession requires time and often money to maintain. Too many or the wrong types of possessions can demand so much time or money that they harm our relationships with the Lord and our families. A quiet, simple life is the safest environment for us to be able to invest enough time to nurture our relationships with the Lord. First Thessalonians 4:11-12 counsels, *"Make it your ambition to lead a quiet life and attend to your own business and work with your hands, just as we commanded you, so that you may behave properly toward outsiders and not be in any need."*

Do not become unduly encumbered with the cares of this life. *"Suffer hardship with me, as a good soldier of Christ Jesus. No soldier in active service entangles himself in the affairs of everyday life, so that he may please the one who enlisted him as a soldier"* (2 Timothy 2:3-4).

> *A quiet, simple life is the safest environment for us to be able to invest enough time to nurture our relationship with the Lord.*

4. Do not be conformed to this world

Romans 12:2 begins with this command, *"Do not be conformed to this world."* The Amplified version reads this way: *"Do not be conformed to this world (this age), [fashioned after and adapted to its external, superficial customs]"* (Romans 12:2). We live in what probably is the most affluent culture in the history of the world. We are constantly bombarded with manipulative advertising to prompt us to spend money. Advertisers usually stress the importance of image rather than function. For example, automobile ads rarely focus on a car as reliable transportation that is economical to operate. Instead, an image of status or sex appeal is projected.

Reflect on the claims of TV commercials. No matter what the product—clothing, deodorants, credit cards, you name it—the message is communicated that the "fulfilling, beautiful, wrinkle-free life" can be ours if we are willing to buy it. Unfortunately, to some extent this media onslaught has influenced all of us. Author George Fooshee so aptly states, "People buy things they do not need with money they do not have to impress people they do not even like."

POVERTY, PROSPERITY, OR STEWARDSHIP?

Some Christians embrace one of two extremes. On one hand are those who believe that godliness can occur only in poverty. However, a number of godly people in Scripture were among the wealthiest people of their day. In the Old Testament the Lord extended the reward of abundance to the children of Israel when they were obedient, but the threat of poverty was one of the consequences of disobedience. Deuteronomy 30:15-16 reads, *"I have set before you today life and prosperity, and death and adversity; in that I command you today to love the Lord your God, to walk in His ways and to keep His commandments . . . that the Lord your God may bless you."*

We may pray for prosperity when our relationship with the Lord is healthy, and we have a proper perspective of possessions. *"Beloved, I pray that in all respects you may prosper and be in good health, just as your soul prospers"* (3 John 2). The Bible does not say that a godly person must live in poverty. A godly person may have material resources.

At the other hand lies the belief that all Christians who truly have faith will always prosper. This extreme is also in error. Study the life of Joseph. He is an example of a faithful person who experienced prosperity and poverty. He was born into a prosperous family, then was thrown into a pit, and finally sold into slavery by his jealous brothers. While Joseph was a slave, his master promoted him to be head of his household. Later he made the righteous decision not to commit adultery with his master's wife, yet was thrown in jail for years because of that decision. In God's timing he was ultimately elevated to prime minister of Egypt.

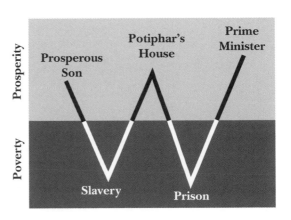

The guideline for prosperity is found in Joshua 1:8. *"This book of the law shall not depart from your mouth, but you shall meditate on it day and night, so that you may be careful to do according to all that is written in it; for then you will make your way prosperous, and then you will have success."*

Two requirements for prosperity become apparent from studying this passage. You must meditate on the Scriptures, engrave them on your mind and heart, and do all that is written in them. Once you have fulfilled these obligations, you place yourself in the position to be blessed financially, but there is no guarantee that the godly will always experience financial prosperity. There are four reasons the godly may not prosper.

1. Violating scriptural principles

Look again at Joshua 1:8. There is the requirement to do according to *all* that is written in the Bible. You may be giving generously but acting dishonestly. You may be honest but not fulfilling your work responsibilities. You may be a faithful employee but head over heels in debt. You may be completely out of debt but not giving. Those who do not understand all the requirements often neglect critical areas of responsibility unknowingly and suffer financially.

2. Building godly character

Romans 5:3-4 reads, *"Tribulation brings about perseverance; and perseverance, proven character."* Many godly people in the Bible went through periods when they were living righteously, yet they lost their possessions. David became a national hero after slaying Goliath, only to be forced to flee for his life from a tormented King Saul. Job lost his children and possessions in the space of a few moments and was described as a *"blameless and upright man, fearing God and turning away from evil"* (Job 1:8). Paul learned the secret of contentment while being held captive in chains, even though he was righteous.

God sometimes molds our character by allowing us to experience difficult circumstances. An example of how the Lord develops character in a people before prospering them is found in Deuteronomy 8:16-18: *"In the wilderness He fed you manna which your fathers did not know, that He might humble you and that He might test you, to do good for you in the end. Otherwise, you may say in your heart, 'My power and the strength of my hand made me this wealth.' But you shall remember the Lord your God, for it is He who is giving you power to make wealth."* The children of Israel needed to be humbled before they could handle wealth. Our Father knows us better than we know ourselves. In His infinite wisdom He knows exactly how much He can entrust to us at any time without it harming our relationship with Him.

3. Our dependence and His discipline

A father was carrying his two-year-old son as he waded in a lake. When they were close to shore, the child was unconcerned because of the apparent safety of the beach, even though the water was deep enough to drown him. He didn't understand his dependence upon his father. However, the farther they moved away from shore, the tighter the child held to his father. Like the child, we are always completely dependent on the Lord to provide for us. However, often we don't recognize our dependence when we are "close to shore," experiencing the apparent security of financial prosperity. But when our possessions are few or none, it is easier to recognize our needs and to cling to our heavenly Father.

Moreover, Hebrews 12:6,10 tells us that, *"Those whom the Lord loves He disciplines, and He scourges every son whom He receives . . . for our good, so that we may share His holiness."* If we have sin in our lives or a wrong attitude toward money, the Lord may discipline us by allowing financial difficulties aimed at encouraging us to forsake our sin.

4. The mystery of God's sovereignty

In Hebrews 11 we find "Faith's Hall of Fame." In verses 1-38 we have a list of people who triumphed miraculously by the exercise of their faith in God. But in verse 39 the writer directs our attention to godly people who gained God's approval, yet *"did not receive what was promised."* God ultimately chooses how much to entrust to each person, and sometimes we simply can't understand His decisions.

Let's summarize. The Scriptures teach neither the necessity of poverty nor uninterrupted prosperity. What the Bible teaches is the responsi-

> *God sometimes molds our character by allowing us to experience difficult circumstances.*

bility of being a faithful steward. Please review this diagram which contrasts the three perspectives.

	Poverty	Stewardship	Prosperity
Possessions are	Evil	A responsibility	A right
I work to	Meet only basic needs	Serve Christ	Become rich
Godly people are	Poor	Faithful	Wealthy
Ungodly people are	Wealthy	Unfaithful	Poor
I give	Because I must	Because I love God	To get
My spending is	Without gratitude to God	Prayerful and responsible	Carefree and consumptive

LIFESTYLE

The Bible does not prescribe one standard of living for everyone. In Scripture, godly people are represented in all walks of life, and the Lord still places His people strategically in every level of society—rich and poor. We encourage you to evaluate your standard of living prayerfully. To stimulate your thinking, let's examine several scriptural principles that should influence your lifestyle.

1. Have an eternal perspective

Recognize and nurture an eternal perspective. Almost everything in our culture implores us to focus on the immediate. Advertisers persuade purchasers to gratify themselves today with no thought of tomorrow. To understand how brief life is on earth, picture life as follows.

Our momentary time on earth is but a dot on the timeline of eternity. Yet we have the opportunity to affect eternity by how we handle money today. We not only have the privilege to lay up treasures for ourselves in heaven but we are able to spend money to influence people for Jesus Christ. Gaining an eternal perspective and eternal values will have a profound effect on your decision making.

Moses is an example. Study Hebrews 11:24-26 carefully, *"By faith*

We can either live with a view toward eternity or live focused on this present world.

Moses, when he had grown up, refused to be called the son of Pharaoh's daughter, choosing rather to endure ill-treatment with the people of God than to enjoy the passing pleasures of sin, considering the reproach of Christ greater riches than the treasures of Egypt; for he was looking to the reward." Moses faced a choice. As Pharaoh's adopted son, he could enjoy the lavish lifestyle of royalty, or he could choose to become a Hebrew slave. Because he had an eternal perspective, he chose the latter and was used by the Lord in a remarkable way. We face a similar decision. We can either live with a view toward eternity or live focused on this present world.

As an adult, have you ever returned to a place you knew as a child? If so, you've probably been shocked to discover how small it really was! Do you remember wanting to get something so much that it consumed all your thoughts? Yet today it means almost nothing to you? We think we will experience something similar when we arrive in heaven. Many things that loom so large and important to us now will fade into insignificance in the light of eternity. We can either live with a view toward eternity or live focused on this present world.

2. Beware of financial bondage

Many people are in financial bondage. Some are in bondage even though they are wealthy because of wrong attitudes toward money. *"He who loves money will not be satisfied with money, nor he who loves abundance with its income. This too is vanity. When good things increase, those who consume them increase. So what is the advantage to their owners except to look on? The sleep of the working man is pleasant, whether he eats little or much; but the full stomach of the rich man does not allow him to sleep"* (Ecclesiastes 5:10-12).

Others are in bondage because of mismanagement of their income or a lack of trusting the Lord to provide.

There are some typical warning signs of financial bondage:

- Worry about financial matters
- Consumed with thinking about money
- No contentment
- Bills overdue
- Overwork
- Lack of savings
- Not able to sleep because of financial matters

- Financial arguments with your spouse
- Being called by your creditors

The only solution to this bondage is learning and applying God's financial principles. Jesus said, *"You will know the truth, and the truth will make you free"* (John 8:32). Encourage your coaching participants to become students of the financial principles revealed in the Scriptures.

YOU CAN KNOW THE LORD

You may coach people who do not yet know Christ as their personal Savior and Lord. The following five steps describe how a person can enter into this relationship with the Lord.

1. God loves you and wants you to experience a meaningful life.

God created us in His own image, and He desires an intimate relationship with each of us. *"For God so loved the world, that He gave His only begotten Son, that whoever believes in Him should not perish, but have eternal life"* (John 3:16). *"I [Jesus] came that they might have life, and might have it abundantly"* (John 10:10). God the Father loved us so much that He gave His only Son, Jesus Christ, to die for us so that we could enjoy eternal life with Him.

2. Unfortunately, we are separated from God.

God is holy, which means God is perfect, and He cannot have a relationship with anyone who is not perfect. Every person has sinned, and the consequence of sin was separation from God. *"For all have sinned and fall short of the glory of God"* (Romans 3:23). *"Your sins have cut you off from God"* (Isaiah 59:2, TLB).

The diagram below illustrates an enormous gap that separates people from God. Individuals try without success to bridge this gap through their own efforts, such as philosophy, religion, material goods, charitable activity, or living a good moral life.

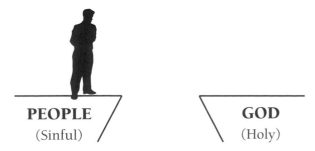

PEOPLE
(Sinful)

GOD
(Holy)

3. God's only provision to bridge this gap is Jesus Christ.

Jesus Christ died on the cross to pay the penalty for our sin. He bridged the gap between us and God. *"Jesus said to him, 'I am the way, and the*

God created us in His own image, and He desires an intimate relationship with each of us.

truth, and the life; no one comes to the Father, but through Me' " (John 14:6). *"God demonstrates His own love toward us, in that while we were yet sinners, Christ died for us"* (Romans 5:8).

This diagram illustrates our union with God through Jesus Christ.

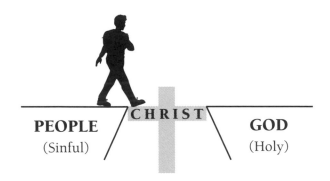

PEOPLE (Sinful) **CHRIST** **GOD** (Holy)

4. This relationship is a gift from God.

By an act of faith we can receive the free gift of a relationship with God. *"For by grace you have been saved through faith; and that not of yourselves, it is the gift of God; not as a result of works, so that no one may boast"* (Ephesians 2:8-9).

5. We must each receive Jesus Christ individually.

We need to ask Jesus Christ to forgive us of our sins and to come into our lives to be our Savior and Lord.

If you are helping coaching participants who are not certain whether they have this relationship, they may receive Christ by praying a prayer similar to this one: "Father God, I need You. I invite Jesus to come into my life as my Savior and Lord and make me the person You want me to be. Thank You for forgiving my sins and giving me the gift of eternal life."

If you are not certain you have a relationship with the Lord, we encourage you to pray that prayer right now. Nothing in life compares to knowing Christ. If you asked Christ into your life, please tell someone from your church or let us know at Crown so that we will be able to assist you in your spiritual growth.

APPLYING THE PRINCIPLES TO MONEY MAP COACHING

Communicate these principles to your coaching participants.

1. The spiritual consequence for ignoring God's direction in our lives is our loss of peace and communion with Him.

2. You can learn to be content regardless of the circumstances. Consider the ways God has blessed you, and accept the situations that cannot be changed.

3. Possessions will not bring real joy; only knowing the Lord will produce this.

4. You can experience the peace of God, because He loves you and cares for you.

5. God made us and knows everything about us. He knows every challenge we will face. He never asks too much of us. His strength and wisdom is sufficient for all of life's circumstances.

6. Do not establish your standard of living by comparing it with others around you.

7. If you do not yet know Jesus Christ as your personal Savior, you can invite Him into your life.

HOW WOULD YOU RESPOND TO A COACHING PARTICIPANT?

The following questions and views are commonly expressed during Money Map coaching sessions. Describe how you would respond to each.

1. No one can possibly understand what I'm going through.

2. There's no hope. I've done everything I can do.

3. It is wrong for a Christian to be wealthy.

4. I'm sure that everyone who is wealthy has been dishonest.

5. Having money makes me feel secure.

6. At times, God will withhold things from us to make us turn to Him.

Please review this section until you are thoroughly familiar with the principles you will use in Money Map coaching sessions.

ANSWERS TO THE QUESTIONS

1. **Read *Luke 3:14; Philippians 4:11-13; and 1 Timothy 6:6-8*.**

   What do each of these passages communicate to you about contentment?

   Luke 3:14—[Be content with your wages.]

   Philippians 4:11-13—[Contentment is not something that occurs naturally; it is learned. We can learn to be content in any circumstance.]

   1 Timothy 6:6-8—[Godliness with contentment is a means of great gain. We cannot take anything with us when we die, and we should be content with our basic needs satisfied.]

2. **Read *Luke 12:15; Ephesians 5:3,5; and Colossians 3:5*.**

   What do each of these passages say about coveting and greed?

   Luke 12:15—[We are warned that there are various forms of greed.]

   Ephesians 5:3,5—[A godly person should not be greedy, and a covetous person is an idolater.]

   Colossians 3:5—[Greed equals idolatry.]

   Define coveting: *[Coveting is wanting something that is owned by another.]*

   Define greed: *[Greed is the excessive desire for a possession.]*

3. **Read *Deuteronomy 30:15-16; Joshua 1:8; and Hebrews 11:36-40*.**

   What do each of these passages communicate to you about financial prosperity for the believer?

   Deuteronomy 30:15-16—[One of the blessings of obedience was prosperity.]

   Joshua 1:8—[Knowing and obeying all of the commands in the Scriptures resulted in prosperity.]

   Hebrews 11:36-40—[Even godly people exercising faith have experienced poverty and difficult circumstances.]

   Reflect on the lives of Job, Joseph, and Paul. Did these men ever experience periods of financial abundance and at other times a lack of financial prosperity?

   [Job, Joseph, and Paul each experienced periods of plenty and times of want.]

   Was their lack of financial prosperity a result of sin and lack of faith?

   [Their times of poverty usually were not a result of sin or a lack of faith.]

Should all Christians always prosper financially? Why?

[Once a person has fulfilled all areas of being a faithful steward, he or she is in a position for the Lord to prosper financially. However, the Lord may not for one of three reasons: (1) He is building our character (Romans 5:3-4). (2) He needs to discipline us in an area of our life where there is sin (Hebrews 12:6,10). (3) God's sovereignty (Hebrews 11:36-40).]

4. **Read *Mark 8:36-37*; *Acts 4:32-37*; and *1 Thessalonians 4:11-12*.**
   What do these passages communicate to you about lifestyle?

   Mark 8:36-37—[A person can become tremendously wealthy, but without Christ it is meaningless.]

   Acts 4:32-37—[An equality of needs being met within the body of Christ led to revival.]

   1 Thessalonians 4:11-12—[We are encouraged to live a quiet, industrious life.]

5. **Read *John 3:16*.**
   Is it possible for an individual to know Jesus Christ as his or her personal Savior and have eternal life?

   [Yes, 1 John 5:11-12 says, "God has given us eternal life, and this life is in His Son. He who has (knows) the Son has the life; he who does not have (knows) the Son of God does not have the life."]

   How does a person enter into this relationship with Jesus Christ?

   [One enters into a relationship with the Lord by inviting Jesus Christ to come into his or her heart as Savior.]

ANSWERS TO: HOW WOULD YOU RESPOND TO A COACHING PARTICIPANT?

1. No one can possibly understand what I'm going through.

   [Jesus understands us completely. Hebrews 4:15 reads, "For we do not have a high priest who cannot sympathize with our weaknesses, but One (Jesus) who has been tempted in all things as we are, yet without sin."]

2. There's no hope. I've done everything I can do.

   [We have certain responsibilities in the handling of our finances, and the Lord has responsibilities. The Lord cares deeply for us. In Hebrews 13:5 we read, "He Himself said, 'I will never desert you, nor will I ever forsake you.' "]

3. Is it wrong for a Christian to be wealthy?

   [Not if we have the proper attitude towards the possessions entrusted to us. First Timothy 6:17-18 is written to the rich: "Instruct those who are rich in this present world not to be con-

ceited or to fix their hope on the uncertainty of riches, but on God, who richly supplies us with all things to enjoy. Instruct them to do good, to be rich in good works, to be generous and ready to share."]

4. I'm sure that everyone who is wealthy has been dishonest.

   [*This is not true. The Lord has entrusted many godly people with resources because they have been faithful and use it for the funding of His kingdom.*]

5. Having money makes me feel secure.

   [*It shouldn't because it is uncertain. The Lord alone is to be our security.*]

6. Is it true that, at times, God will withhold things from us to make us turn to Him?

   [*Yes, because the Lord is more interested in the development of our godly character than He is in our comfort.*]

THE COACHING PROCESS

Approach

Analyze

I. Approach to Money Map coaching

Prerequisites to becoming a Money Map Coach

Coaching information you need to know

II. Analyze

Journey to Financial Freedom

SESSION ONE

    1. Open in prayer

    2. Personal Information sheet

    3. Commitment to Coaching Form

    4. Information Gathering Forms

    5. Diagnosis of financial health

    6. Goals setting

    7. Actions steps

    8. Close in prayer

SESSION TWO

    1. Open in prayer

    2. Share conversation

    3. Review Session One

    4. Introduce budgeting concepts

    5. Actions steps

    6. Close in prayer

APPROACH

You have now studied the biblical financial principles, completed your personal budget, and learned about your personality and different personality types. In this section, you will discover how to approach Money Map coaching. How you approach situations sometimes helps determine the outcome. The information in this section will be very helpful as you serve your coaching participants.

Crown Financial Ministries has been training volunteer Money Map Coaches since the late 1970s. Our training is not intended to equip people to become professional counselors.

As a volunteer Money Map Coach, it is imperative that you live on a budget and understand the financial principles presented in this course. It is not a requirement for you to be totally debt free before you can coach others.

As a Money Map Coach, your main task is to introduce people to God's financial principles. Your secondary function is to help with budgeting and the pressures of debt. We've learned that unless people understand and apply these financial principles they will be back in financial difficulty. Without first dealing with the underlying issues, just learning the mechanics of how to budget is not a long-term solution.

PREREQUISITES TO BECOMING A MONEY MAP COACH

1. Have a personal relationship with the Lord Jesus Christ.
2. Be an active member of a church that teaches that salvation comes only through the Lord Jesus Christ.
3. Complete this *Money Map Coach Training Course.*
4. Live on a budget.
5. Have the approval of your pastor, bishop, or priest.
6. Be certain your church leadership understands that your Money Map coaching is a ministry of the church and that you serve under the church leadership.

COACHING INFORMATION YOU NEED TO KNOW

You are an instrument of God to help change lives. It has been said, "To the world you might be one person, but to one person you might be the world." This section of the course focuses on the biblical concepts of coaching. You will begin to learn the techniques of coaching others, as well as the challenges. There will be great rewards as the Lord uses you to impact lives. Earlier you learned about the unique personality that God has given you and what strengths and weaknesses are inherent in your personality type. Ask the Lord to give you insight into how you present yourself to others, as well as how to deal with different personalities of the coaching participants.

THE SWs OF COACHING

- **SOME WILL**

  Some coaching participants will listen to your counsel and will follow through and do what is necessary to balance their budgets and begin to pay off debt.

- **SOME WAIT**

  Some coaching participants will meet with you once and then won't communicate with you for awhile. Then, sometimes even a year later, they will again ask for help. These people need more time to struggle with their problems before they are willing to be serious about solving them.

- **SOME WON'T**

  Some participants will ask for help. Unfortunately, when they learn the discipline, and in some cases the sacrifice that will be required, they will never be heard from again.

- **SO WHAT**

  So what does this mean to you as a coach? People have different commitment levels. **Do not take things personally.** When people don't seem to care, pray for them. When some are initially excited and then drop out of coaching, pray for them. When some delay coming to get help, pray for them. Always remember to pray. You can't force a person to be faithful, but you can always encourage them and pray.

COACHING ETIQUETTE

When working with participants, there are certain things you will need to remember.

- Always reply to any request for Money Map coaching. You may be busy and have no appointments available, but to ignore a request for a week or longer is not Christ-like.

- Take time to pray for your coaching participants before you meet them. Ask God to give you His love and compassion, so that you can be a minister of Christ to them.

- Always start your session with prayer.

- Be sure to stay calm even when faced with serious needs. Your body language communicates a great deal. Remember how Christ responded to those who came to Him for help. He did not shake His head in disbelief of their circumstances. He did not sigh when they told Him how severe their circumstances were. He loved them.

- Take some time to build a relationship with those who are seeking help. Show that you care about them. *"Everyone must be quick to hear, slow to speak and slow to anger; for the anger of man does not achieve the righteousness of God"* (James 1:19-20). Take time to talk but, more importantly, *listen!*

Before you can help someone else you need to want to be used by God as His servant. You will need God's direction and help as you work with people. Someone once said, "Three things in life are important. The first is to be kind. The second is to be kind. And the third is to be kind." You will regret many things in life but you will never regret being too kind or too fair.

Jesus said it this way, *"Treat people the same way you want them to treat you"* (Matthew 7:12). And Paul wrote, *"Do nothing from selfishness or empty conceit, but with humility of mind regard one another as more important than yourselves; do not merely look out for your own personal interests, but also for the interests of others"* (Philippians 2:3-4).

The most important thing to communicate to the coaching participants is that you truly care about them and what they are experiencing. If you are distracted or busy with the other issues, your participants will sense that you don't really care about them. People want to know you care before they care what you know.

Remember that everyone who came to the Lord seeking help knew without a doubt that He cared about them. He asked them to turn from their sin and, with His help, seek righteousness. This will happen with your coaching participants. They will need to make changes in their lifestyles or spending habits. It will take tough love to offer suggestions, but if they are going to handle money God's way, changes will have to be made. Your job is to offer them godly advice. It is the responsibility of the participants to be faithful to act. Good financial habits are not developed overnight. Some coaching participants will need to be brought along slowly, some will respond quickly, and some will refuse to turn their financial lives over to the Lord.

LEARNING TO BE A GOOD COACH

As you begin to serve, you will quickly learn that the Lord has much to teach you. There will be times when you will be tired and will not be looking forward to the coaching session, and the Lord will encourage you by the attitude of your coaching participants.

Other times coaching participants will not be willing to change enough to succeed. In situations like this, you need to communicate that there are no quick and painless solutions to their problems. If they are unwilling, they fall into the categories of "Some Wait" or "Some Won't." When this happens ask yourself, "Did I pray for this person? Did I pray for God's direction?" If the answer is no, take time to pray, because it gives the Lord the maximum freedom to change their lives.

What makes a good coach may surprise you. Age, income, profession, or social status don't make a good Money Map Coach. Maturity in Christ, a calling to this ministry, commitment, and a willingness to study (2 Timothy 2:15) are far more important. Some of the best coaches have experienced their own financial difficulties and have seen God guide and provide as they yielded their decisions to Him.

We have learned that a successful Money Map coaching experience depends largely on how committed the coaching participants are to the process of learning and implementing what they learn.

Coaches faithfulness

For there to be success, it's essential that the coach do the following.

- Pray for the coaching participant.
- Coaches must identify their own personality strengths and weaknesses.
- The coach must be sensitive to those who come for help.
- Humbly serve the coaching participant.
- Demonstrate that you care for the coaching participant.

Flexibility

The Money Map coaching process will rarely be the same every time. Different needs will require you to be flexible. This will require patience. Learning to ask pertinent questions (coaches should always ask "what" questions and not "why" questions) and learning to listen are two skills you will refine as you gain experience.

As a representative of Christ, it is imperative that you respond promptly to each request for a session. Remember that many who call are under stress. A delayed response from you will increase their stress. The worst possible response is no response. If your schedule is full, and you are unable to take any more referrals, let them know. If the referral came from Crown, send them back to us for another referral.

GENERAL COACHING INFORMATION

Initial meeting

Your *initial meeting* with a coaching participant should run about one and one-half hours. More difficult cases may take two hours, but set a time limit and keep it. Be sure to communicate to the participant the time needed for the session. Generally, sessions should stop no later than 10 P.M. If time is available during the day, do not hesitate to use it. A *neutral location* is best. If your church does not have a room available, you may choose a public place, where there are few distractions. When you are meeting with a single person of the opposite sex, have a third party in the building with a clear view of the room in which you meet. Failure to do this will place everyone in a potentially compromising position. One alternative is for a husband and wife to do the coaching together when the participant is single.

Number of cases

The ideal number of active coaching cases is two coaching participants per coach. However, you may have a schedule that will allow more. Be sure that you do not spend so much time ministering that your family suffers. To be effective, you need the support of your family.

Generally speaking, it is better to coach people who are not close friends or family members. Total honesty is essential, and often friends or family will not reveal the total situation. Because of a lack of information, this leads to a faulty assessment.

Coaching married couples

If you are working with a married couple, it is always best to coach them together. A budget will involve both. Genesis 2:24 tells us God made man and woman to be one in marriage. They must learn to work as a unit, rather than as individuals. Unfortunately, in some cases one spouse will not agree to Money Map coaching. This is a clear indication of the spiritual condition of the marriage. Your response must be one of compassion. Do not say, "I'm sorry, but since your spouse will not come with you I cannot help you." A good suggestion would be to meet once or twice with the spouse who desires help. Be sure to have a third party with you when you meet with the coaching participant. Marriage coaching may be discussed with the participant's pastor. If possible, get someone of the same sex to be a prayer partner with the spouse who desires help. Remember, turning away someone in need without ministering to him or her is not Christ-like. Do not exclude non-Christians from coaching. This will be a good opportunity for evangelism. Be alert to opportunities. Remember that Christ died for their salvation, so be sure to show Christ's love through your concern. Be sensitive, not judgmental.

Record keeping

Record keeping is vital for an effective ministry. Coaches and churches have their own ways of record keeping. Good records will accomplish the following things.

1. Will provide complete information on the coaching participant and his or her family.
2. Will provide a reminder of when and how to follow up on a previous session.
3. Will provide a quick review before your next session.
4. Will provide an evaluation of progress and problems.
5. Will provide a way of assessing the thoroughness of the coach.
6. Will *not* contain original copies belonging to the coaching participant.
7. Will provide a secure place for the information.

If you are working as the sole Money Map Coach for your church, be sure that someone else (other than your spouse) knows where you keep your files in case of emergency.

Telephone contact

Telephone contact is usually the first way the coaching participant will communicate with you. An effective screening system can greatly enhance your ministry. The same system should answer all your calls. If the church office is the contact point, all calls should be referred there, assuming there's a way to leave a message when no one is in the office.

Nearly everyone who calls will say that he or she is in a crisis. However, a crisis does not usually occur overnight; it happens over time. Therefore, few crises require immediate attention. They should be dealt with within the established coaching schedule. Asking some pertinent questions while on the telephone with the coaching participant will help determine the need and may, in some cases, take care of the participant who is not in need of coaching. These are some questions you might ask.

—Are your creditors contacting you or calling you?

—Do you have outstanding bills you cannot pay?

—Have you or your spouse lost your job?

—Have you ever declared bankruptcy?

—Is your checkbook balanced?

Some situations do demand immediate attention, and a system must be available to handle these. Try not to discourage anyone by indicating that he or she is not as important as others. Everyone is important in God's eyes.

Planning information

Planning information is important for the first session to be most effective. You will want to communicate to coaching participants what they will need to bring to the session. Also, ask the participant to bring copies of important documents, rather than the originals, if possible. Some suggestions of information to bring are (1) two or three monthly checking statements, (2) the checkbook and check record, (3) tax returns for two years, and (4) pay stubs.

If you are a trained professional in an area that would be helpful to coaching participants, refer them to another professional who is not closely associated with you. There must be no question of your motives. When working with a participant, you may have to suggest actions that are difficult. Coaching participants should have such confidence in your desire to help, without any self-serving interest, that they will be willing to consider those options. Also, do not charge for your time. If participants want to reimburse you for the materials you provide, that is acceptable. However, participants should determine what materials they will use and pay for. If a participant cannot afford the material, the church may offer a scholarship to cover this cost.

Under no circumstances should you take the coaching participant's checkbook and pay the bills. You also should not keep the participant's original documents in your file. If they are lost, you are liable.

GOALS

Setting goals is an important step in the process. As Christians our goals should be centered around what Jesus would have us do. Goals should be established for all your coaching participants. When a goal is reached, no matter how small, it should be celebrated and will be an encouragement even if there are significant challenges to be faced.

Be realistic when setting goals with your coaching participants. Be sure to make the initial goals obtainable so you can encourage them. Later you can suggest that they establish long-term and life goals. Participants must set the goals; however, you can help direct them so that the goals are realistic. The goals can be set by week, month, year, or any other time frame that fits the need.

There are a number of categories that can be goal oriented. The coaching participant can set goals regarding bill payment, eliminating debt, giving, savings, future purchases, and so on. At the end of the year (or each month) review the goals, celebrate the ones achieved, and discuss why any goals were not accomplished. Be sure to point out how God has provided.

Financial goals for the _____ family

Category	Specific Goal	Time Frame	Goal Successfully Met
Savings	We will save $5 a week toward a lamp replacement.	6 weeks	1-June
Debt Retirement	We will reduce our consumer debt by $100 per month until it is gone.	Monthly	1/31, 2/29, 3/31, 4/31
Offering	We will give an additional $25 per month to the church for missionary work.	Ongoing as God provides	1/31, 2/29,

Personal and spiritual goals for the _____ family

Category	Specific Goal	Time Frame	Goal Successfully Met
Personal Goals			
Spiritual Goals			

SPIRITUAL SENSITIVITY

There are reasons why people find themselves in difficult financial situations. It's your job to lead them to solutions and reinforce God's principles in their lives. It will be important to remember that what you talk coaching participants into someone else can talk them out of, unless what you share is based on God's eternal Word.

Whether the coaching participants get on budgets pales in the light of their eternal destiny. As you work with participants, it's most important to confirm that your participants know Christ as Savior. If not, at the appropriate time share the salvation message. Your personal testimony is a powerful way to communicate the need for salvation. However, if you are too aggressive in witnessing, you may do more damage than good.

Unless you have a very unusual situation, the first words you say to the coaching participant when you meet should *not* be "Do you know where you will spend eternity?" Gently probe to determine whether he or she knows Jesus Christ as Savior.

You may be hesitant to share the Gospel with your coaching participant, but God will give you the opportunity if you ask Him. Sharing the Gospel with others is not complicated. God promises that His Word will not return to us void, but it is the power of God through His Word that leads to salvation. Please refer to pages 109 and 110.

Don't assume new Christians will go to church; don't assume they will read the Bible; and don't assume they know what they are supposed to do. Care for them spiritually as you help them develop good financial habits.

Please let us know if you lead a coaching participant to the Lord. Contact the Money Map Coaching department at Crown and let us rejoice with you.

DIAGNOSIS OF FINANCIAL HEALTH

Most of the time you will find that coaching participants spend more than they earn each month. It is your job to determine the extent of the financial difficulty and to communicate that there is hope.

In general, there are four levels of financial difficulty:

1. Fixable with minor expense cutting
2. Fixable with increased income and expense cutting
3. Not immediately fixable
4. Not humanly fixable.

The same basic steps are applicable for each level. For instance, in Level 1 insurance and wills are addressed. Insurance and wills should be addressed for each level, even though we've not mentioned it on Levels 2-4. One level builds on the other. In most cases, the coaching participant should agree to no more borrowing. Borrowing is not biblically prohibited, but it is labeled unwise. We have included a deed on page 136 to help people recognize that God owns everything. This is not legally binding.

LEVEL #1

FIXABLE WITH MINOR EXPENSE CUTTING

- At this level two or three sessions may be sufficient. *(If you choose to use the percentage guideline chart, remember that these are guidelines and not inflexible percentages that cannot be adjusted. For instance, housing in some areas is significantly higher than in others.*

- As you work with the coaching participant and evaluate each expense category, you probably will be able to suggest options for reducing expenses. Most of the time the Food and Miscellaneous categories can be reduced. Be sure to address the subject of sufficient life insurance coverage and the need for a will.

- You may want to assign homework #1 and #2 in the *Journey to Financial Freedom* manual to help them learn God's way of handling money.

LEVEL #2

FIXABLE WITH INCREASED INCOME AND EXPENSE CUTTING

- If unsecured debt is not a problem, then proceed with evaluating the actual monthly expenses. After each expense category has been reduced as much as possible, if there is still a negative monthly balance, address the possibility of additional income. Part-time work is an option. There may be opportunities for ministry in a local church that could be explored. Many times elderly people in the church need some "handyman" or housekeeping help. Working for the elderly can help meet their needs, as well as provide additional income. If this is not an option, and every other avenue of earning additional income has been explored, then church benevolence may be discussed. The pastor or the benevolence committee may request your assistance in this process.

- If unsecured debt is a problem, suggest that the coaching participant visit the Financial Hope Web site. After visiting this site, the participant should be able to determine if he or she should pursue a debt management plan, based on the information found within the Financial Hope Web site. If the coaching participant begins a debt management plan, your role is to give long-term care as you teach God's financial principles and lifetime budgeting. This combination really serves those who need help.

- Homework should be assigned as outlined in the *Journey to Financial Freedom* manual. If possible, have the coaching participant complete all homework assignments before you stop coaching them.

LEVEL #3

NOT IMMEDIATELY FIXABLE

- Most of the time, unsecured debt will be a serious problem. Suggest that the coaching participant visit the Financial Hope Web site to investigate if a debt management plan would be an option for him or her.

- Many times coaching participants will have a car lease, rather than a car loan. This can be difficult to solve. Check your state's laws dealing with leases to see if there are any options available to them. Research the Internet or check with your state attorney general's office. Selling the car may be an option. However, the payoff of the lease may be more than the market value of the car. There may be a possibility of someone else assuming the lease. If the participant has no options and must keep the car through the remainder of the lease period, other categories may have to be reduced to meet the payment.

- After all alternatives have been exhausted, church benevolence may be addressed.

- If the debt has been incurred due to an illness or other uncontrollable circumstance, keep the coaching participant's pastor informed. Obtain the participant's permission before talking to his or her pastor. Your concern and care will provide hope and comfort. There may be agencies in your area that can help those who have medical needs. Christian radio stations, Chambers of Commerce, and churches are good sources of information. Be sure to check the reliability of each organization before you suggest that the participant consider any of them.

LEVEL #4

NOT HUMANLY FIXABLE

- This situation will require the most emotional help. Giving hope to the hopeless is vital. Coaching participants usually will be under extreme stress and often will not react or think clearly. If a participant is forced into bankruptcy, be sure to give as much support as you can. Have people in your church pray for the participant (by first name only) and for you regularly. Encourage the participant by sharing that God is still in control and He understands all their needs. Homework assignments may be a possibility, but it will depend on the coaching participant's stress level. You may want to work on the assignments with the participants, or you may just want to encourage them through Scripture and remind them of the promises of God. If the coaching participants do not have pastors, it would be wise to introduce your pastor or another pastor who will help them spiritually.

- An this level, survival may be the goal for a while. Living from paycheck to paycheck will be a challenge. Weekly meetings may be necessary to help the coaching participant decide how the paycheck will be spent. Eliminating small debts and obtaining second or third jobs should be a priority. Once the participant's finances have stabilized a little, you will be able to begin establishing a budget.

- Review the "Bankruptcy" section on the enclosed CD before you meet with someone who may be forced into bankruptcy. You cannot be the coaching participant's legal counsel, but be familiar with what may happen and the terms that will be used.

The following is a brief guide to help you work through the steps when you deal with what appears to be a hopeless situation.

STEP ONE: Work out a negotiated repayment plan with all creditors. You may need to contact some of the creditors yourself and explain that you will meet regularly with the participant and that a workable budget has been developed. Ask to talk to a supervisor in the creditor's office. Explain that the participant has been to a credit counseling agency and no help could be offered. It may be necessary for the participant to be on the telephone as you talk to the creditor. The creditor may not work with you without the participant.

Tell the creditor that you volunteer your time through the ministry of your church, that you do not charge for your time, and that you encourage people to pay all of their debts. If you are asked about your training, say that you were trained by Crown Financial Ministries, a nonprofit, Christian teaching and educational ministry, whose goal is to teach people scriptural principles of becoming financially free.

STEP TWO: You may discover that the coaching participants have ignored the creditors or made promises that they have not kept. The creditors may have already labeled them irresponsible and not to be trusted. If this is the case, some of the creditors may refuse to negotiate a repayment plan that you present to them. They may threaten legal action.

At this point all assets should be examined for possible liquidation. This would include automobiles, houses, recreational equipment, and even retirement plans. The creditors need to know that you are not trying to hide assets from them. This can be communicated in your cover letter and the Financial Statement.

STEP THREE: If you have been unsuccessful in securing approval for an acceptable repayment plan, talk to the creditors again. They will either initiate legal action or they will wait. If they hold it off, then there still may be an opportunity for negotiation. Psalm 50:15 says, *"Call upon Me in the day of trouble."* The coaching participants should be looking to the Lord for His solution to this problem. Many times the Lord will change creditors' hearts, and what looked like an impossibility will become a workable plan. On the other hand, the Lord may have lessons for the participants to learn through their creditors.

If the creditors take legal action, they will ask for a garnishment of wages or a judgment. Most states have garnishment provisions. This allows the creditor, upon court approval, to attach up to 25 percent of a wage earner's paycheck until the full amount is paid. A judgment is a legal assignment of damages by a creditor that may allow for the accumulation of interest on the balance owed, plus legal fees. Judgments normally are in force for seven years and then may be renewed by the creditor. The individual would not be able to sell or purchase certain assets during this period, unless the creditor is paid first.

At this point, three options are available. First, the coaching participants immediately contact the creditors and ask for another chance to prove themselves. (If you enter a coaching situation at this point, it can be beneficial for you to call the creditor.) At times the creditors may release the legal action if they feel that, with the help of the coach, payments will be forthcoming.

The second option is to allow the garnishment and adjust the budget, allowing for the 25 percent reduction in income. This option only works when the other creditors are willing to work with the coaching participants. It may be that all of the creditors will begin legal action, asking for garnishment of wages. If this is the case, then they must wait in line, because only one creditor at a time may garnish a paycheck. The question here is, can the participant survive a 25 percent reduction in income? If both husband and wife work and the debts are in both names, it's feasible for the creditors to attach both of their paychecks.

The third option is to seek bankruptcy protection; specifically, Chapter 13 personal reorganization. This provides a way for the court to assign specified payments to creditors who previously may have denied such a repayment plan. If Chapter 13 is not an option, then Chapter 7 is the last option. Review the "Bankruptcy" section on the CD for more details. At this point, an attorney will need to be contacted. If you sense that the coaching participant may be suicidal, get professional help immediately. Work through your pastor and professionals. If you or your pastor are not familiar with coaching professionals, you may want to contact Focus on the Family at 1-800-A-FAMILY for a referral in your area.

REPAYMENT PLANS

When you have computed a coaching participant's repayment plan, it is important that you send information to each creditor. Sample letters are included in this course. This plan should include four items: the letter to the creditor signed by the coaching participant, a Monthly Income and Expense Statement, a Debt Payment Computation that shows how much can be paid on each debt, and a current Financial Statement. A check for the amount specified should be signed, attached, and sent (return receipt requested) to each creditor. Make sure participants understand that the cover letter contains a commitment not to use credit while they are repaying these debts. It is not proper to ask creditors to accept a lower payment while the participants continue to borrow. The cover letter also commits coaching participants to use any windfall money to repay the debts earlier. Once the initial plan has been sent, the participant must follow up with a check each month, as promised, until paid. This is a spiritual matter (self-discipline) and a lesson participants need to learn. Your sending the checks will only cause more dependence on you. If you do decide to send the checks, you will need to be bonded.

ANALYZE

You are now ready to begin an important phase: How to analyze the coaching participant's financial situation. This is sometimes challenging. It helps to have a plan of evaluation before you begin coaching. This section presents the necessary steps to evaluate the coaching participant's financial condition using the *Journey to Financial Freedom Manual*.

The *Journey to Financial Freedom Manual* has been developed to assist Money Map Coaches organize and schedule the coaching process. It provides easy access to forms and homework assignments. Work through the manual as if you were the coaching participant. Most of this work you have already completed. Do not skip the step of reviewing this from the coaching participant's viewpoint. To be a good teacher, you must first be a student.

This exercise will help you understand how to use this manual in your coaching. You will use it as a homework and coaching tool. Remember, every coaching participant is unique and will require flexibility. Additional *Journey to Financial Freedom Manuals* may be ordered by calling 1-800-722-1976 or by visiting www.crown.org.

JOURNEY TO FINANCIAL FREEDOM
Practical steps to Money Map coaching

Please have your Journey to Financial Freedom Manual *open as you work through this section.*

SESSION ONE

1. **Open in Prayer**

   This is the most important step in Money Map coaching. Prayer is your key to discover God's direction during your sessions. Prayer acknowledges God is really in charge. Pray for wisdom and direction, both for you and for your coaching participants. Pray that there will be a united spirit as decisions are made. You lead in the prayer during the first session. In future sessions you will be able to sense whether your coaching participants should join in spoken prayer.

2. **Personal Information sheet**

   Fill out this sheet with your coaching participants. This is a good time to get to know the people with whom you are working. Find out about their families, their interests, and as unoffensibly as possible their church affiliation and frequency of attendance. As you complete this form, listen carefully to the coaching participants. Listen to the small things: the moments of hesitation, the sighs, the way things are phrased. You will learn more about your participants by listening than by talking. After you have finished the information sheet, make a copy of it for your files. Be sure to share your contact information as well. This is a good time to develop a trust relationship.

3. **Commitment to Coaching Form**

   This form is designed for you and the coaching participant to make certain commitments. It communicates that the Money Map coaching experience should not be taken lightly. You may need to be flexible with this form. One spouse may be a Christian and the other may not be. Ask for God's guidance in handling special circumstances. Remember that people who have been offended are hard to influence for Christ.

4. **Information Gathering Forms**

   List of Debts

   Fill out this form as completely as possible. List all debts: credit card debt, debts owed to family or friends, debts to doctors and dentists, mortgages, and student loans.

   Financial Statement

   Use this form to learn the coaching participant's overall financial position. This form lists assets and liabilities. If assets are greater than liabilities, it is a good indication that becoming debt free may be possible.

   Monthly Income and Expenses

   This form is where your Money Map coaching "lives." General budget categories are listed and lines are provided for specific categories for the coaching participant's situation. When this form is initially filled out, it will not be completely accurate. After tracking spending for 30 days, revise this form.

5. **Diagnosis of financial health**

   Financial Hope

   Earlier in the approach section, you studied the four levels of financial difficulty. In rare cases, you will find that the participant is doing everything right and only needs affirmation. Beginning with level 2, you may decide to suggest that the participant visit the Financial Hope Web site. Financial Hope will be able to help only those who (1) have an income, (2) are willing to work within a debt-management plan that does not allow for adding more debt, and (3) have a sincere desire to be debt free.

   Spending decisions

   At this stage, discuss how the coaching participants make spending decisions. How do they determine what will be purchased? If the coaching participants are a married couple, do they discuss major purchases? Do they have separate checking accounts? Who keeps the checkbook?

6. Goals setting

This step is designed to give hope by identifying achievable goals. You will concentrate on financial goals, but it may find be helpful to consider personal goals (education, relationships) and spiritual goals (Bible reading, prayer, church attendance). You may ask them to set weekly or daily goals so that they can experience success. Suggest they attend a Crown Small Group Study or seminar.

7. Actions steps

30-day diary

This is designed to help coaching participants determine exactly how much they spend. This is an eye-opening experience to all who will commit to this process.

Balance budget using the Monthly Income and Expense form

Ask the participant to review and balance his or her budget, using this form.

Quit Claim Deed

Assign the Quit Claim Deed for review in Session Two.

Additional recommendations

You may suggest additional action steps for the coaching participant to consider as he or she revises the spending plan.

Homework Assignment #1

Assign this section to be completed before the next session.

Set date for next meeting

Set a definite time and location to meet. It is important that you and the coaching participant know how to contact each other if you need to reschedule a session.

8. Close in prayer

This is a time for thanksgiving to God for what has been accomplished and for guidance and strength for the future.

SESSION TWO

1. Open in prayer

2. Share conversation

Take some time to talk about how things have progressed since your last session. Be sure to *listen* to the coaching participant. Talking too soon may communicate to the coaching participant that you don't really care what he or she has to say.

3. Review Session One

Begin with the 30-day diary. If the diary has been completed, ask the coaching participants what they learned from this exercise. If they have not completed it, place this on the Actions Steps list to be accomplished before the next session.

You may want to bring a copy of the appropriate percentage guideline form to give to the coaching participant. Begin by asking for the revised budget. If not completed, then work with him or her to accomplish this either during session two or place on the Actions Steps list. If the revised budget is completed, review it and ask the participant to explain the changes. Discuss the spending decisions. Note any changes that still need to be made in the Actions Steps list and adjust goals if needed.

If the coaching participants have significant unsecured debt and have not addressed their debts, review the possibility of using Financial Hope. If they have begun a debt management plan, discuss the outcome and how it will impact their budgets.

Review homework assignment #1 and the Deed. Ask the participants what they found interesting and discuss how they will implement God's financial principles.

4. Introduce budgeting concepts

Coaching participants have different levels of experience in budgeting. Some will be knowledgeable in the use of budgeting software. By now you are familiar with the different budgeting systems. Determine the budget that will best suit your coaching participant. You can offer the spreadsheet format from the Crown Small Group Study; the envelope system in the *Family Financial Workbook;* or budgeting software, such as *Money Matters.* You may show the coaching participant the different helpful tools that are available through Crown in the materials catalog or on the Web site.

5. Actions steps

Have the coaching participant write down all the action steps that need to be accomplished before the next session. Make certain that the coaching participant clearly understands the instructions. Be sure to include the date and time of the next session.

6. Close in prayer

This is a time to thank God for what has been accomplished and for guidance and strength for the future.

Follow the outlines in the manual for the future coaching sessions. You will work with coaching participants as they make decisions, adjust spending, and learn what the Bible says about handling money. Their progress will largely be determined by their faithfulness. You will want to encourage the participants, but you cannot do their work for them. Provide information on how to attend Crown's Small Group Study or seminar or view Crown's video.

You may use the Post-Coaching Review form on the next page to keep record of each session.

POST-COACHING REVIEW

Participant's name _____ Telephone (____)_____

Date of session _____

Date of next session _____ Time _____

Location _____

Homework assigned _____

Recommendations given

_____

_____

_____

Goals set

_____

_____

Evaluation of financial status

_____

_____

Special needs

_____

_____

Action steps

_____

_____

Additional information

_____

_____

WEEK SEVEN

Quit Claim Deed

This Quit Claim Deed, Made the _____ day of _____

From: _____

To: The Lord

I (we) hereby transfer to the Lord the ownership of the following possessions:

Witnesses who hold me (us) accountable in the recognition of the Lord's ownership:

_____

_____

Stewards of the possessions above:

_____

_____

This instrument is not a binding legal document and cannot be used to transfer property.

CASE STUDIES
ONE AND TWO

ASSIGNMENT

1. Review the Suggested Percentage Guidelines on pages 138 to 142.

2. Review *SnapShot Gold*® on the CD.

3. Complete the Case Studies One and Two on pages 143 to 154.

You have learned God's financial principles, developed your personal budget, and studied the process of Money Map coaching. Now you will begin to complete 12 case studies. Each consists of a brief description of the financial situation, along with a completed Monthly Income and Expense form, List of Debts form, and Financial Statement.

Complete a revised budget for each case study by applying the biblical principles and budgeting techniques you've learned. Suggested percentage guidelines are provided for you to use as a reference. The goal is to balance the budget by allocating appropriate funds in each category.

You can assume that the financial information in the case studies has been gathered by using the *Journey to Financial Freedom* manual. You will often discover that gathering accurate financial information will be a challenge.

SUGGESTED PERCENTAGE GUIDELINES FOR FAMILY INCOME
(Family of Four)
(The Net Spendable percentages are applicable to Head of Household family of three, as well)

Gross Household Income	25,000 or less	35,000	45,000	55,000	65,000	85,000	115,000
1. Tithe	10%	10%	10%	10%	10%	10%	10%
2. Taxes[1]	*2.7%	11.2%	14.8%	17.2%	18.8%	23.5%	26.3%
Net Spendable percentages below add to 100%							
NET SPENDABLE INCOME	21,825	27,580	33,840	40,040	46,280	58,475	73,255
3. Housing	39%	36%	32%	30%	30%	30%	29%
4. Food	15%	12%	13%	12%	11%	11%	11%
5. Transportation	15%	12%	13%	14%	14%	13%	13%
6. Insurance	5%	5%	5%	5%	5%	5%	5%
7. Debts	5%	5%	5%	5%	5%	5%	5%
8. Entertainment/Recreation	3%	5%	5%	7%	7%	7%	8%
9. Clothing	4%	5%	5%	6%	6%	7%	7%
10. Savings	5%	5%	5%	5%	5%	5%	5%
11. Medical/Dental	5%	6%	6%	5%	5%	5%	5%
12. Miscellaneous	4%	4%	6%	6%	7%	7%	7%
13. Investments[2]	—	5%	5%	5%	5%	5%	5%
EXTRA EXPENSE—If you have this expense below, the percentage shown must be deducted from other budget categories.							
14. School/Child Care[3]	8%	6%	5%	5%	5%	5%	5%
15. Unallocated Surplus Income[4]	—	—	—	—	—	—	—

[1] Guideline percentages for tax category include taxes for Social Security, federal, and a small estimated amount for state, based on 2002 rates. The tax code changes regularly. Please be sure to insert your actual tax into this category.

[2] This category is used for long-term investment planning, such as college education or retirement.

[3] This category is added as a guide only. If you have this expense, the percentage shown must be deducted from other budget categories.

[4] This category is used when surplus income is received. This would be kept in the checking account to be used within a few weeks; otherwise, it should be transferred to an allocated category.

* In some cases earned income credit will apply. It may be possible to increase the number of deductions to lessen the amount of tax paid per month. Review the last tax return for specific information.

SUGGESTED PERCENTAGE GUIDELINES FOR FAMILY INCOME
(Family of Two—Married Couple)

Gross Household Income	15,000 or less	25,000	35,000	45,000	55,000	65,000	115,000
1. Tithe	10%	10%	10%	10%	10%	10%	10%
2. Taxes[1]	8.8%	14.3%	18%	20.2%	21.5%	23.3%	28.8%
Net Spendable percentages below add to 100%							
NET SPENDABLE INCOME	**12,180**	**18,925**	**25,200**	**31,410**	**37,675**	**43,355**	**70,380**
3. Housing	40%	36%	32%	30%	30%	30%	29%
4. Food	15%	12%	13%	12%	11%	11%	11%
5. Transportation	15%	12%	13%	14%	14%	13%	13%
6. Insurance	5%	5%	5%	5%	5%	5%	5%
7. Debts	5%	5%	5%	5%	5%	5%	5%
8. Entertainment/Recreation	3%	5%	5%	6%	7%	7%	8%
9. Clothing	4%	5%	5%	6%	6%	7%	7%
10. Savings	4%	5%	5%	5%	5%	5%	5%
11. Medical/Dental	6%	6%	6%	6%	5%	5%	5%
12. Miscellaneous	3%	4%	6%	6%	7%	7%	7%
13. Investments[2]	—	5%	5%	5%	5%	5%	5%
EXTRA EXPENSE—If you have this expense below, the percentage shown must be deducted from other budget categories.							
14. School/Child Care[3]	—	—	—	—	—	—	—
15. Unallocated Surplus Income[4]	—	—	—	—	—	—	—

[1] Guideline percentages for tax category include taxes for Social Security, federal, and a small estimated amount for state, based on 2002 rates. The tax code changes regularly. Please be sure to insert your actual tax into this category.

[2] This category is used for long-term investment planning, such as college education or retirement.

[3] This category is added as a guide only. If you have this expense, the percentage shown must be deducted from other budget categories.

[4] This category is used when surplus income is received. This would be kept in the checking account to be used within a few weeks; otherwise, it should be transferred to an allocated category.

SUGGESTED PERCENTAGE GUIDELINES
FOR FAMILY INCOME
(Single Parent—One Child)

Gross Income	15,000	20,000	25,000
1. Tithe	10%	10%	10%
2. Taxes[1]	*3.2%	6.7%	11.8%
Net Spendable percentages below add to 100%			
NET SPENDABLE INCOME	**13,020**	**16,660**	**19,550**
3. Housing	40%	39%	39%
4. Food[2]	15%	14%	14%
5. Transportation	15%	14%	14%
6. Insurance	3%	3%	4%
7. Debts	4%	5%	5%
8. Entertainment/Recreation	3%	4%	4%
9. Clothing	5%	5%	5%
10. Savings	5%	5%	5%
11. Medical/Dental	7%	7%	6%
12. Miscellaneous	3%	4%	4%
13. Investments[3]	—	—	—
EXTRA EXPENSE—If you have this expense below, the percentage shown must be deducted from other budget categories.			
14. School/Child Care[4]	—	—	—
15. Unallocated Surplus Income[5]	—	—	—

[1] This percentage is based on year 2002 rates for Social Security, federal, and state taxes. This does not factor the Earned Income Credit, which may alter this figure considerably. The tax code changes regularly. Please be sure to insert your actual tax into this category.

[2] This percentage is for money spent on food and does not include the reduction that would result by food stamp or food bank use.

[3] Considering the obligations at this income level, there may be no surplus funds for investing long term.

[4] This percentage has not been factored into the budget. If you must pay for child care, all other categories must be reduced to provide funds for this expense. Although this is a real need, many single parents have alternate arrangements to meet the need through family or scholarship programs.

[5] This category is used when surplus income is received, such as irregular child support. This would be kept in the checking account to be used within a few weeks; otherwise, it should be transferred to an allocated category.

* In some cases earned income credit will apply. It may be possible to increase the number of deductions to lessen the amount of tax paid per month. Review the last tax return for specific information.

SUGGESTED PERCENTAGE GUIDELINES
FOR INDIVIDUAL INCOME
(Single Adults)

	Living Alone	With Roommate	Living Alone	With Roommate
Gross Income	**23,000**	**23,000**	**32,000**	**32,000**
1. Tithe	10%	10%	10%	10%
2. Taxes[1]	19.7%	21%	21.9%	24%
Net Spendable percentages below add to 100%				
NET SPENDABLE INCOME	**16,169**	**15,870**	**21,792**	**21,120**
3. Housing	39%	25%	38%	22%
4. Food	9%	9%	8%	8%
5. Transportation	14%	19%	14%	19%
6. Insurance	4%	4%	4%	4%
7. Debts	5%	5%	5%	5%
8. Entertainment/Recreation	7%	9%	6%	9%
9. Clothing	5%	7%	5%	6%
10. Savings	5%	8%	5%	13%
11. Medical/Dental	5%	5%	4%	3%
12. Miscellaneous	5%	5%	6%	6%
13. Investments[2]	2%	5%	5%	5%
EXTRA EXPENSE—If you have this expense below, the percentage shown must be deducted from other budget categories.				
14. Education[3]	3%	10%	7%	10%
15. Unallocated Surplus Income[4]	—	—	—	—

[1] Guideline percentages for tax category include taxes for Social Security, federal, and a small estimated amount for state, based on 2002 rates. The tax code changes regularly. Please be sure to insert your actual tax into this category.

[2] This category is used for long-term investment planning, such as retirement.

[3] This category is added as a guide only. If you have this expense, the percentage shown must be deducted from other budget categories.

[4] This category is used when surplus income is received. This would be kept in the checking account to be used within a few weeks; otherwise, it should be transferred to an allocated category.

SUGGESTED PERCENTAGE GUIDELINES
FOR FAMILY INCOME
(Family of Six)

Gross Income	25,000 or less	35,000	45,000	55,000	65,000
1. Tithe	10%	10%	10%	10%	10%
2. Taxes[1]	*1.7%	9%	9.8%	12.8%	15.1%
Net Spendable percentages below add to 100%					
NET SPENDABLE INCOME	22,075	28,350	36,090	42,460	48,685
3. Housing	38%	38%	34%	33%	32%
4. Food	15%	15%	14%	14%	14%
5. Transportation	14%	14%	12%	12%	11%
6. Insurance	5%	5%	5%	5%	5%
7. Debts	5%	5%	5%	5%	5%
8. Entertainment/Recreation	3%	4%	4%	5%	5%
9. Clothing	5%	5%	6%	6%	7%
10. Savings	4%	4%	5%	5%	5%
11. Medical/Dental	8%	7%	7%	7%	7%
12. Miscellaneous	3%	3%	5%	5%	5%
13. Investments[2]	—	—	3%	3%	4%
EXTRA EXPENSE—If you have this expense below, the percentage shown must be deducted from other budget categories.					
14. School/Child Care[3]	10%	8%	6%	6%	5%
15. Unallocated Surplus Income[4]	—	—	—	—	—

[1] Guideline percentages for tax category include taxes for Social Security, federal, and a small estimated amount for state, based on 2002 rates. The tax code changes regularly. Please be sure to insert your actual tax into this category.

[2] This category is used for long-term investment planning, such as college education or retirement.

[3] This category is added as a guide only. If you have this expense, the percentage shown must be deducted from other budget categories.

[4] This category is used when surplus income is received. This would be kept in the checking account to be used within a few weeks; otherwise, it should be transferred to an allocated category.

* In some cases earned income credit will apply. It may be possible to increase the number of deductions to lessen the amount of tax paid per month. Review the last tax return for specific information.

CASE STUDY ONE

Background Information: Stan Jones, age 48, is a permanently disabled veteran. Penny Jones, age 46, works as a convenience store clerk, making $900 per month. They have two grown children, ages 19 and 21, living at home, but the children contribute nothing financially to the household. The other children are ages 5 and 8. The 8-year-old has speech therapy twice per week; insurance does not pay for this expense. As a permanently disabled veteran, Stan was able to receive a partial grant from the V.A, which allowed them to purchase a four-bedroom house that was adapted for wheelchair use. They also received an automobile grant, which allowed them to purchase a used van with adaptive driving equipment. Health benefits are provided for Stan, Penny, and the two younger children through the V.A. Stan has $100,000 of term life insurance on himself, and neither he nor Penny have wills.

Assignment: Explain how you would coach the Jones family. Include key Scriptures that you would offer for Stan and Penny to consider as they make decisions. Show how you would help them balance their budget, repay their debts, and prevent future indebtedness.

CASE STUDY ONE—AS IS
MONTHLY INCOME AND EXPENSES

GROSS INCOME PER MONTH		$2,700
Salary	900	
Interest		
Dividends		
Social Security	700	
VA benefits	1,100	

LESS:

1. **Tithe**		$270
2. **Tax** (Est. - Incl. Fed., State, FICA)		$259
NET SPENDABLE INCOME		$2,171

3. **Housing**		$805
Mortgage (rent)	650	
Insurance	(incl.)	
Taxes	(incl.)	
Electricity	55	
Gas	45	
Water	15	
Sanitation		
Telephone	40	
Maintenance		
Other (_____)		
Other (_____)		

4. **Food**		$425

5. **Automobile(s)**		$545
Payments	395	
Gas and Oil	80	
Insurance	70	
License/Taxes		
Maint./Repair/Replace		

6. **Insurance**		$25
Life ($100,000 term)	25	
Medical		
Other (_____)		

7. **Debts**		$553
Credit Card	193	
Loans and Notes	360	
Other (_____)		
Other (_____)		

8. **Enter./Recreation**		$230
Eating Out	80	
Baby Sitters	20	
Activities/Trips	30	
Vacation	100	
Other (_____)		
Other (_____)		

9. **Clothing**		$100
10. **Savings**		$0

11. **Medical Expenses**		$275
Doctor	25	
Dentist		
Credit Card		
Speech Therapy	250	

12. **Miscellaneous**		$185
Toiletry, cosmetics	5	
Beauty, barber		
Laundry, cleaning		
Allowances, lunches	50	
Subscriptions	5	
Gifts (incl. Christmas)	75	
Cash	50	
Cable/Internet		
Other (_____)		
Other (_____)		

13. **Investments**		$0

14. **School/Child Care**		$0
Tuition		
Materials		
Transportation		
Day Care		
Other (_____)		

TOTAL EXPENSES		$3,143

INCOME VERSUS EXPENSES

Net Spendable Income	$2,171
Less Expenses	$3,143
	-972

15. **Unallocated Surplus Income**[1]

---

[1] This category is used when surplus income is received. This would be kept in the checking account to be used within a few weeks; otherwise, it should be transferred to an allocated category.

FINANCIAL STATEMENT

ASSETS

Liquid Assets[1]

Checking Acct.	$125
Savings Acct.	55
Total Liquid Assets	**$180**

Invested Assets[2]

IRA	$6,000
Total Invested	**$6,000**

Use Assets[3]

Furniture	$3,000
Personal Items	15,000
Ford Van	8,000
Residence	100,000
Honda Accord	20,000
Total Use Assets	**$146,000**
TOTAL ASSETS	**$152,180**

LIABILITIES[4]

Credit Cards	$7,000
1st Nat. Bank	4,000
Preferred Finance	5,000
Hometown Furn.	3,000
1st Bank (Residence)	65,000
2nd Bank (Honda)	15,000
TOTAL LIABILITIES	**$99,000**

NET WORTH	**$53,180**
(Assets-Liabilities)	

TOTAL LIABILITIES AND NET WORTH	**$152,180**

[1] Cash, Savings Accounts, Checking Accounts
[2] IRAs, TSAs, 401(k)s, Investment, Real Estate, CDs, Antiques presented at fair market value.
[3] Residence, Autos, Personal Belongings presented at fair market value.
[4] Outstanding Real Estate Loans, Credit Cards, Auto Loans, Personal Loans.

LIST OF DEBTS
CASE STUDY ONE

To Whom Owed	Contact Name Phone Number	Pay Off	Payments Left	Monthly Payment	Date Due	Interest Rate
VISA		$2,500	55	$69	25th	19%
MasterCard		$4,500	59	$124	15th	20%
1st National Bank		$4,000	44	$120	25th	16%
Preferred Finance Co.		$5,000	47	$150	15th	18%
Hometown Furniture		$3,000	44	$90	1st	16%
1st Bank		$65,000	240	$650	1st	11.6%
2nd Bank		$15,000	38	$395	15th	8%

CASE STUDY ONE—WORKSHEET
MONTHLY INCOME AND EXPENSES

GROSS INCOME PER MONTH _____

    Salary _____

    Interest _____

    Dividends _____

    Other (_____) _____

    Other (_____) _____

LESS:

  1. Tithe _____

  2. Tax (Est. - Incl. Fed., State, FICA) _____

    NET SPENDABLE INCOME _____

  3. Housing _____

    Mortgage (rent) _____

    Insurance _____

    Taxes _____

    Electricity _____

    Gas _____

    Water _____

    Sanitation _____

    Telephone _____

    Maintenance _____

    Other (_____) _____

    Other (_____) _____

  4. Food _____

  5. Automobile(s) _____

    Payments _____

    Gas and Oil _____

    Insurance _____

    License/Taxes _____

    Maint./Repair/Replace _____

  6. Insurance _____

    Life _____

    Medical _____

    Other (_____) _____

  7. Debts _____

    Credit Card _____

    Loans and Notes _____

    Other (_____) _____

    Other (_____) _____

8. Enter./Recreation _____

    Eating Out _____

    Baby Sitters _____

    Activities/Trips _____

    Vacation _____

    Other (_____) _____

    Other (_____) _____

9. Clothing _____

10. Savings _____

11. Medical Expenses _____

    Doctor _____

    Dentist _____

    Credit Card _____

    Other (_____) _____

12. Miscellaneous

    Toiletry, cosmetics _____

    Beauty, barber _____

    Laundry, cleaning _____

    Allowances, lunches _____

    Subscriptions _____

    Gifts (incl. Christmas) _____

    Cash _____

    Cable/Internet _____

    Other (_____) _____

    Other (_____) _____

13. Investments _____

14. School/Child Care _____

    Tuition _____

    Materials _____

    Transportation _____

    Day Care _____

    Other (_____) _____

TOTAL EXPENSES _____

INCOME VERSUS EXPENSES

  Net Spendable Income _____

  Less Expenses _____

  _____

15. Unallocated Surplus Income[1] _____

---

[1] This category is used when surplus income is received. This would be kept in the checking account to be used within a few weeks; otherwise, it should be transferred to an allocated category.

CASE STUDY ONE
COMMENTS

CASE STUDY TWO

Background Information: Peter and Shelly Smith are 29 and 27, respectively. They have two children, ages 4 and 6. Peter is a sales representative for an agricultural supply company and currently makes $2,100 per month. They live in a rented two-bedroom house in a small rural town. There are no real monthly financial problems, except that no surplus is being accumulated. They owe $4,000 to a family member who must be repaid eventually, although there is no immediate pressure. The Smiths receive about $2,400 from income tax refunds each year, which they spend frivolously. When their first child was born, they purchased life insurance and had wills written. Medical insurance is provided through Peter's employer for a small monthly amount.

Assignment: Peter and Shelly have basically been keeping within their income. How would you advise them to increase their budget surplus, pay off the debts, and prevent future indebtedness?

CASE STUDY TWO—AS IS
MONTHLY INCOME AND EXPENSES

GROSS INCOME PER MONTH $2,100

Salary	2,100
Interest	
Dividends	
Other (_____)	
Other (_____)	

LESS:

1. **Tithe** $210

2. **Tax** (Est. - Incl. Fed., State, FICA) $225

   NET SPENDABLE INCOME $1,665

3. **Housing** $513

Mortgage (rent)	375
Insurance	
Taxes	
Electricity	55
Gas	40
Water	13
Sanitation	5
Telephone	25
Maintenance	
Other (_____)	
Other (_____)	

4. **Food** $350

5. **Automobile(s)** $182

Payments	
Gas and Oil	80
Insurance	50
License/Taxes	12
Maint./Repair/Replace	40

6. **Insurance** $60

Life ($30,000 Whole Life)	60
Medical	
Other (_____)	

7. **Debts** $20

Credit Card	20
Loans and Notes	
Other (_____)	
Other (_____)	

8. **Enter./Recreation** $230

Eating Out	80
Baby Sitters	20
Activities/Trips	55
Vacation	75
Other (_____)	
Other (_____)	

9. **Clothing** $50

10. **Savings** $25

11. **Medical Expenses** $50

Doctor	20
Dentist	20
Drugs	10
Other (_____)	

12. **Miscellaneous** $178

Toiletry, cosmetics	10
Beauty, barber	10
Laundry, cleaning	10
Allowances, lunches	35
Subscriptions	3
Gifts (incl. Christmas)	40
Cash	70
Cable/Internet	
Other (_____)	
Other (_____)	

13. **Investments** $0

14. **School/Child Care** $0

Tuition	
Materials	
Transportation	
Day Care	
Other (_____)	

TOTAL EXPENSES $1,658

INCOME VERSUS EXPENSES

Net Spendable Income	$1,665
Less Expenses	$1,658

15. **Unallocated Surplus Income**[1] $7

[1] This category is used when surplus income is received. This would be kept in the checking account to be used within a few weeks; otherwise, it should be transferred to an allocated category.

CASE STUDY TWO
FINANCIAL STATEMENT

ASSETS

Liquid Assets[1]	
Checking Acct.	$75
Savings Acct.	45
Total Liquid Assets	$120

Invested Assets[2]	
Life Ins. Cash Value	$385
Total Invested	$385

Use Assets[3]	
Ford	$3,000
Personal Items	10,000
Total Use Assets	$13,000
TOTAL ASSETS	$13,505

LIABILITIES[4]

Loan to parents	$4,000
VISA	800
TOTAL LIABILITIES	$4,800

NET WORTH	$8,705
(Assets-Liabilities)	

TOTAL LIABILITIES AND NET WORTH	$13,505

[1] Cash, Savings Accounts, Checking Accounts
[2] IRAs, TSAs, 401(k)s, Investment, Real Estate, CDs, Antiques presented at fair market value.
[3] Residence, Autos, Personal Belongings presented at fair market value.
[4] Outstanding Real Estate Loans, Credit Cards, Auto Loans, Personal Loans.

LIST OF DEBTS
CASE STUDY TWO

To Whom Owed	Contact Name Phone Number	Pay Off	Payments Left	Monthly Payment	Date Due	Interest Rate
VISA		$800	52	$20	25th	13%
Parents		$4,000	—	—	—	N/A

CASE STUDY TWO—WORKSHEET
MONTHLY INCOME AND EXPENSES

GROSS INCOME PER MONTH _____

    Salary _____

    Interest _____

    Dividends _____

    Other (_____) _____

    Other (_____) _____

LESS:

  1. Tithe _____

  2. Tax (Est. - Incl. Fed., State, FICA) _____

    NET SPENDABLE INCOME _____

  3. Housing

    Mortgage (rent) _____

    Insurance _____

    Taxes _____

    Electricity _____

    Gas _____

    Water _____

    Sanitation _____

    Telephone _____

    Maintenance _____

    Other (_____) _____

    Other (_____) _____

  4. Food _____

  5. Automobile(s) _____

    Payments _____

    Gas and Oil _____

    Insurance _____

    License/Taxes _____

    Maint./Repair/Replace _____

  6. Insurance _____

    Life _____

    Medical _____

    Other (_____) _____

  7. Debts _____

    Credit Card _____

    Loans and Notes _____

    Other (_____) _____

    Other (_____) _____

8. Enter./Recreation _____

    Eating Out _____

    Baby Sitters _____

    Activities/Trips _____

    Vacation _____

    Other (_____) _____

    Other (_____) _____

9. Clothing _____

10. Savings _____

11. Medical Expenses _____

    Doctor _____

    Dentist _____

    Credit Card _____

    Other (_____) _____

12. Miscellaneous

    Toiletry, cosmetics _____

    Beauty, barber _____

    Laundry, cleaning _____

    Allowances, lunches _____

    Subscriptions _____

    Gifts (incl. Christmas) _____

    Cash _____

    Cable/Internet _____

    Other (_____) _____

    Other (_____) _____

13. Investments _____

14. School/Child Care _____

    Tuition _____

    Materials _____

    Transportation _____

    Day Care _____

    Other (_____) _____

TOTAL EXPENSES _____

INCOME VERSUS EXPENSES

    Net Spendable Income _____

    Less Expenses _____

15. Unallocated Surplus Income[1] _____

---

[1] This category is used when surplus income is received. This would be kept in the checking account to be used within a few weeks; otherwise, it should be transferred to an allocated category.

CASE STUDY TWO
COMMENTS

CASE STUDY ONE ANSWERS

When reviewing the suggested answers to the case studies, keep in mind that taxes are estimates. When working with coaching participants, be sure to refer to their paycheck stubs or ask the participants to check with their employers or a tax professional.

This case posed several problems. The debt situation put significant pressure on the marriage, caused in part by the two grown children living at home and paying nothing toward expenses. The practice of a child finishing school, getting a job, but not contributing anything to the household expenses is unwise. Children need to learn to be responsible.

First, there had to be an absolute commitment to no more borrowing, so all credit cards were destroyed. An arrangement was made with Hometown Furniture Company to take back the furniture that was only six weeks old. This reduced their liability by $3,000. Replacement furniture was provided through surpluses from church families.

The Joneses decided to withdraw their IRA, setting aside what they would owe in penalties and taxes. With the proceeds, they paid off Preferred Finance. A debt management plan was established to pay creditors a total of $220 per month.

Other changes:

1. The two older children will be required to pay $200 each for living expenses.
2. They sold the Honda and financed an older used car at $150 per month.
3. They decreased Entertainment/Recreation to $100 per month.
4. They increased Savings to $150 per month for contingencies.
5. They made minor adjustments to Miscellaneous.
6. It was pointed out to them that they needed more life insurance. The Joneses acted on this advice and increased Stan's coverage to $250,000 and purchased a $100,000 policy on Penny.
7. They decided to take more tax deductions instead of getting a large refund. This increased their monthly income significantly.
8. They were encouraged to secure wills as soon as they could afford it.

CASE STUDY ONE—ANSWER
MONTHLY INCOME AND EXPENSES

GROSS INCOME PER MONTH $3,100

Salary	900
Interest	
Other	400
Social Security	700
VA benefits	1,100

LESS:

1. Tithe $310

*2. Tax (Est. - Incl. Fed., State, FICA) $69

NET SPENDABLE INCOME $2,721

3. Housing $870

Mortgage (rent)	650
Insurance	(incl.)
Taxes	(incl.)
Electricity	75
Gas	45
Water	20
Sanitation	5
Telephone	40
Maintenance	35
Other (_____)	
Other (_____)	

4. Food $431

5. Automobile(s) $305

Payments	150
Gas and Oil	80
Insurance	35
License/Taxes	5
Maint./Repair/Replace	35

6. Insurance $60

Life ($250,000 term) Stan	40
Life ($100,000 term) Penny	20
Other (_____)	

7. Debts $220

Credit Card	140
Loans and Notes	80
Other (_____)	
Other (_____)	

8. Enter./Recreation $100

Eating Out	40
Baby Sitters	
Activities/Trips	20
Vacation	40
Other (_____)	
Other (_____)	

9. Clothing $100

10. Savings $150

11. Medical Expenses $295

Doctor	20
Dentist	25
Drugs	
Speech Therapy	250

12. Miscellaneous $190

Toiletry, cosmetics	15
Beauty, barber	10
Laundry, cleaning	15
Allowances, lunches	50
Subscriptions	5
Gifts (incl. Christmas)	50
Cash	45
Cable/Internet	
Other (_____)	
Other (_____)	

13. Investments $0

14. School/Child Care $0

Tuition	
Materials	
Transportation	
Day Care	
Other (_____)	

TOTAL EXPENSES $2,721

INCOME VERSUS EXPENSES

Net Spendable Income	$2,721
Less Expenses	$2,721

15. Unallocated Surplus Income[1]

---

[1] This category is used when surplus income is received. This would be kept in the checking account to be used within a few weeks; otherwise, it should be transferred to an allocated category.

* Earned Income Credit <334>

CASE STUDY TWO ANSWERS

The tax refund is needed now in their monthly budget. They decided to take more deductions and reduced their taxes. With this additional monthly income, the credit card payments can be accelerated and some payments to the parents can begin. There were other changes made.

1. The Smiths purchased renter's insurance for $15 per month.

2. They increased Automobile Maintenance/Repair/Replace to $120 per month.

3. They converted the existing $30,000 whole life policy to a term policy of $250,000 on Peter for $30 per month and added a $100,000 term policy for Shelly for $15 per month. The $385 cash value proceeds were applied toward credit card debt. (They shared their concerns with their life insurance agent. He agreed to convert the present policy to a term policy.)

4. They reduced Entertainment/Recreation to $156 per month.

5. The Smiths increased Clothing to $60 per month.

6. They established a Savings of $75 per month for contingencies.

7. They increased Medical Expenses to $60 per month.

8. They reduced their Food bill by $70 per month.

This case required follow-up of only two months. Already convinced that they should be good stewards, the couple just needed to be shown how. By committing to a no-borrowing policy in the future and the establishment of savings, the Smiths should avoid any further debt problem.

CASE STUDY TWO—ANSWERS
MONTHLY INCOME AND EXPENSES

GROSS INCOME PER MONTH — $2,100

Salary	2,100
Interest	
Dividends	
Other (_____)	
Other (_____)	

LESS:

1. Tithe — $210

*2. Tax (Est. - Incl. Fed., State, FICA) — $161

NET SPENDABLE INCOME — $1,729

3. Housing — $528

Mortgage (rent)	350
Insurance	15
Taxes	
Electricity	75
Gas	40
Water	18
Sanitation	
Telephone	30
Maintenance	
Other (_____)	
Other (_____)	

4. Food — $280

5. Automobile(s) — $262

Payments	
Gas and Oil	80
Insurance	50
License/Taxes	12
Maint./Repair/Replace	120

6. Insurance — $45

Life ($250,000 term) Peter	30
Life ($100,000 term) Shelly	15
Other (_____)	

7. Debts — $120

Credit Card	70
Loans and Notes	50
Other (_____)	
Other (_____)	

8. Enter./Recreation — $156

Eating Out	65
Baby Sitters	20
Activities/Trips	25
Vacation	46
Other (_____)	
Other (_____)	

9. Clothing — $60

10. Savings — $75

11. Medical Expenses — $60

Doctor	30
Dentist	20
Drugs	10
Other (_____)	

12. Miscellaneous — $143

Toiletry, cosmetics	10
Beauty, barber	10
Laundry, cleaning	10
Allowances, lunches	30
Subscriptions	3
Gifts (incl. Christmas)	20
Cash	60
Cable/Internet	
Other (_____)	
Other (_____)	

13. Investments — $0

14. School/Child Care — $0

Tuition	
Materials	
Transportation	
Day Care	
Other (_____)	

TOTAL EXPENSES — $1,729

INCOME VERSUS EXPENSES

Net Spendable Income	$1,729
Less Expenses	$1,729

15. Unallocated Surplus Income[1]

---

[1] This category is used when surplus income is received. This would be kept in the checking account to be used within a few weeks; otherwise, it should be transferred to an allocated category.

* Earned Income Credit <146>

WEEK

ASSIGNMENT

Complete Case Studies Three, Four, and Five.

CASE STUDY THREE

Background Information: Kathy Thomas is 84. She has been a widow for one year and has no living relatives. For the past six months she has been trying to decide where to live. She currently lives in a two-bedroom apartment and has considered trying to find a room-mate. Kathy has excellent health for her age. She has two dogs that she takes for a one-mile walk everyday. Her deceased husband had a retirement benefit, but he had chosen the single-life pay option. He left her with $15,000 of life insurance proceeds. After funeral expenses she had only $3,000 left. She has almost exhausted this. Her pastor has referred her to you, knowing that Kathy will need help with some difficult decisions in the near future.

Assignment: This is a challenging case because of Kathy's age. Make a list of all the suggestions you would give to Kathy and any action items you would be responsible for, considering her age. Comment on how you would advise Kathy to develop a budget and plan for her future.

CASE STUDY THREE—AS IS
MONTHLY INCOME AND EXPENSES

GROSS INCOME PER MONTH		$650
Salary		
Interest		
Dividends		
Social Security	650	
Other (_____)		

LESS:

1. **Tithe**		$65
2. **Tax** (Est. - Incl. Fed., State, FICA)		

NET SPENDABLE INCOME		$585

3. **Housing**		$515
Mortgage (rent)	385	
Insurance	10	
Taxes		
Electricity	60	
Gas	25	
Water	15	
Sanitation		
Telephone	20	
Maintenance		
Other (_____)		
Other (_____)		

4. **Food**		$75

5. **Automobile(s)**		$0
Payments		
Gas and Oil		
Insurance		
License/Taxes		
Maint./Repair/Replace		

6. **Insurance**		$0
Life		
Medical		
Other (_____)		

7. **Debts**		$0
Credit Card		
Loans and Notes		
Other (_____)		
Other (_____)		

8. **Enter./Recreation**		$20
Eating Out	10	
Baby Sitters		
Activities/Trips	10	
Vacation		
Other (_____)		
Other (_____)		

9. **Clothing**		$15
10. **Savings**		$0
11. **Medical Expenses**		$60
Doctor	25	
Dentist	10	
Drugs	25	
Other (_____)		

12. **Miscellaneous**		$35
Toiletry, cosmetics	5	
Beauty, barber		
Laundry, cleaning	10	
Allowances, lunches		
Subscriptions	5	
Gifts (incl. Christmas)	5	
Cash	10	
Cable/Internet		
Other (_____)		
Other (_____)		

13. **Investments**		$0

14. **School/Child Care**		$0
Tuition		
Materials		
Transportation		
Day Care		
Other (_____)		

TOTAL EXPENSES		$720

INCOME VERSUS EXPENSES

Net Spendable Income	$585
Less Expenses	$720
	-$135

15. **Unallocated Surplus Income**[1]

---

[1] This category is used when surplus income is received. This would be kept in the checking account to be used within a few weeks; otherwise, it should be transferred to an allocated category.

CASE STUDY THREE
FINANCIAL STATEMENT

ASSETS

Liquid Assets[1]

Checking Acct.	$55
Savings Acct.	380

Total Liquid Assets	$435

Invested Assets[2]

Total Invested	$0

Use Assets[3]

Personal Items	$7,000

Total Use Assets	$7,000
TOTAL ASSETS	$7,435

LIABILITIES[4]

TOTAL LIABILITIES	$0

NET WORTH (Assets-Liabilities)	$7,435

TOTAL LIABILITIES AND NET WORTH	$7,435

[1] Cash, Savings Accounts, Checking Accounts
[2] IRAs, TSAs, 401(k)s, Investment, Real Estate, CDs, Antiques presented at fair market value.
[3] Residence, Autos, Personal Belongings presented at fair market value.
[4] Outstanding Real Estate Loans, Credit Cards, Auto Loans, Personal Loans.

LIST OF DEBTS
CASE STUDY THREE

To Whom Owed	Contact Name Phone Number	Pay Off	Payments Left	Monthly Payment	Date Due	Interest Rate
NO DEBTS						

CASE STUDY THREE—WORKSHEET
MONTHLY INCOME AND EXPENSES

GROSS INCOME PER MONTH _____

    Salary _____

    Interest _____

    Dividends _____

    Other (_____) _____

    Other (_____) _____

LESS:

  1. Tithe _____

  2. Tax (Est. - Incl. Fed., State, FICA) _____

     NET SPENDABLE INCOME _____

  3. Housing

    Mortgage (rent) _____

    Insurance _____

    Taxes _____

    Electricity _____

    Gas _____

    Water _____

    Sanitation _____

    Telephone _____

    Maintenance _____

    Other (_____) _____

    Other (_____) _____

  4. Food _____

  5. Automobile(s)

    Payments _____

    Gas and Oil _____

    Insurance _____

    License/Taxes _____

    Maint./Repair/Replace _____

  6. Insurance _____

    Life _____

    Medical _____

    Other (_____) _____

  7. Debts _____

    Credit Card _____

    Loans and Notes _____

    Other (_____) _____

    Other (_____) _____

8. Enter./Recreation

    Eating Out _____

    Baby Sitters _____

    Activities/Trips _____

    Vacation _____

    Other (_____) _____

    Other (_____) _____

9. Clothing _____

10. Savings _____

11. Medical Expenses

    Doctor _____

    Dentist _____

    Credit Card _____

    Other (_____) _____

12. Miscellaneous _____

    Toiletry, cosmetics _____

    Beauty, barber _____

    Laundry, cleaning _____

    Allowances, lunches _____

    Subscriptions _____

    Gifts (incl. Christmas) _____

    Cash _____

    Cable/Internet _____

    Other (_____) _____

    Other (_____) _____

13. Investments _____

14. School/Child Care _____

    Tuition _____

    Materials _____

    Transportation _____

    Day Care _____

    Other (_____) _____

TOTAL EXPENSES _____

INCOME VERSUS EXPENSES

  Net Spendable Income

  Less Expenses

       _____

15. Unallocated Surplus Income[1] _____

[1] This category is used when surplus income is received. This would be kept in the checking account to be used within a few weeks; otherwise, it should be transferred to an allocated category.

CASE STUDY THREE
COMMENTS

CASE STUDY FOUR

Background Information: Mike Pierce is 30 years old and his wife Ann is 26. They have been married eight years and have a 2-year-old son and a 4-month-old daughter. They rent a three-bedroom apartment.

Mike has worked for five years as a cook for a restaurant. Ann is a homemaker. They received more than $2,900 from their tax return last year, which they spent on a summer vacation and a second car.

They attend a small community church in town. Ann is a very committed Christian, but Mike is not. This has led to disagreements about tithing: Ann would like to give, but Mike says it is impossible.

Ann has been under a great deal of pressure because of lack of money for clothing and entertainment. She is also the one who pays the bills and handles the checking account. They own two cars with debts on both.

Mike's employer pays for family health insurance coverage. The Pierces used their VISA card to finance recently obtained wills.

Assignment: Ignorance and mismanagement in many areas is evidenced in this couple. After reviewing their following Monthly Income and Expenses form, Financial Statement, and List of Debts, balance the Pierce's budget and give appropriate recommendations.

CASE STUDY FOUR—AS IS
MONTHLY INCOME AND EXPENSES

GROSS INCOME PER MONTH $1,650

- Salary   1,650
- Interest
- Dividends
- Other
- Other (_____)

LESS:

1. **Tithe** $0

2. **Tax** (Est. - Incl. Fed., State, FICA) $115

   NET SPENDABLE INCOME $1,535

3. **Housing** $640
   - Mortgage (rent)   400
   - Insurance
   - Taxes
   - Electricity   140
   - Gas   25
   - Water
   - Sanitation
   - Telephone   75
   - Maintenance
   - Other (_____)
   - Other (_____)

4. **Food** $355

5. **Automobile(s)** $440
   - Payments   230
   - Gas and Oil   140
   - Insurance   50
   - License/Taxes   20
   - Maint./Repair/Replace

6. **Insurance** $60
   - Life (25,000 Whole Life)   60
   - Medical
   - Other (_____)

7. **Debts** $150
   - Credit Card   75
   - Loans and Notes   75
   - Other (_____)
   - Other (_____)

8. **Enter./Recreation** $0
   - Eating Out
   - Baby Sitters
   - Activities/Trips
   - Vacation
   - Other (_____)
   - Other (_____)

9. **Clothing** $0

10. **Savings** $0

11. **Medical Expenses** $0
    - Doctor
    - Dentist
    - Drugs
    - Other (_____)

12. **Miscellaneous** $60
    - Toiletry, cosmetics
    - Beauty, barber
    - Laundry, cleaning
    - Allowances, lunches
    - Subscriptions
    - Gifts (incl. Christmas)
    - Cash   60
    - Cable/Internet
    - Other (_____)
    - Other (_____)

13. **Investments** $0

14. **School/Child Care** $0
    - Tuition
    - Materials
    - Transportation
    - Day Care
    - Other (_____)

    TOTAL EXPENSES $1,705

INCOME VERSUS EXPENSES

Net Spendable Income	$1,535
Less Expenses	$1,705
	-$170

15. **Unallocated Surplus Income**[1]

[1] This category is used when surplus income is received. This would be kept in the checking account to be used within a few weeks; otherwise, it should be transferred to an allocated category.

CASE STUDY FOUR
FINANCIAL STATEMENT

ASSETS

Liquid Assets[1]

Checking Acct.	$64

Total Liquid Assets $64

Invested Assets[2]

Life Insurance	
Cash value	$500

Total Invested $500

Use Assets[3]

Toyota	$7,000
Ford	3,500
Personal Items	10,000

Total Use Assets $20,500

TOTAL ASSETS $21,064

LIABILITIES[4]

First Bank (Toyota)	$1,500
Community Bk. (Ford)	1,000
Sears	300
J.C. Penney	450
VISA	200
Finance Co.	3,100

TOTAL LIABILITIES $6,550

NET WORTH $14,514
(Assets-Liabilities)

**TOTAL LIABILITIES
AND NET WORTH** $21,064

[1] Cash, Savings Accounts, Checking Accounts
[2] IRAs, TSAs, 401(k)s, Investment, Real Estate, CDs, Antiques presented at fair market value.
[3] Residence, Autos, Personal Belongings presented at fair market value.
[4] Outstanding Real Estate Loans, Credit Cards, Auto Loans, Personal Loans.

LIST OF DEBTS
CASE STUDY FOUR

To Whom Owed	Contact Name Phone Number	Pay Off	Payments Left	Monthly Payment	Date Due	Interest Rate
Sears		$300	14	$25	25th	14%
J. C. Penney		$450	21	$25	22nd	18%
VISA		$200	8	$25	18th	20%
Finance Co.		$3,100	65	$75	15th	18%
First Bank		$1,500	14	$125	1st	14%
Community Bank		$1,000	11	$105	15th	16%

CASE STUDY FOUR—WORKSHEET
MONTHLY INCOME AND EXPENSES

GROSS INCOME PER MONTH _____
    Salary _____
    Interest _____
    Dividends _____
    Other (_____) _____
    Other (_____) _____

LESS:

1. Tithe _____

2. Tax (Est. - Incl. Fed., State, FICA) _____

    NET SPENDABLE INCOME _____

3. Housing _____
    Mortgage (rent) _____
    Insurance _____
    Taxes _____
    Electricity _____
    Gas _____
    Water _____
    Sanitation _____
    Telephone _____
    Maintenance _____
    Other (_____) _____
    Other (_____) _____

4. Food _____

5. Automobile(s) _____
    Payments _____
    Gas and Oil _____
    Insurance _____
    License/Taxes _____
    Maint./Repair/Replace _____

6. Insurance _____
    Life _____
    Medical _____
    Other (_____) _____

7. Debts _____
    Credit Card _____
    Loans and Notes _____
    Other (_____) _____
    Other (_____) _____

8. Enter./Recreation _____
    Eating Out _____
    Baby Sitters _____
    Activities/Trips _____
    Vacation _____
    Other (_____) _____
    Other (_____) _____

9. Clothing _____

10. Savings _____

11. Medical Expenses _____
    Doctor _____
    Dentist _____
    Credit Card _____
    Other (_____) _____

12. Miscellaneous _____
    Toiletry, cosmetics _____
    Beauty, barber _____
    Laundry, cleaning _____
    Allowances, lunches _____
    Subscriptions _____
    Gifts (incl. Christmas) _____
    Cash _____
    Cable/Internet _____
    Other (_____) _____
    Other (_____) _____

13. Investments _____

14. School/Child Care _____
    Tuition _____
    Materials _____
    Transportation _____
    Day Care _____
    Other (_____) _____

TOTAL EXPENSES _____

INCOME VERSUS EXPENSES

    Net Spendable Income _____
    Less Expenses _____

15. Unallocated Surplus Income[1] _____

---

[1] This category is used when surplus income is received. This would be kept in the checking account to be used within a few weeks; otherwise, it should be transferred to an allocated category.

CASE STUDY FOUR
COMMENTS

CASE STUDY FIVE

Background Information: Terry Smith is 35 years old and his wife Mindy is 33. They recently celebrated their 10-year wedding anniversary. They have three children, ages 3, 5, and 8. Terry is a CPA. Mindy has never worked outside of the home, although she completed one year of college.

Terry and Mindy have been attending a large church since they were married. Terry sings in the choir; Mindy is active in children's Sunday school.

On the surface it appears that this is a happy, well-adjusted family. They have a comfortable house, new cars, and enjoy good health.

Last week Terry announced to Mindy that he wanted a divorce. He said he did not love her any longer and that he wanted to marry Cindy, a lady he sings with in the choir. He has already met with an attorney to begin divorce proceedings.

The church quickly responded by following the steps outlined in Matthew 18:15-17. But Terry and Cindy are not repentant and want nothing to do with the church. They will be moving to another state next month.

When the divorce becomes final, Mindy has the following situation.

1. She was awarded the $110,000 house.

2. She was awarded all personal belongings—furniture, toys, clothes.

3. She will receive child support of $200 per month per child until each child reaches age 18.

4. She was given the Honda Accord, which has a loan against it.

5. She will be responsible for half of the credit cards and personal loans, totaling $40,000, which were acquired jointly.

6. Terry is responsible for providing health insurance for the children. He is also responsible for all medical expenses the health insurance doesn't pay, plus all dental and prescription drug expenses for the children.

7. Terry is to carry life insurance on himself in the amount of $250,000 with the children as the beneficiaries until the youngest child reaches age 21.

8. No alimony was awarded.

9. Mindy was awarded the exemptions of the children for income tax purposes.

Mindy is working 40 hours per week at a bookstore, where she earns $6.50 an hour. Mindy's sister has offered to watch the children while Mindy works. The church has helped with food and utility bills.

Assignment: You have been asked to assist the church leadership in coaching Mindy about her financial situation. A Monthly Income and Expenses form, Financial Statement, and List of Debts provide additional information. What would be your advice to Mindy?

This is a difficult situation. When basic scriptural principles are violated, God's best is not possible. Since the marriage ended, you will only be working with Mindy.

CASE STUDY FIVE—AS IS
MONTHLY INCOME AND EXPENSES

GROSS INCOME PER MONTH ___$1,835___

Salary	1,235
Interest	_____
Dividends	_____
Child Support	600
Other (_____)	

LESS:

1. Tithe ___$10___

2. Tax (Est. - Incl. Fed., State, FICA) ___$95.00___

NET SPENDABLE INCOME ___$1,730___

3. Housing ___$1,000___

Mortgage (rent)	660
Insurance	30
Taxes	90
Electricity	150
Gas	_____
Water	25
Sanitation	_____
Telephone	45
Maintenance	_____
Other (_____)	_____
Other (_____)	_____

4. Food ___$300___

5. Automobile(s) ___$479___

Payments	341
Gas and Oil	100
Insurance	28
License/Taxes	10
Maint./Repair/Replace	_____

6. Insurance ___$0___

Life	_____
Medical	_____
Other (_____)	_____

7. Debts ___$560___

Credit Card	328
Loans and Notes	232
Other (_____)	_____
Other (_____)	_____

8. Enter./Recreation ___$0___

Eating Out	_____
Baby Sitters	_____
Activities/Trips	_____
Vacation	_____
Other (_____)	_____
Other (_____)	_____

9. Clothing ___$0___

10. Savings ___$0___

11. Medical Expenses ___$0___

Doctor	_____
Dentist	_____
Drugs	_____
Other (_____)	_____

12. Miscellaneous ___$30___

Toiletry, cosmetics	10
Beauty, barber	10
Laundry, cleaning	10
Allowances, lunches	_____
Subscriptions	_____
Gifts (incl. Christmas)	_____
Cash	_____
Cable/Internet	_____
Other (_____)	_____
Other (_____)	_____

13. Investments ___$0___

14. School/Child Care ___$0___

Tuition	_____
Materials	_____
Transportation	_____
Day Care	_____
Other (_____)	_____

TOTAL EXPENSES ___$2,369___

INCOME VERSUS EXPENSES

Net Spendable Income	$1,730
Less Expenses	$2,369
	-$639

15. Unallocated Surplus Income[1] _____

---

[1] This category is used when surplus income is received. This would be kept in the checking account to be used within a few weeks; otherwise, it should be transferred to an allocated category.

CASE STUDY FIVE
FINANCIAL STATEMENT

ASSETS

Liquid Assets[1]

Checking Acct.	$125

Total Liquid Assets $125

Invested Assets[2]

Total Invested $0

Use Assets[3]

Residence	$110,000
Honda	12,000
Personal Items	20,000

Total Use Assets $142,000

TOTAL ASSETS $142,125

LIABILITIES[4]

1st Mortgage (Residence)	$89,600
Thrifty Auto Loan (Honda)	10,000
Credit Cards	12,000
Best Finance Co.	8,000

TOTAL LIABILITIES $119,600

NET WORTH $22,525
(Assets-Liabilities)

TOTAL LIABILITIES AND NET WORTH $142,125

---

[1] Cash, Savings Accounts, Checking Accounts
[2] IRAs, TSAs, 401(k)s, Investment, Real Estate, CDs, Antiques presented at fair market value.
[3] Residence, Autos, Personal Belongings presented at fair market value.
[4] Outstanding Real Estate Loans, Credit Cards, Auto Loans, Personal Loans.

LIST OF DEBTS
CASE STUDY FIVE

To Whom Owed	Contact Name Phone Number	Pay Off	Payments Left	Monthly Payment	Date Due	Interest Rate
Sears		$4,000	53	$112	18th	18%
VISA		$5,500	48	$148	25th	13%
MasterCard		$2,500	47	$68	28th	12.8%
Best Finance Co.		$8,000	48	$232	10th	17%
Thrift Auto Loans		$10,000	37	$341	15th	16%
First Mortgage		$89,600	340	$660	1st	8%

CASE STUDY FIVE—WORKSHEET
MONTHLY INCOME AND EXPENSES

GROSS INCOME PER MONTH _____

    Salary _____

    Interest _____

    Dividends _____

    Other (_____) _____

    Other (_____) _____

LESS:

  1. Tithe _____

  2. Tax (Est. - Incl. Fed., State, FICA) _____

    NET SPENDABLE INCOME _____

  3. Housing _____

    Mortgage (rent) _____

    Insurance _____

    Taxes _____

    Electricity _____

    Gas _____

    Water _____

    Sanitation _____

    Telephone _____

    Maintenance _____

    Other (_____) _____

    Other (_____) _____

  4. Food _____

  5. Automobile(s) _____

    Payments _____

    Gas and Oil _____

    Insurance _____

    License/Taxes _____

    Maint./Repair/Replace _____

  6. Insurance _____

    Life _____

    Medical _____

    Other (_____) _____

  7. Debts _____

    Credit Card _____

    Loans and Notes _____

    Other (_____) _____

    Other (_____) _____

8. Enter./Recreation _____

    Eating Out _____

    Baby Sitters _____

    Activities/Trips _____

    Vacation _____

    Other (_____) _____

    Other (_____) _____

9. Clothing _____

10. Savings _____

11. Medical Expenses _____

    Doctor _____

    Dentist _____

    Credit Card _____

    Other (_____) _____

12. Miscellaneous _____

    Toiletry, cosmetics _____

    Beauty, barber _____

    Laundry, cleaning _____

    Allowances, lunches _____

    Subscriptions _____

    Gifts (incl. Christmas) _____

    Cash _____

    Cable/Internet _____

    Other (_____) _____

    Other (_____) _____

13. Investments _____

14. School/Child Care _____

    Tuition _____

    Materials _____

    Transportation _____

    Day Care _____

    Other (_____) _____

TOTAL EXPENSES _____

INCOME VERSUS EXPENSES

  Net Spendable Income _____

  Less Expenses _____

15. Unallocated Surplus Income[1] _____

---

[1] This category is used when surplus income is received. This would be kept in the checking account to be used within a few weeks; otherwise, it should be transferred to an allocated category.

CASE STUDY FIVE
COMMENTS

CASE STUDY THREE ANSWERS

This was a difficult case because the income was so small, but fortunately Kathy is seeking help now. Her age and lack of living relatives contributes to this difficulty. The church is responsible for her care. Kathy needs fellowship, transportation, and someone to check on her needs. She needs to find a roommate or a less expensive place to live. She will need someone to help her pay her monthly bills and assist her with paperwork.

Answer Part One

1. She applied for winter heat assistance and was granted $10 per month.

2. She increased the food budget to $100 per month and received help from a member of the church with wise shopping skills.

3. She decreased Entertainment/Recreation to $18 per month.

4. Kathy increased Clothing to $25 per month.

5. She established a contingency Savings of $30 per month.

6. She decreased Miscellaneous to $27 per month.

After her budget was set up, there was a shortfall of $200. The benevolence ministry of the church agreed to provide this until a roommate was found or a less expensive apartment was located. It was agreed that someone from the church would call Kathy daily and watch over her.

Answer Part Two

Unfortunately, churches are not always faithful to care for the widows. If the church is unwilling to help, you may need to suggest that she apply for food stamps and any government benevolence that may be available. This is not an ideal answer and certainly not the way God would prefer. No matter what the church does, be sure to have others join you in praying for Kathy.

CASE STUDY THREE—ANSWER
MONTHLY INCOME AND EXPENSES

GROSS INCOME PER MONTH $850

Salary	
Interest	
Dividends	
Social Security	650
Church Benevolence	200

LESS:

1. Tithe $85

2. Tax (Est. - Incl. Fed., State, FICA) _____

NET SPENDABLE INCOME $765

3. Housing $505

Mortgage (rent)	385
Insurance	10
Taxes	
Electricity	60
Gas	15
Water	15
Sanitation	
Telephone	20
Maintenance	
Other (_____)	
Other (_____)	

4. Food $100

5. Automobile(s) $0

Payments	
Gas and Oil	
Insurance	
License/Taxes	
Maint./Repair/Replace	

6. Insurance $0

Life	
Medical	
Other (_____)	

7. Debts $0

Credit Card	
Loans and Notes	
Other (_____)	
Other (_____)	

8. Enter./Recreation $18

Eating Out	8
Baby Sitters	
Activities/Trips	5
Vacation	5
Other (_____)	
Other (_____)	

9. Clothing $25

10. Savings $30

11. Medical Expenses $60

Doctor	25
Dentist	10
Drugs	25
Other (_____)	

12. Miscellaneous $27

Toiletry, cosmetics	7
Beauty, barber	
Laundry, cleaning	10
Allowances, lunches	
Subscriptions	
Gifts (incl. Christmas)	
Cash	10
Cable/Internet	
Other (_____)	
Other (_____)	

13. Investments $0

14. School/Child Care $0

Tuition	
Materials	
Transportation	
Day Care	
Other (_____)	

TOTAL EXPENSES $765

INCOME VERSUS EXPENSES

Net Spendable Income	$765
Less Expenses	$765

15. Unallocated Surplus Income[1] _____

---

[1] This category is used when surplus income is received. This would be kept in the checking account to be used within a few weeks; otherwise, it should be transferred to an allocated category.

CASE STUDY FOUR ANSWERS

The Pierces had no idea they were spending $170 more each month than Mike was making. After two sessions, Mike's attitude became more positive. He even recommitted his life to the Lord. He began to see that there was hope for their situation, and he even wanted to tithe to the church.

They committed to keep their phone calls to a minimum and write letters or e-mail friends and relatives. This saved $50 per month.

By eliminating junk food and eating wisely, they were able to save $65 per month and drastically reduce their Food budget.

The Ford was sold for $3,500. After paying off the $1,000 loan, the balance was applied to paying off the Sears, J.C. Penney, and VISA credit cards and the $1,500 balance on the Toyota. They even had $50 left over to deposit in Savings.

The Pierces realized they needed more life insurance but could not afford $60 per month. They shared this with their agent, who assisted them in the purchase of a term policy with a death benefit of $250,000 for $20 per month. Their whole life policy was cash surrendered, and the $500 received was applied against the finance company loan.

Debts were reduced to $75 per month, and funds were allocated to Entertainment/ Recreation, Clothing, Savings, Medical, and Miscellaneous. Mike and Ann each agreed to only $10 cash for monthly spending money.

When the Pierces examined their tax return, they discovered they qualified for the earned income tax credit. They reduced the amount they pay each month in taxes by increasing their deductions.

The possibility of Ann working was also discussed. This was an issue they will pray about and address later.

CASE STUDY FOUR—ANSWER
MONTHLY INCOME AND EXPENSES

GROSS INCOME PER MONTH $1,650

Salary	1,650
Interest	
Dividends	
Other	
Other (_____)	

LESS:

1. Tithe $165

*2. Tax (Est. - Incl. Fed., State, FICA) $126

NET SPENDABLE INCOME $1,359

3. Housing $579

Mortgage (rent)	400
Insurance	
Taxes	
Electricity	119
Gas	25
Water	10
Sanitation	
Telephone	25
Maintenance	
Other (_____)	
Other (_____)	

4. Food $290

5. Automobile(s) $180

Payments	
Gas and Oil	100
Insurance	30
License/Taxes	10
Maint./Repair/Replace	40

6. Insurance $20

Life ($250,000 term) Mike	20
Medical	
Other (_____)	

7. Debts $75

Credit Card	75
Loans and Notes	
Other (_____)	
Other (_____)	

8. Enter./Recreation $30

Eating Out	15
Baby Sitters	5
Activities/Trips	
Vacation	10
Other (_____)	
Other (_____)	

9. Clothing $40

10. Savings $52

11. Medical Expenses $30

Doctor	20
Dentist	10
Drugs	
Other (_____)	

12. Miscellaneous $63

Toiletry, cosmetics	8
Beauty, barber	10
Laundry, cleaning	13
Allowances, lunches	
Subscriptions	
Gifts (incl. Christmas)	12
Cash	20
Cable/Internet	
Other (_____)	
Other (_____)	

13. Investments $0

14. School/Child Care $0

Tuition	
Materials	
Transportation	
Day Care	
Other (_____)	

TOTAL EXPENSES $1,359

INCOME VERSUS EXPENSES

Net Spendable Income	$1,359
Less Expenses	$1,359

15. Unallocated Surplus Income[1]

---

[1] This category is used when surplus income is received. This would be kept in the checking account to be used within a few weeks; otherwise, it should be transferred to an allocated category.

* Earned Income Credit <298>

CASE STUDY FIVE ANSWERS

This is a difficult case. At least Mindy has $20,000 equity in a house; most in her situation do not. Realistically, Mindy must sell the house and pay off her creditors (Proverbs 3:27). Many friends with the best of intentions recommended that Mindy file for a Chapter 7 bankruptcy. Much time was taken in coaching her on the scriptural principles regarding bankruptcy (Psalm 37:21; Ecclesiastes 5:4-5; Proverbs 22:7).

Following normal coaching procedures, a balanced budget was developed to provide some funds in each category, and the creditors were contacted. The credit card providers and the finance company agreed to reduced payments.

After being apprised of the total financial picture, the church leadership approved financial assistance in the amount of $200 per month. Since Mindy was more than willing to be held accountable to the church and was willing to sell her home as soon as possible to pay the debts, she displayed a good attitude in a difficult situation. Because of this attitude, another member of the church offered to trade an old automobile for Mindy's car and to pay off Mindy's loan. Mindy got an older but reliable and debt-free car. This also lowered her automobile insurance premiums.

It was determined that Mindy should apply for a major medical health policy for herself. She found a $2,000 deductible plan for $75 per month.

Due to the earned income credit, she is taking more deductions and reducing her monthly tax paid.

Mindy will require more than financial assistance from members of the church as she adjusts to a new lifestyle. They will need to be sensitive to her emotions—bitterness, loneliness, depression—and be available to encourage and minister to her.

She hopes to be able to sell the house within a couple of months. If this happens, she can pay off her debts and begin to look for a better job or training in a skill or trade.

Many things could go wrong, however.

- What if her ex-husband declares bankruptcy?
- What if the ex-husband doesn't pay child support?
- What if the creditors garnish her wages?
- What if she can't sell her house for $110,000 but receives an offer for $85,000?

If the support stops, Mindy must consider the option of suing her ex-husband. Does Mindy have the right to sue? Yes, she has the legal right, but is that what the Lord would want her to do?

Mindy must examine her attitude and compare it to God's word. She will need to search her own heart for the Lord's will in this situation and find peace about whether to sue Terry.

While a wife would find no biblical basis for taking her ex-husband to court for non-payment of alimony support, we believe the issue of child support is a different matter. Unlike the parents, children have no choice in their circumstances. They did not choose to be born; they were given into our care by God. A father cannot refuse his responsibility to the children simply because it is inconvenient. Paul wrote in 1 Timothy 5:8, *"If anyone does not provide for his own, and especially for those of his household, he has denied the faith and is worse than an unbeliever."*

If the father is an unbeliever, it makes no difference; the rules are the same. If he has fathered children, he must support them. If it's necessary to use the law for him to meet his responsibility, then use it. We recommend doing everything possible outside of filing for abandonment. If his reason for failure to pay is beyond his control (illness, out of work), that should be taken into consideration. But remember, almost everybody can pay something, even if it is not all that is required.

The final decision of whether to sue must be made prayerfully and on the basis of actual need, not anger or greed. Be certain that all other means of negotiating have been exhausted before appealing to the courts for assistance.

MONTHLY INCOME AND EXPENSES

GROSS INCOME PER MONTH		$2,035
Salary	1,235	
Interest		
Dividends		
Benevolence	200	
Child Support	600	

LESS:

1. Tithe		$40
*2. Tax (Est. - Incl. Fed., State, FICA)		$95
NET SPENDABLE INCOME		$1,900

3. Housing		$958
Mortgage (rent)	660	
Insurance	30	
Taxes	90	
Electricity	125	
Gas		
Water	18	
Sanitation		
Telephone	35	
Maintenance		
Other (_____)		
Other (_____)		

4. Food		$200

5. Automobile(s)		$140
Payments		
Gas and Oil	100	
Insurance	15	
License/Taxes	5	
Maint./Repair/Replace	20	

6. Insurance		$75
Life		
Medical	75	
Other (_____)		

7. Debts		$390
Credit Card	240	
Loans and Notes	150	
Other (_____)		
Other (_____)		

8. Enter./Recreation		$30
Eating Out	15	
Baby Sitters		
Activities/Trips	15	
Vacation		
Other (_____)		
Other (_____)		

9. Clothing		$22
10. Savings		$25
11. Medical Expenses		$10
Doctor	10	
Dentist		
Drugs		
Other (_____)		

12. Miscellaneous		$50
Toiletry, cosmetics	10	
Beauty, barber	10	
Laundry, cleaning	10	
Allowances, lunches		
Subscriptions		
Gifts (incl. Christmas)	10	
Cash	10	
Cable/Internet		
Other (_____)		
Other (_____)		

13. Investments		$0

14. School/Child Care		$0
Tuition		
Materials		
Transportation		
Day Care		
Other (_____)		

TOTAL EXPENSES		$1,900

INCOME VERSUS EXPENSES

Net Spendable Income	$1,900
Less Expenses	$1,900

15. Unallocated Surplus Income[1]

---

[1] This category is used when surplus income is received. This would be kept in the checking account to be used within a few weeks; otherwise, it should be transferred to an allocated category.

* Earned Income Credit <304>

ASSIGNMENT

Complete Case Studies Six, Seven, Eight, and Nine.

Background Information: Jim Crenshaw is 32 years old and his wife Katie is 28. They have been married for nine years.

Jim has worked for a building supply company 10 years. Katie is a homemaker and takes care of their 2-year-old handicapped son.

They are both committed Christians who desire to tithe but just don't see how they can on Jim's salary, especially with the extra expenses for the special needs of their son. They also would like to have more children but believe their financial situation does not allow it.

They own a house and car, which are both financed. Jim's employer pays for their health insurance. They both have wills.

Assignment: This coaching session could be emotional. It will be important to approach this situation tenderly with the healing balm of God's Word. List the steps and Scripture you would use to encourage the Crenshaws as they make decisions about their financial future. Using the Monthly Income and Expenses form, Financial Statement, and List of Debts, balance the Crenshaw's budget and give appropriate recommendations.

CASE STUDY SIX—AS IS
MONTHLY INCOME AND EXPENSES

GROSS INCOME PER MONTH		$3,300	
Salary	3,300		
Interest			
Dividends			
Other (_____)			
Other (_____)			

LESS:

1. Tithe		$50
2. Tax (Est. - Incl. Fed., State, FICA)		$544
NET SPENDABLE INCOME		$2,706

3. Housing		$817
Mortgage (rent)	550	
Insurance	25	
Taxes	65	
Electricity	75	
Gas	40	
Water	15	
Sanitation	7	
Telephone	40	
Maintenance		
Other (_____)		
Other (_____)		
4. Food		$400
5. Automobile(s)		$545
Payments	340	
Gas and Oil	100	
Insurance	50	
License/Taxes	5	
Maint./Repair/Replace	50	
6. Insurance		$0
Life		
Medical		
Other (_____)		
7. Debts		$620
Credit Card	516	
Loans and Notes		
Other (_____)	104	
Other (_____)		

8. Enter./Recreation		$100
Eating Out	30	
Baby Sitters	10	
Activities/Trips	10	
Vacation	50	
Other (_____)		
Other (_____)		
9. Clothing		$50
10. Savings		$0
11. Medical Expenses		$55
Doctor	35	
Dentist	10	
Drugs	10	
Other (_____)		
12. Miscellaneous		$177
Toiletry, cosmetics	10	
Beauty, barber	10	
Laundry, cleaning	15	
Allowances, lunches	40	
Subscriptions	12	
Gifts (incl. Christmas)	30	
Cash	60	
Cable/Internet		
Other (_____)		
Other (_____)		
13. Investments		$0
14. School/Child Care		$0
Tuition		
Materials		
Transportation		
Day Care		
Other (_____)		
TOTAL EXPENSES		$2,764

INCOME VERSUS EXPENSES

Net Spendable Income	$2,706
Less Expenses	$2,764
	-$58

15. Unallocated Surplus Income[1]

---

[1] This category is used when surplus income is received. This would be kept in the checking account to be used within a few weeks; otherwise, it should be transferred to an allocated category.

CASE STUDY SIX
FINANCIAL STATEMENT

ASSETS

Liquid Assets[1]

Checking Acct.	$325
Savings Acct.	195

Total Liquid Assets	$520

Invested Assets[2]

Retirement Plan	$28,000

Total Invested	$28,000

Use Assets[3]

Residence	$89,000
Pontiac	12,000
Personal Items	26,000

Total Use Assets	$127,000
TOTAL ASSETS	$155,520

LIABILITIES[4]

Home Mortgage Co. (Res.)	$65,000
1st National (Pontiac)	10,000
Credit Cards	18,000
Parents	2,500
Medical	3,825

TOTAL LIABILITIES	$99,325

NET WORTH (Assets-Liabilities)	$56,195

TOTAL LIABILITIES AND NET WORTH	$155,520

[1] Cash, Savings Accounts, Checking Accounts
[2] IRAs, TSAs, 401(k)s, Investment, Real Estate, CDs, Antiques presented at fair market value.
[3] Residence, Autos, Personal Belongings presented at fair market value.
[4] Outstanding Real Estate Loans, Credit Cards, Auto Loans, Personal Loans.

LIST OF DEBTS
CASE STUDY SIX

To Whom Owed	Contact Name Phone Number	Pay Off	Payments Left	Monthly Payment	Date Due	Interest Rate
Sears		$400	24	$20	8th	18%
J.C. Penney		$600	31	$25	22nd	18%
VISA		$2,800	54	$78	10th	19%
MasterCard		$3,500	50	$95	15th	14%
Discover		$1,100	48	$30	28th	14%
MasterCard #2		$1,800	58	$50	5th	21%
VISA #2		$4,600	53	$130	10th	18%
VISA #3		$3,200	55	$88	25th	19%
Community Hosp.		$2,950	40	$82	5th	7%
Medical Clinic		$875	46	$22	25th	7%
Home Mortgage Co.		$65,000	310	$550	1st	9%
First National		$10,000	33	$340	5th	8%
Parents		$2,500			when able	N/A

CASE STUDY SIX—WORKSHEET
MONTHLY INCOME AND EXPENSES

GROSS INCOME PER MONTH _____

    Salary _____

    Interest _____

    Dividends _____

    Other (_____) _____

    Other (_____) _____

LESS:

  1. Tithe _____

  2. Tax (Est. - Incl. Fed., State, FICA) _____

    NET SPENDABLE INCOME _____

  3. Housing _____

    Mortgage (rent) _____

    Insurance _____

    Taxes _____

    Electricity _____

    Gas _____

    Water _____

    Sanitation _____

    Telephone _____

    Maintenance _____

    Other (_____) _____

    Other (_____) _____

  4. Food _____

  5. Automobile(s) _____

    Payments _____

    Gas and Oil _____

    Insurance _____

    License/Taxes _____

    Maint./Repair/Replace _____

  6. Insurance _____

    Life _____

    Medical _____

    Other (_____) _____

  7. Debts _____

    Credit Card _____

    Loans and Notes _____

    Other (_____) _____

    Other (_____) _____

8. Enter./Recreation _____

    Eating Out _____

    Baby Sitters _____

    Activities/Trips _____

    Vacation _____

    Other (_____) _____

    Other (_____) _____

9. Clothing _____

10. Savings _____

11. Medical Expenses _____

    Doctor _____

    Dentist _____

    Credit Card _____

    Other (_____) _____

12. Miscellaneous _____

    Toiletry, cosmetics _____

    Beauty, barber _____

    Laundry, cleaning _____

    Allowances, lunches _____

    Subscriptions _____

    Gifts (incl. Christmas) _____

    Cash _____

    Cable/Internet _____

    Other (_____) _____

    Other (_____) _____

13. Investments _____

14. School/Child Care _____

    Tuition _____

    Materials _____

    Transportation _____

    Day Care _____

    Other (_____) _____

TOTAL EXPENSES _____

INCOME VERSUS EXPENSES

    Net Spendable Income _____

    Less Expenses _____

    _____

15. Unallocated Surplus Income[1] _____

[1] This category is used when surplus income is received. This would be kept in the checking account to be used within a few weeks; otherwise, it should be transferred to an allocated category.

CASE STUDY SIX
COMMENTS

CASE STUDY SEVEN

Background Information: Matthew Thornton is 45 years old and his wife Sharron is 39. They have two children: a son 14 and a daughter 12. The Thorntons have been happily married for 16 years. They live in an average three-bedroom, two-bath house. Matthew has worked in sales for a national food distribution company for 15 years. Sharron is a very satisfied homemaker.

The Thorntons are active in church and desire to give more. They give what is left over each month, if anything.

They always take family vacations and view their tax refund as vacation money. Last year they received a $1,200 refund.

They have two immediate objectives: to begin saving for their children's college education and to begin a retirement plan.

They own two cars, one of which is paid for, and Matthew uses a company vehicle for work. His employer provides family health insurance. He and Sharron do not have wills.

Assignment: This is a typical Money Map coaching situation. This family has no extreme spending habits but are dealing with everyday expenses and modest debt. Remember that your goal in Money Map coaching is to teach them the financial scriptural principles so that they will continue to handle money God's way after your coaching is completed. Review their Monthly Income and Expenses form, Financial Statement, and List of Debts; then balance the Thornton's budget and give appropriate recommendations.

CASE STUDY SEVEN—AS IS
MONTHLY INCOME AND EXPENSES

GROSS INCOME PER MONTH $3,000

Salary	3,000
Interest	
Dividends	
Other (_____)	
Other (_____)	

LESS:

1. Tithe $100

2. Tax (Est. - Incl. Fed., State, FICA) $557

NET SPENDABLE INCOME $2,343

3. Housing $734

Mortgage (rent)	450
Insurance	25
Taxes	75
Electricity	75
Gas	50
Water	12
Sanitation	7
Telephone	40
Maintenance	
Other (_____)	
Other (_____)	

4. Food $400

5. Automobile(s) $470

Payments	225
Gas and Oil	140
Insurance	50
License/Taxes	5
Maint./Repair/Replace	50

6. Insurance $150

Life ($100,000 WL)	150
Medical	
Other (_____)	

7. Debts $230

Credit Card	55
Loans and Notes	175
Other (_____)	
Other (_____)	

8. Enter./Recreation $240

Eating Out	80
Baby Sitters	
Activities/Trips	60
Vacation	100
Other (_____)	
Other (_____)	

9. Clothing $100

10. Savings $0

11. Medical Expenses $30

Doctor	10
Dentist	20
Drugs	
Other (_____)	

12. Miscellaneous $450

Toiletry, cosmetics	5
Beauty, barber	15
Laundry, cleaning	10
Allowances, lunches	100
Subscriptions	20
Gifts (incl. Christmas)	100
Cash	200
Cable/Internet	
Other (_____)	
Other (_____)	

13. Investments $0

14. School/Child Care $0

Tuition	
Materials	
Transportation	
Day Care	
Other (_____)	

TOTAL EXPENSES $2,804

INCOME VERSUS EXPENSES

Net Spendable Income	$2,343
Less Expenses	$2,804
	-$461

15. Unallocated Surplus Income[1]

---

[1] This category is used when surplus income is received. This would be kept in the checking account to be used within a few weeks; otherwise, it should be transferred to an allocated category.

CASE STUDY SEVEN
FINANCIAL STATEMENT

ASSETS

Liquid Assets[1]

Checking Account	$125
Money Market	3,000

Total Liquid Assets	$3,125

Invested Assets[2]

Life Insurance	
Cash Value	$1,000

Total Invested	$1,000

Use Assets[3]

Residence	$70,000
Toyota	3,000
Chevrolet	7,000
Personal Items	20,000

Total Use Assets	$100,000
TOTAL ASSETS	$104,125

LIABILITIES[4]

First Mortgage (Residence)	$40,000
United Federal (Chevrolet)	2,700
Credit Cards	1,650
Credit Union	500
1st Bank & Trust	600

TOTAL LIABILITIES	$45,450

NET WORTH	$58,675
(Assets-Liabilities)	

TOTAL LIABILITIES AND NET WORTH	$104,125

[1] Cash, Savings Accounts, Checking Accounts
[2] IRAs, TSAs, 401(k)s, Investment, Real Estate, CDs, Antiques presented at fair market value.
[3] Residence, Autos, Personal Belongings presented at fair market value.
[4] Outstanding Real Estate Loans, Credit Cards, Auto Loans, Personal Loans.

LIST OF DEBTS
CASE STUDY SEVEN

To Whom Owed	Contact Name Phone Number	Pay Off	Payments Left	Monthly Payment	Date Due	Interest Rate
MasterCard		$750	33	$25	25th	12%
VISA		$900	37	$30	28th	14%
Credit Union		$500	8	$65	15th	10%
First Bank & Trust		$600	7	$100	1st	11%
First Mortgage		$40,000	264	$450	1st	12%
Credit Union		$2,700	13	$225	15th	14%

CASE STUDY SEVEN—WORKSHEET
MONTHLY INCOME AND EXPENSES

GROSS INCOME PER MONTH _____
- Salary _____
- Interest _____
- Dividends _____
- Other (_____) _____
- Other (_____) _____

LESS:

1. **Tithe** _____

2. **Tax** (Est. - Incl. Fed., State, FICA) _____

   NET SPENDABLE INCOME _____

3. **Housing** _____
   - Mortgage (rent) _____
   - Insurance _____
   - Taxes _____
   - Electricity _____
   - Gas _____
   - Water _____
   - Sanitation _____
   - Telephone _____
   - Maintenance _____
   - Other (_____) _____
   - Other (_____) _____

4. **Food** _____

5. **Automobile(s)** _____
   - Payments _____
   - Gas and Oil _____
   - Insurance _____
   - License/Taxes _____
   - Maint./Repair/Replace _____

6. **Insurance** _____
   - Life _____
   - Medical _____
   - Other (_____) _____

7. **Debts** _____
   - Credit Card _____
   - Loans and Notes _____
   - Other (_____) _____
   - Other (_____) _____

8. **Enter./Recreation** _____
   - Eating Out _____
   - Baby Sitters _____
   - Activities/Trips _____
   - Vacation _____
   - Other (_____) _____
   - Other (_____) _____

9. **Clothing** _____

10. **Savings** _____

11. **Medical Expenses** _____
    - Doctor _____
    - Dentist _____
    - Credit Card _____
    - Other (_____) _____

12. **Miscellaneous** _____
    - Toiletry, cosmetics _____
    - Beauty, barber _____
    - Laundry, cleaning _____
    - Allowances, lunches _____
    - Subscriptions _____
    - Gifts (incl. Christmas) _____
    - Cash _____
    - Cable/Internet _____
    - Other (_____) _____
    - Other (_____) _____

13. **Investments** _____

14. **School/Child Care** _____
    - Tuition _____
    - Materials _____
    - Transportation _____
    - Day Care _____
    - Other (_____) _____

    TOTAL EXPENSES _____

INCOME VERSUS EXPENSES

   Net Spendable Income
   Less Expenses _____

15. **Unallocated Surplus Income**[1] _____

[1] This category is used when surplus income is received. This would be kept in the checking account to be used within a few weeks; otherwise, it should be transferred to an allocated category.

CASE STUDY SEVEN
COMMENTS

CASE STUDY EIGHT

Background Information: Linda Smith is a single parent with two teenage children. She has been divorced for 10 years. She had a tumultuous marriage. Her husband was an alcoholic, and he abused the children. He left when Linda sought coaching. She began attending church with friends and became a Christian during their separation. That was more than her husband could handle, so he filed for divorce.

The first year after the divorce, Linda's ex-husband was involved with the children but paid little financial support. The court ordered that she receive alimony for six months, but it was not paid regularly. Since she had not worked outside the home and she lived in an area with a distressed economy, she could not find work. She depended on welfare during this time. She was uncomfortable being on welfare, because her parents had been on welfare and she had sworn that that would never happen to her. However, because she was on welfare, she was a priority with the child support collection office. A year and a half after the divorce, she had a court date to have the child support deducted from her ex-husband's pay. By that time, the support had almost disappeared and so had her ex-husband, except for an occasional phone call. She left welfare after taking a secretarial course at a local community college.

Linda went to the church for coaching because her youngest child was turning 18 and she was about to lose the child support. She was only earning $15,000 a year working as a secretary, but she was handling her budget very well. Her income was supplemented by the $60-a-week child support check, and she received a large Earned Income Credit (EIC) each year. She didn't budget the EIC for the year; she usually spent it to get her car fixed, replace worn out things, and to take a trip to see her family. She has tithed on her income and her child support for several years, and she believes that is why she has been able to make ends meet.

Linda's son is 19 years old but has not yet graduated from high school. Her daughter is graduating early at 17 and hoping to attend college in the fall. The children work part-time to pay for some of their own expenses, such as clothing, shoes, and entertainment. Linda disciplined herself to cut back in some areas to pay off credit card debt, but she doesn't have any reserve. Therefore, anytime something breaks or an emergency arises, she uses the credit card.

Linda's rent is very modest for her area and her only "extras" are long-distance phone charges and cable TV. She has a six-year-old car that she bought on credit because she felt she needed dependable transportation. She had been given old cars in the past and was grateful for the gifts, but when they broke down she didn't have anyone to fix them. She had to depend on area garages, and she had to pay for the repairs with her credit card.

Since she has no investments or savings to help her children go to college, she is carrying $50,000 life insurance. She also has a modest premium charge for family medical coverage and dental coverage through her employer. Linda does not have a will.

Linda's debt situation has tremendously improved from her earlier years as a single parent. At one point, she was facing bankruptcy. With hard work and sacrifice, she has whittled a debt of $8,000 down to under $2,000. She also has a school loan that she is still paying.

Her family has few funds for entertainment. Most of the money is spent on driving once or twice a year to her hometown to see family. Eating out is her only time to socialize with other adults at work or at church. Her clothing budget is small, since her kids buy most of their own things, and she shops at second-hand or discount stores for bargains. She puts a small amount in savings each month, but it usually doesn't stay there.

Her only medical expenses are co-pays. Her Miscellaneous category is high due to the amount she spends on gifts. She feels the need to buy something for every shower or wedding, graduation, or birthday that she is invited to celebrate. Because she is part of a singles' group at church, there are quite a few celebrations. In addition, she always makes Christmas and birthdays special for her children so they won't feel poor.

Since her budget is so tight, she doesn't know how to adjust to the $260-per-month drop that is coming.

Assignment: Dealing with a single parent is multifaceted. Often, outside help is necessary to balance the budget. It will be vital for you to provide strong support and confident leadership as you work with single parents. In your Money Map coaching sessions, only address those financial principles that have been violated. Ask the pastor or professional counselor to deal with the other issues. After reviewing her Monthly Income and Expenses form, Financial Statement, and List of Debts, balance Linda's budget to allow for the loss of $260 per month and give any other appropriate recommendations.

CASE STUDY EIGHT—AS IS
MONTHLY INCOME AND EXPENSES

GROSS INCOME PER MONTH $1,760

Salary	1,500
Interest	
Dividends	
Child Support	260
Other (_____)	

LESS:

1. **Tithe** $150

2. **Tax** (Est. - Incl. Fed., State, FICA) $150

NET SPENDABLE INCOME $1,460

3. **Housing** $583

Mortgage (rent)	395
Insurance	8
Taxes	
Electricity	90
Gas	
Water	10
Sanitation	5
Telephone	40
Maintenance	
Cable TV	35
Other (_____)	

4. **Food** $250

5. **Automobile(s)** $273

Payments	128
Gas and Oil	80
Insurance	50
License/Taxes	5
Maint./Repair/Replace	10

6. **Insurance** $40

Life (50,000 Term)	10
Medical	25
Dental	5

7. **Debts** $62

Credit Card	50
Loans and Notes	12
Other (_____)	
Other (_____)	

8. **Enter./Recreation** $67

Eating Out	20
Baby Sitters	
Activities/Trips	25
Vacation	22
Other (_____)	
Other (_____)	

9. **Clothing** $25

10. **Savings** $23

11. **Medical Expenses** $30

Doctor	20
Dentist	10
Drugs	
Other (_____)	

12. **Miscellaneous** $107

Toiletry, cosmetics	10
Beauty, barber	10
Laundry, cleaning	10
Allowances, lunches	10
Subscriptions	3
Gifts (incl. Christmas)	37
Cash	27
Cable/Internet	
Other (_____)	
Other (_____)	

13. **Investments** $0

14. **School/Child Care** $0

Tuition	
Materials	
Transportation	
Day Care	
Other (_____)	

TOTAL EXPENSES $1,460

INCOME VERSUS EXPENSES

Net Spendable Income	$1,460
Less Expenses	$1,460

15. **Unallocated Surplus Income**[1]   _____

---

[1] This category is used when surplus income is received. This would be kept in the checking account to be used within a few weeks; otherwise, it should be transferred to an allocated category.

CASE STUDY EIGHT
FINANCIAL STATEMENT

ASSETS			LIABILITIES[4]		
Liquid Assets[1]			Fast Finance Co. (Ford)		$1,280
Checking Account		$65	Credit Card		1,685
Money Market		35	Student Loans		324
Total Liquid Assets		$100	**TOTAL LIABILITIES**		$3,289
Invested Assets[2]					
			NET WORTH		$8,811
			(Assets-Liabilities)		
Total Invested		$0			
Use Assets[3]					
Ford		$2,000			
Personal Items		10,000			
			TOTAL LIABILITIES		
			AND NET WORTH		$12,100
Total Use Assets		$12,000			
TOTAL ASSETS		$12,100			

[1] Cash, Savings Accounts, Checking Accounts
[2] IRAs, TSAs, 401(k)s, Investment, Real Estate, CDs, Antiques presented at fair market value.
[3] Residence, Autos, Personal Belongings presented at fair market value.
[4] Outstanding Real Estate Loans, Credit Cards, Auto Loans, Personal Loans.

LIST OF DEBTS
CASE STUDY EIGHT

To Whom Owed	Contact Name / Phone Number	Pay Off	Payments Left	Monthly Payment	Date Due	Interest Rate
First Bank VISA		$1,685	39	$50	25th	9%
American Student Finance		$324	30	$12	28th	8%
Fast Finance Co.		$1,280	11	$128	15th	18%

CASE STUDY EIGHT—WORKSHEET
MONTHLY INCOME AND EXPENSES

GROSS INCOME PER MONTH _____

    Salary _____

    Interest _____

    Dividends _____

    Other (_____) _____

    Other (_____) _____

LESS:

  1. Tithe _____

  2. Tax (Est. - Incl. Fed., State, FICA) _____

    NET SPENDABLE INCOME _____

  3. Housing

    Mortgage (rent) _____

    Insurance _____

    Taxes _____

    Electricity _____

    Gas _____

    Water _____

    Sanitation _____

    Telephone _____

    Maintenance _____

    Other (_____) _____

    Other (_____) _____

  4. Food _____

  5. Automobile(s) _____

    Payments _____

    Gas and Oil _____

    Insurance _____

    License/Taxes _____

    Maint./Repair/Replace _____

  6. Insurance _____

    Life _____

    Medical _____

    Other (_____) _____

  7. Debts _____

    Credit Card _____

    Loans and Notes _____

    Other (_____) _____

    Other (_____) _____

8. Enter./Recreation _____

    Eating Out _____

    Baby Sitters _____

    Activities/Trips _____

    Vacation _____

    Other (_____) _____

    Other (_____) _____

9. Clothing _____

10. Savings _____

11. Medical Expenses _____

    Doctor _____

    Dentist _____

    Credit Card _____

    Other (_____) _____

12. Miscellaneous _____

    Toiletry, cosmetics _____

    Beauty, barber _____

    Laundry, cleaning _____

    Allowances, lunches _____

    Subscriptions _____

    Gifts (incl. Christmas) _____

    Cash _____

    Cable/Internet _____

    Other (_____) _____

    Other (_____) _____

13. Investments _____

14. School/Child Care _____

    Tuition _____

    Materials _____

    Transportation _____

    Day Care _____

    Other (_____) _____

TOTAL EXPENSES _____

INCOME VERSUS EXPENSES

    Net Spendable Income

    Less Expenses _____

15. Unallocated Surplus Income[1]

---

[1] This category is used when surplus income is received. This would be kept in the checking account to be used within a few weeks; otherwise, it should be transferred to an allocated category.

CASE STUDY EIGHT
COMMENTS

CASE STUDY NINE

Background Information: Both Ralph and Elizabeth Boling are 66 years old and have been married 46 years. They met while working at a lumber mill. Since neither one graduated from high school, they both were content to continue working at the mill. When they turned 65 and were required to retire from the mill, they began living on Social Security and savings.

The Bolings never had children and have no living relatives. They have been active in the same church for their entire married lives. While working at the mill they were able to rent a small house owned by the mill. After retirement they purchased a new mobile home and leased a new car. Using some of their savings, they purchased an acre of land on which to place the mobile home. They also paid for a well and a septic tank.

They purchased new furniture on credit cards and took several long trips around the United States, again using their credit cards. They both purchased life insurance when they married but they have no wills.

After exhausing all of their savings, they approached the pastor for help. He referred them to you for financial coaching.

Assignment: After reviewing their Monthly Income and Expenses form, Financial Statement, and List of Debts, balance the Boling's budget and give appropriate recommendations.

CASE STUDY NINE—AS IS
MONTHLY INCOME AND EXPENSES

GROSS INCOME PER MONTH $1,726

Salary	
Interest	
Dividends	
Social Security	1,726
Other (_____)	

LESS:

1. Tithe $172

2. Tax (Est. - Incl. Fed., State, FICA) $0

NET SPENDABLE INCOME $1,554

3. Housing $685

Mortgage (rent)	466
Insurance	29
Taxes	50
Electricity	35
Gas	65
Water	
Sanitation	
Telephone	40
Maintenance	
Cable TV	
Other (_____)	

4. Food $250

5. Automobile(s) $805

Payments	650
Gas and Oil	75
Insurance	65
License/Taxes	15
Maint./Repair/Replace	

6. Insurance $54

Life (2,000 WL each)	10
Medicare Part B	44
Other (_____)	

7. Debts $563

Credit Card	483
Loans and Notes	
Other (_____)	80
Other (_____)	

8. Enter./Recreation $80

Eating Out	30
Baby Sitters	
Activities/Trips	50
Vacation	
Other (_____)	
Other (_____)	

9. Clothing $0

10. Savings $0

11. Medical Expenses $0

Doctor	
Dentist	
Drugs	
Other (_____)	

12. Miscellaneous $115

Toiletry, cosmetics	10
Beauty, barber	10
Laundry, cleaning	10
Allowances, lunches	
Subscriptions	25
Gifts (incl. Christmas)	20
Cash	40
Cable/Internet	
Other (_____)	
Other (_____)	

13. Investments $0

14. School/Child Care $0

Tuition	
Materials	
Transportation	
Day Care	
Other (_____)	

TOTAL EXPENSES $2,552

INCOME VERSUS EXPENSES

Net Spendable Income	$1,554
Less Expenses	$2,552
	-$998

15. Unallocated Surplus Income[1] _____

---

[1] This category is used when surplus income is received. This would be kept in the checking account to be used within a few weeks; otherwise, it should be transferred to an allocated category.

CASE STUDY NINE
FINANCIAL STATEMENT

ASSETS

Liquid Assets[1]

Checking Acct.	$75
Savings Acct.	100

Total Liquid Assets $175

Invested Assets[2]

IRA	$3,000
Whole Life CV	4,000
Whole Life CV	4,000

Total Invested $11,000

Use Assets[3]

Mobile Home	$38,000
Honda	15,000
Oldsmobile	8,000

Total Use Assets $61,000

TOTAL ASSETS $72,175

LIABILITIES[4]

First Mortgage (Residence)	$35,000
First Leasing Co. (Honda)	15,500
MasterCard	5,000
Discover	4,500
VISA	4,000
Sears	3,500
Hospital	3,000
First Natl. Bank (Olds)	1,500
Physicians	850

TOTAL LIABILITIES $72,850

NET WORTH -$675
(Assets-Liabilities)

TOTAL LIABILITIES AND NET WORTH $72,175

---

[1] Cash, Savings Accounts, Checking Accounts
[2] IRAs, TSAs, 401(k)s, Investment, Real Estate, CDs, Antiques presented at fair market value.
[3] Residence, Autos, Personal Belongings presented at fair market value.
[4] Outstanding Real Estate Loans, Credit Cards, Auto Loans, Personal Loans.

LIST OF DEBTS
CASE STUDY NINE

To Whom Owed	Contact Name Phone Number	Pay Off	Payments Left	Monthly Payment	Date Due	Interest Rate
First Mortgage		$35,000	170	$466	25th	13%
First Leasing Co.		$15,500	48	$450	28th	17%
MasterCard		$5,000	47	$150	15th	18%
Discover		$4,500	45	$135	1st	16%
VISA		$4,000	51	$110	1st	16%
Sears		$3,500	60	$88	15th	18%
Hospital		$3,000	58	$60	8th	6%
First Natl. Bank		$1,500	8	$200	12th	17%
Physicians		$850	49	$20	10th	7%

CASE STUDY NINE—WORKSHEET
MONTHLY INCOME AND EXPENSES

GROSS INCOME PER MONTH _____

    Salary _____

    Interest _____

    Dividends _____

    Other (_____) _____

    Other (_____) _____

LESS:

  1. Tithe _____

  2. Tax (Est. - Incl. Fed., State, FICA) _____

    NET SPENDABLE INCOME _____

  3. Housing

    Mortgage (rent) _____

    Insurance _____

    Taxes _____

    Electricity _____

    Gas _____

    Water _____

    Sanitation _____

    Telephone _____

    Maintenance _____

    Other (_____) _____

    Other (_____) _____

  4. Food _____

  5. Automobile(s) _____

    Payments _____

    Gas and Oil _____

    Insurance _____

    License/Taxes _____

    Maint./Repair/Replace _____

  6. Insurance _____

    Life _____

    Medical _____

    Other (_____) _____

  7. Debts _____

    Credit Card _____

    Loans and Notes _____

    Other (_____) _____

    Other (_____) _____

  8. Enter./Recreation _____

    Eating Out _____

    Baby Sitters _____

    Activities/Trips _____

    Vacation _____

    Other (_____) _____

    Other (_____) _____

  9. Clothing _____

  10. Savings _____

  11. Medical Expenses _____

    Doctor _____

    Dentist _____

    Credit Card _____

    Other (_____) _____

  12. Miscellaneous _____

    Toiletry, cosmetics _____

    Beauty, barber _____

    Laundry, cleaning _____

    Allowances, lunches _____

    Subscriptions _____

    Gifts (incl. Christmas) _____

    Cash _____

    Cable/Internet _____

    Other (_____) _____

    Other (_____) _____

  13. Investments _____

  14. School/Child Care _____

    Tuition _____

    Materials _____

    Transportation _____

    Day Care _____

    Other (_____) _____

  TOTAL EXPENSES _____

  INCOME VERSUS EXPENSES

    Net Spendable Income _____

    Less Expenses _____

  15. Unallocated Surplus Income[1] _____

[1] This category is used when surplus income is received. This would be kept in the checking account to be used within a few weeks; otherwise, it should be transferred to an allocated category.

CASE STUDY NINE
COMMENTS

CASE STUDY SIX ANSWERS

The Crenshaws have been discouraged. Finances have always been tight, and with their son's handicap they have no hope for improving in the future. They have used credit cards to pay for medical expenses.

After spending time in the Scriptures and examining the hope that is available through Christ, the Crenshaws began to realize how their situation could be changed.

They began by committing to give the full 10 percent of Jim's salary. The Housing category was reduced by $16 per month.

Food was reduced to $300 per month. The Automobile category was only reduced by $35, until they could sell the car and obtain one with a smaller payment.

The Crenshaws had no life insurance. After reviewing their needs, they purchased a $250,000 death benefit of term insurance for $20 a month on Jim and a $100,000 death benefit of term insurance for $10 a month on Katie.

They began a debt management plan to reduce credit card payments from $516 per month to $360 per month. This was of major importance.

Entertainment/Recreation was reduced to $80 per month and Clothing to $30 per month.

A monthly plan for Savings was added, which totaled $40. This isn't much, but it is a start.

Medical Expenses remained the same, and Miscellaneous was decreased to $116 per month.

With this plan and the understanding of God's principles of finance, the Crenshaws have begun to experience freedom from financial bondage. Money will remain tight until they sell the car or the house, but eventually they should be out of debt.

Follow-up appointments will be necessary, but eventually the Crenshaws should be in a position to help others.

MONTHLY INCOME AND EXPENSES

GROSS INCOME PER MONTH			$3,300
Salary	3,300		
Interest			
Dividends			
Other (_____)			
Other (_____)			

LESS:

1. **Tithe**		$330
2. **Tax** (Est. - Incl. Fed., State, FICA)		$544
NET SPENDABLE INCOME		$2,426

3. **Housing**		$801
Mortgage (rent)	550	
Insurance	25	
Taxes	66	
Electricity	70	
Gas	40	
Water	15	
Sanitation	5	
Telephone	30	
Maintenance		
Other (_____)		
Other (_____)		
4. **Food**		$300
5. **Automobile(s)**		$510
Payments	340	
Gas and Oil	75	
Insurance	50	
License/Taxes	5	
Maint./Repair/Replace	40	
6. **Insurance**		$30
Life ($250,000 term) Jim	20	
Life ($100,000 term) Katie	10	
Other (_____)		
7. **Debts**		$464
Credit Card	360	
Loans and Notes		
Other (_____)	104	
Other (_____)		

8. **Enter./Recreation**		$80
Eating Out	25	
Baby Sitters	10	
Activities/Trips	20	
Vacation	25	
Other (_____)		
Other (_____)		
9. **Clothing**		$30
10. **Savings**		$40
11. **Medical Expenses**		$55
Doctor	35	
Dentist	10	
Drugs	10	
Other (_____)		
12. **Miscellaneous**		$116
Toiletry, cosmetics	15	
Beauty, barber	10	
Laundry, cleaning	15	
Allowances, lunches	16	
Subscriptions		
Gifts (incl. Christmas)	30	
Cash	30	
Cable/Internet		
Other (_____)		
Other (_____)		
13. **Investments**		$0
14. **School/Child Care**		$0
Tuition		
Materials		
Transportation		
Day Care		
Other (_____)		
TOTAL EXPENSES		$2,426

INCOME VERSUS EXPENSES

Net Spendable Income	$2,426
Less Expenses	$2,426

15. **Unallocated Surplus Income**[1] _____

[1] This category is used when surplus income is received. This would be kept in the checking account to be used within a few weeks; otherwise, it should be transferred to an allocated category.

CASE STUDY SEVEN ANSWERS

The Thorntons were shocked when they were shown that they spent $461 more each month than they made. Both Matthew and Sharron were eager to change their habits of handling finances. Their first change was to tithe $300 per month because they wanted to put God first in their lives.

Matthew changed his tax exemptions so that less taxes would be deducted from his paycheck.

A review of their Housing expenses revealed there was no excess spending. The only change was to place some money in the Maintenance category.

Food was reduced from $400 to $350 per month. Matthew and Sharron agreed they purchased too much junk food and that they needed to become more health conscious.

They decided they could get by with one car, so they sold the Toyota and used the proceeds to pay off their Chevrolet. By doing this they reduced other Automobile categories as well.

They took a hard look at their Life Insurance and realized they needed a $250,000 death benefit. They had also been struggling to meet the monthly premium, so after discussing this situation with their life insurance agent they decided to drop the whole life policy, which was only 3 years old, and purchase a term policy with a $250,000 death benefit for $25 per month. The $1,000 cash value from the whole life policy was used to reduce credit card debt.

The remaining Debts were totally paid off with the proceeds from the money market account. This decision relieved a tremendous burden.

Entertainment/Recreation was reduced to $180 per month. Clothing stayed the same, and a Savings plan was started by setting aside $165 per month.

The Medical Expenses category was increased to $40 per month. Miscellaneous was cut to $295 per month by reducing the Gift, Lunch, and Cash categories.

With the remaining $185 in their budget, they started an investment program for retirement and college funds for their children.

They were also advised to see an attorney to discuss the need for wills.

The Thorntons are very excited because they now have a plan that provides a path for them to become free of financial bondage. As they continue to study what God's Word says about money, they will be capable of helping others in this area.

CASE STUDY SEVEN—ANSWER
MONTHLY INCOME AND EXPENSES

GROSS INCOME PER MONTH $3,000

Salary	3,000	
Interest		
Dividends		
Other (_____)		
Other (_____)		

LESS:

1. Tithe $300

2. Tax (Est. - Incl. Fed., State, FICA) $429

NET SPENDABLE INCOME $2,271

3. Housing $756

Mortgage (rent)	450
Insurance	25
Taxes	75
Electricity	75
Gas	50
Water	16
Sanitation	10
Telephone	30
Maintenance	25
Other (_____)	
Other (_____)	

4. Food $350

5. Automobile(s) $175

Payments	
Gas and Oil	80
Insurance	40
License/Taxes	5
Maint./Repair/Replace	50

6. Insurance $25

Life ($250,000 term) Matt	25
Medical	
Other (_____)	

7. Debts $0

Credit Card	
Loans and Notes	
Other (_____)	
Other (_____)	

8. Enter./Recreation $180

Eating Out	60
Baby Sitters	
Activities/Trips	20
Vacation	100
Other (_____)	
Other (_____)	

9. Clothing $100

10. Savings $165

11. Medical Expenses $40

Doctor	20
Dentist	20
Drugs	
Other (_____)	

12. Miscellaneous $295

Toiletry, cosmetics	10
Beauty, barber	15
Laundry, cleaning	10
Allowances, lunches	90
Subscriptions	10
Gifts (incl. Christmas)	85
Cash	75
Cable/Internet	
Other (_____)	
Other (_____)	

13. Investments $185

14. School/Child Care $0

Tuition	
Materials	
Transportation	
Day Care	
Other (_____)	

TOTAL EXPENSES $2,271

INCOME VERSUS EXPENSES

Net Spendable Income	$2,271
Less Expenses	$2,271

15. Unallocated Surplus Income[1]

[1] This category is used when surplus income is received. This would be kept in the checking account to be used within a few weeks; otherwise, it should be transferred to an allocated category.

CASE STUDY EIGHT ANSWERS

First the coach looked at the Earned Income Credit. Since Linda had been spending the lump sum, it was not helping her throughout the year. The coach encouraged her to apply for the credit on a quarterly basis instead of once a year. This will make it easier for Linda to include it in her budget.

Although she loses child support, her children will be able to work full-time during the summer to help her and to save for school.

Since she is already paying a modest mortgage, few adjustments could be made in her Housing costs. She has decided to have her family call her to reduce her long-distance charges, and her children will pay for their long-distance calls. She is dropping from full cable service to basic cable service. She is keeping that because she cannot receive TV signals in her area without cable.

The Food category will decrease to $190. It is a very modest budget for two teenagers and a mother. The kids will contribute to the food budget when they can.

In the Automobile category, Linda was encouraged to take advantage of the church's car care ministry for oil changes and to share rides when possible.

Linda will drop the additional life insurance, since her children are now adults and the purpose was to pay for college. With low family income, the children should be able to obtain scholarships and grants and work to pay for their education. Dental coverage on the children ends when they become 18, so that will be dropped. The family medical coverage will continue as long as the children are under age 24 and still in school.

In the Debt category, the credit card payment was dropped to $32 per month. Linda had made great progress in cutting down her debt, so the coach felt confident that she would continue to pay it off with any extra that became available. The biggest problem was accumulating enough reserve so that Linda would not have to rely on credit again. Obviously, her budget still does not allow for much saving, so she will have to depend on her family and the church to help in times of emergency. If she can avoid using credit, she will eventually have $32 more per month to build a savings.

Linda has agreed to decrease the Entertainment area by only visiting her family once a year. The coach encouraged Linda either to have her family visit her or ask them to pay for her second visit. With her children busy working and attending college, she will not need as much money for entertainment.

The Clothing category remained at $20 per month. The coach suggested that Linda may need the help of a clothing closet or donations of work clothes from women in the church.

Since the church does not already have a way of distributing clothing, Linda decided that she would provide space in her basement to start such a ministry.

Savings and Medical expenses remained the same.

The Miscellaneous category was cut from $107 per month to $53 per month. Linda agreed to make some of her gifts, to partner with others on gifts for church members, and to limit gifts to her children. She is cutting laundry expenses by buying larger sizes of off-brand detergents. She is discontinuing her subscriptions and will ask friends to pass on their magazines when they've finished reading them.

CASE STUDY EIGHT—ANSWER
MONTHLY INCOME AND EXPENSES

GROSS INCOME PER MONTH　　$1,500

Salary	1,500
Interest	
Dividends	
Other (_____)	
Other (_____)	

LESS:

1. Tithe　　$150

*2. Tax (Est. - Incl. Fed., State, FICA)　　$115

NET SPENDABLE INCOME　　$1,235

3. Housing　　$551

Mortgage (rent)	395
Insurance	8
Taxes	
Electricity	80
Gas	
Water	10
Sanitation	5
Telephone	30
Maintenance	
Cable TV	23
Other (_____)	

4. Food　　$190

5. Automobile(s)　　$262

Payments	128
Gas and Oil	70
Insurance	50
License/Taxes	5
Maint./Repair/Replace	9

6. Insurance　　$25

Life	
Medical	25
Other (_____)	

7. Debts　　$44

Credit Card	32
Loans and Notes	12
Other (_____)	
Other (_____)	

8. Enter./Recreation　　$40

Eating Out	15
Baby Sitters	
Activities/Trips	10
Vacation	15
Other (_____)	
Other (_____)	

9. Clothing　　$20

10. Savings　　$20

11. Medical Expenses　　$30

Doctor	20
Dentist	8
Drugs	2
Other (_____)	

12. Miscellaneous　　$53

Toiletry, cosmetics	10
Beauty, barber	10
Laundry, cleaning	5
Allowances, lunches	
Subscriptions	
Gifts (incl. Christmas)	13
Cash	15
Cable/Internet	
Other (_____)	
Other (_____)	

13. Investments　　$0

14. School/Child Care　　$0

Tuition	
Materials	
Transportation	
Day Care	
Other (_____)	

TOTAL EXPENSES　　$1,235

INCOME VERSUS EXPENSES

Net Spendable Income	$1,235
Less Expenses	$1,235

15. Unallocated Surplus Income[1]

---

[1] This category is used when surplus income is received. This would be kept in the checking account to be used within a few weeks; otherwise, it should be transferred to an allocated category.

* Earned Income Credit <314>

CASE STUDY NINE ANSWERS

The Bolings are a hard-working couple. Though they didn't spend much money on themselves while they were working, they did go overboard at retirement. Though they both worked at the same mill for over 40 years, the mill provided no retirement plan. Ralph did manage to start an IRA, but he never contributed much.

Their situation is typical for some of the retired elderly who only have Social Security to live on. As the population ages, the church will be faced with more situations like this.

Their situation embarrassed the Bolings but they were willing to follow counsel. It was determined that their Housing was pretty much set. Although they could sell the mobile home and land, this would be a last resort. Rents were equivalent to their mortgage payment. Their telephone bill was reduced by $10 per month. By using menus when shopping, the Bolings felt they could reduce the Food category by $50.

Now for the difficult part. The leased Honda was a relatively new lease and not one to get out of easily. They advertised the car and found a buyer willing to pay the market value of $15,000. With this $15,000 and $500 from cashing in their IRA, they bought out the lease. They took another $1,500 from IRA money and paid off the Oldsmobile loan. This reduced their insurance and all other car expenses so that the monthly auto expense was now $73. They placed the balance of the IRA money in Savings.

The coach requested an insurance agent to review the life insurance policies. The agent informed them that they could stop paying the premiums, because the dividends were large enough to pay the premiums. He also found that there was $1,750 of accumulated dividends on each policy. They decided to cash in the accumulated dividends on each policy and use this to pay off the Sears credit card completely. The life insurance policies would be kept for death and burial expenses.

The balance of the credit card payments were reduced by negotiating with the creditors. The old medical expenses remained.

Entertainment/Recreation were cut in half and money was added to the Clothing, Savings, and Medical categories in amounts of $25, $32, and $45 respectively.

Miscellaneous was reduced to $70 by dropping some magazine subscriptions, gift money, and basic spending money.

This was a difficult case and not one that was handled quickly. This required several months to complete. The Bolings requested additional accountability with their budget and they used an attorney from their church to draft their wills. They also discussed finding some odd jobs that would generate income to help pay off their debts faster.

CASE STUDY NINE—ANSWER
MONTHLY INCOME AND EXPENSES

GROSS INCOME PER MONTH $1,726

Salary	
Interest	
Dividends	
Social Security	1,726
Other (_____)	

LESS:

1. Tithe $172

2. Tax (Est. - Incl. Fed., State, FICA) $0

NET SPENDABLE INCOME $1,554

3. Housing $675

Mortgage (rent)	466
Insurance	29
Taxes	50
Electricity	35
Gas	65
Water	
Sanitation	
Telephone	30
Maintenance	
Cable TV	
Other (_____)	

4. Food $200

5. Automobile(s) $73

Payments	
Gas and Oil	35
Insurance	18
License/Taxes	5
Maint./Repair/Replace	15

6. Insurance $44

Life	
Medicare Part B	44
Other (_____)	

7. Debts $350

Credit Card	270
Loans and Notes	
Other (_____)	80
Other (_____)	

8. Enter./Recreation $40

Eating Out	20
Baby Sitters	
Activities/Trips	20
Vacation	
Other (_____)	
Other (_____)	

9. Clothing $25

10. Savings $32

11. Medical Expenses $45

Doctor	15
Dentist	10
Drugs	20
Other (_____)	

12. Miscellaneous $70

Toiletry, cosmetics	10
Beauty, barber	10
Laundry, cleaning	10
Allowances, lunches	
Subscriptions	5
Gifts (incl. Christmas)	15
Cash	20
Cable/Internet	
Other (_____)	
Other (_____)	

13. Investments $0

14. School/Child Care $0

Tuition	
Materials	
Transportation	
Day Care	
Other (_____)	

TOTAL EXPENSES $1,554

INCOME VERSUS EXPENSES

Net Spendable Income	$1,554
Less Expenses	$1,554

15. Unallocated Surplus Income[1]

---

[1] This category is used when surplus income is received. This would be kept in the checking account to be used within a few weeks; otherwise, it should be transferred to an allocated category.

ASSIGNMENT

1. Complete Case Studies Ten, Eleven, and Twelve.

2. Answer the Review Questions on page 248.

CASE STUDY TEN

Background Information: Mark and Bonnie Currey are both 38 years old. They each have advanced degrees from college and are earning a good living. Mark is an engineer in a respected engineering firm, and Bonnie is a school vice principal. They have one child, a daughter 5, and are expecting twins within the next three months. It is Bonnie's desire to be a stay-at-home mom; however, their lifestyle would have to change significantly due to the loss of Bonnie's income. At the present time, Bonnie's mom is caring for their daughter after school.

The Curreys are active in church, and Mark is in leadership. They tithe regularly and take joy in assisting with the special needs of missionaries.

They have two cars, but they need to purchase a van before the twins arrive. Mark purchased his car with the bonus stock option he received. They both have wills. Mark has adequate life insurance through his company, and Bonnie has a policy she will lose when she is no longer with the school system.

Assignment: After reviewing their Monthly Income and Expenses form, Financial Statement, and List of Debts, balance the Currey's budget and give appropriate recommendations about their budget in light of Bonnie's desire to stay at home with their children.

CASE STUDY TEN—AS IS
MONTHLY INCOME AND EXPENSES

GROSS INCOME PER MONTH		$10,416
Salary	10,416	
Interest		
Dividends		
Other (_____)		
Other (_____)		

LESS:

1. Tithe		$1,250
2. Tax (Est. - Incl. Fed., State, FICA)		$3,425
NET SPENDABLE INCOME		**$5,741**

3. Housing		$2,030
Mortgage (rent)	1,575	
Insurance		
Taxes		
Electricity	165	
Gas	50	
Water	30	
Sanitation	10	
Telephone	100	
Maintenance	100	
Other (_____)		
Other (_____)		

4. Food		$400

5. Automobile(s)		$925
Payments	450	
Gas and Oil	150	
Insurance	200	
License/Taxes	25	
Maint./Repair/Replace	100	

6. Insurance		$0
Life		
Medical		
Other (_____)		

7. Debts		$255
Credit Card	55	
Loans and Notes	200	
Other (_____)		
Other (_____)		

8. Enter./Recreation		$800
Eating Out	250	
Baby Sitters	50	
Activities/Trips	200	
Vacation	300	
Other (_____)		
Other (_____)		

9. Clothing		$150

10. Savings		$150

11. Medical Expenses		$70
Doctor	20	
Dentist	30	
Drugs	20	
Other (_____)		

12. Miscellaneous		$720
Toiletry, cosmetics	50	
Beauty, barber	70	
Laundry, cleaning	75	
Allowances, lunches	30	
Subscriptions	25	
Gifts (incl. Christmas)	100	
Cash	250	
Cable/Internet	50	
Cell Phone	70	
Other (_____)		

13. Investments		$200

14. School/Child Care		$50
Tuition		
Materials		
Transportation		
Day Care		
Pay grandmother	50	

TOTAL EXPENSES		**$5,750**

INCOME VERSUS EXPENSES

Net Spendable Income	$5,741
Less Expenses	$5,750
	-$9

15. **Unallocated Surplus Income**[1]

---

[1] This category is used when surplus income is received. This would be kept in the checking account to be used within a few weeks; otherwise, it should be transferred to an allocated category.

FINANCIAL STATEMENT

ASSETS			**LIABILITIES**[4]	
Liquid Assets[1]			Bank of America (Res.)	$200,000
Checking Account	$3,500		First Choice (BMW)	16,000
Money Market	1,500		Credit Card	2,000
			School Loans	10,000
Total Liquid Assets	$5,000		**TOTAL LIABILITIES**	$228,000
Invested Assets[2]				
CD's	$2,000			
Stock	45,000			
			NET WORTH	$160,000
			(Assets-Liabilities)	
Total Invested	$47,000			
Use Assets[3]				
Residence	$250,000			
Ford Mustang	25,000			
BMW	36,000			
Personal Items	25,000		**TOTAL LIABILITIES**	
			AND NET WORTH	$388,000
Total Use Assets	$336,000			
TOTAL ASSETS	$338,000			

[1] Cash, Savings Accounts, Checking Accounts
[2] IRAs, TSAs, 401(k)s, Investment, Real Estate, CDs, Antiques presented at fair market value.
[3] Residence, Autos, Personal Belongings presented at fair market value.
[4] Outstanding Real Estate Loans, Credit Cards, Auto Loans, Personal Loans.

LIST OF DEBTS
CASE STUDY TEN

To Whom Owed	Contact Name Phone Number	Pay Off	Payments Left	Monthly Payment	Date Due	Interest Rate
VISA		$2,000	46	$55	15th	13%
First National		$10,000	62	$200	1st	8%
Bank of America		$220,000	324	$1,575	1st	7%
First Union		$16,000	45	$450	10th	13%

CASE STUDY TEN—WORKSHEET
MONTHLY INCOME AND EXPENSES

GROSS INCOME PER MONTH _____

    Salary _____

    Interest _____

    Dividends _____

    Other (_____) _____

    Other (_____) _____

LESS:

  1. Tithe _____

  2. Tax (Est. - Incl. Fed., State, FICA) _____

    NET SPENDABLE INCOME _____

  3. Housing _____

    Mortgage (rent) _____

    Insurance _____

    Taxes _____

    Electricity _____

    Gas _____

    Water _____

    Sanitation _____

    Telephone _____

    Maintenance _____

    Other (_____) _____

    Other (_____) _____

  4. Food _____

  5. Automobile(s) _____

    Payments _____

    Gas and Oil _____

    Insurance _____

    License/Taxes _____

    Maint./Repair/Replace _____

  6. Insurance _____

    Life _____

    Medical _____

    Other (_____) _____

  7. Debts _____

    Credit Card _____

    Loans and Notes _____

    Other (_____) _____

    Other (_____) _____

8. Enter./Recreation _____

    Eating Out _____

    Baby Sitters _____

    Activities/Trips _____

    Vacation _____

    Other (_____) _____

    Other (_____) _____

9. Clothing _____

10. Savings _____

11. Medical Expenses _____

    Doctor _____

    Dentist _____

    Credit Card _____

    Other (_____) _____

12. Miscellaneous _____

    Toiletry, cosmetics _____

    Beauty, barber _____

    Laundry, cleaning _____

    Allowances, lunches _____

    Subscriptions _____

    Gifts (incl. Christmas) _____

    Cash _____

    Cable/Internet _____

    Other (_____) _____

    Other (_____) _____

13. Investments _____

14. School/Child Care _____

    Tuition _____

    Materials _____

    Transportation _____

    Day Care _____

    Other (_____) _____

TOTAL EXPENSES _____

INCOME VERSUS EXPENSES

    Net Spendable Income _____

    Less Expenses _____

15. Unallocated Surplus Income[1]

[1] This category is used when surplus income is received. This would be kept in the checking account to be used within a few weeks; otherwise, it should be transferred to an allocated category.

CASE STUDY TEN
COMMENTS

CASE STUDY ELEVEN

Background Information: Mike and Carrie Williams have come to you for help. This is a second marriage for both Mike and Carrie. Mike is 35 with three children from his previous marriage. Carrie is 32 with two children from her first marriage. Mike and Carrie are expecting their first child in four months. Mike works as a grocery store manager and Carrie is a clerk at a local mall.

Mike pays monthly child support and is required to carry health insurance for his children, as well as a minimum of $200,000 of life insurance. He has been awarded the children as tax exemptions if he does what is required of him. He owes no alimony. Carrie's first husband is not paying the child support he owes, and when Carrie tried to track him down through her lawyer he could not be located.

Mike and Carrie want to start tithing, but Carrie now wants to be a stay-at-home mother. There are many challenges. Mike has a will, but Carrie does not. There is no life insurance on Carrie.

Assignment: After reviewing their Monthly Income and Expenses form, Financial Statement, and List of Debts, balance the Williams's budget and give appropriate recommendations.

CASE STUDY ELEVEN—AS IS
MONTHLY INCOME AND EXPENSES

GROSS INCOME PER MONTH		$5,834
Salary (Mike's 4,167)	5,834	
Interest		
Dividends		
Other (_____)		
Other (_____)		

LESS:

1. **Tithe**		$0
2. **Tax** (Est. - Incl. Fed., State, FICA)		$653
NET SPENDABLE INCOME		$5,181
3. **Housing**		$1,400
Mortgage (rent)	1,050	
Insurance	(incl)	
Taxes	(incl)	
Electricity	160	
Gas	50	
Water	25	
Sanitation	10	
Telephone	55	
Maintenance	50	
Other (_____)		
Other (_____)		
4. **Food**		$475
5. **Automobile(s)**		$892
Payments	585	
Gas and Oil	150	
Insurance	97	
License/Taxes	20	
Maint./Repair/Replace	40	
6. **Insurance**		$235
Life	75	
Medical	160	
Other (_____)		
7. **Debts**		$154
Credit Card	154	
Loans and Notes		
Other (_____)		
Other (_____)		

8. **Enter./Recreation**		$425
Eating Out	200	
Baby Sitters	50	
Activities/Trips	100	
Vacation	75	
Other (_____)		
Other (_____)		
9. **Clothing**		$200
10. **Savings**		$50
11. **Medical Expenses**		$55
Doctor	30	
Dentist	15	
Drugs	10	
Other (_____)		
12. **Miscellaneous**		$920
Toiletry, cosmetics	25	
Beauty, barber	25	
Laundry, cleaning	25	
Allowances, lunches	30	
Subscriptions	5	
Gifts (incl. Christmas)	50	
Cash	175	
Cable/Internet	60	
Child Support	525	
Other (_____)		
13. **Investments**		$75
14. **School/Child Care**		$400
Tuition		
Materials		
Transportation		
Day Care	400	
Other (_____)		
TOTAL EXPENSES		$5,281

INCOME VERSUS EXPENSES

Net Spendable Income	$5,181
Less Expenses	$5,281
	-$100

15. **Unallocated Surplus Income**[1]

[1] This category is used when surplus income is received. This would be kept in the checking account to be used within a few weeks; otherwise, it should be transferred to an allocated category.

FINANCIAL STATEMENT

ASSETS			LIABILITIES[4]	
Liquid Assets[1]			Bank of America (Chevy)	$14,000
Checking Account		$955	Bank of America (Ford)	9,500
Savings Account		450	First Union (Residence)	89,000
			VISA	3,000
			MasterCard	3,200
Total Liquid Assets		$1,405	**TOTAL LIABILITIES**	$118,700
Invested Assets[2]				
Stocks		$7,500		
			NET WORTH	$32,705
			(Assets-Liabilities)	
Total Invested		$7,500		
Use Assets[3]				
Residence		$105,000		
Chevy Van		20,000		
Ford		17,500		
			TOTAL LIABILITIES	
			AND NET WORTH	$151,405
Total Use Assets		$142,500		
TOTAL ASSETS		$151,405		

[1] Cash, Savings Accounts, Checking Accounts
[2] IRAs, TSAs, 401(k)s, Investment, Real Estate, CDs, Antiques presented at fair market value.
[3] Residence, Autos, Personal Belongings presented at fair market value.
[4] Outstanding Real Estate Loans, Credit Cards, Auto Loans, Personal Loans.

LIST OF DEBTS
CASE STUDY ELEVEN

To Whom Owed	Contact Name Phone Number	Pay Off	Payments Left	Monthly Payment	Date Due	Interest Rate
First Union		$89,000	342	$850	10th	11%
Bank of America		$14,000	48	$360	15th	11%
Bank of America		$9,500	49	$225	1st	7.4%
VISA		$3,000	52	$75	15th	13%
MasterCard		$3,200	49	$79	5th	12%

CASE STUDY ELEVEN—WORKSHEET
MONTHLY INCOME AND EXPENSES

GROSS INCOME PER MONTH _____

    Salary _____

    Interest _____

    Dividends _____

    Other (_____) _____

    Other (_____) _____

LESS:

  1. Tithe _____

  2. Tax (Est. - Incl. Fed., State, FICA) _____

      NET SPENDABLE INCOME _____

  3. Housing _____

    Mortgage (rent) _____

    Insurance _____

    Taxes _____

    Electricity _____

    Gas _____

    Water _____

    Sanitation _____

    Telephone _____

    Maintenance _____

    Other (_____) _____

    Other (_____) _____

  4. Food _____

  5. Automobile(s) _____

    Payments _____

    Gas and Oil _____

    Insurance _____

    License/Taxes _____

    Maint./Repair/Replace _____

  6. Insurance _____

    Life _____

    Medical _____

    Other (_____) _____

  7. Debts _____

    Credit Card _____

    Loans and Notes _____

    Other (_____) _____

    Other (_____) _____

8. Enter./Recreation _____

    Eating Out _____

    Baby Sitters _____

    Activities/Trips _____

    Vacation _____

    Other (_____) _____

    Other (_____) _____

9. Clothing _____

10. Savings _____

11. Medical Expenses _____

    Doctor _____

    Dentist _____

    Credit Card _____

    Other (_____) _____

12. Miscellaneous _____

    Toiletry, cosmetics _____

    Beauty, barber _____

    Laundry, cleaning _____

    Allowances, lunches _____

    Subscriptions _____

    Gifts (incl. Christmas) _____

    Cash _____

    Cable/Internet _____

    Other (_____) _____

    Other (_____) _____

13. Investments _____

14. School/Child Care _____

    Tuition _____

    Materials _____

    Transportation _____

    Day Care _____

    Other (_____) _____

TOTAL EXPENSES _____

INCOME VERSUS EXPENSES

    Net Spendable Income _____

    Less Expenses _____

15. Unallocated Surplus Income[1] _____

---

[1] This category is used when surplus income is received. This would be kept in the checking account to be used within a few weeks; otherwise, it should be transferred to an allocated category.

CASE STUDY ELEVEN
COMMENTS

CASE STUDY TWELVE

Background Information: Ron and Stacie Hollinger have been married for eight years and have no children. Ron holds a job in upper management in a Fortune 500 company, and Stacie is a CPA with a local accounting office. Ron and Stacie enjoy an active lifestyle and treat themselves to many vacations. Ron and Stacie are Christians, attend a large church, and tithe, but they had not been convicted to become good stewards until last month. They attended a Crown Financial Ministries seminar and learned what God teaches about money. They now want their lifestyle to represent a life that is pleasing to God. Ron and Stacie have current wills.

Assignment: After reviewing their Monthly Income and Expenses form, Financial Statement, and List of Debts, work on the Hollinger's budget and give appropriate recommendations about their lifestyle.

CASE STUDY TWELVE—AS IS
MONTHLY INCOME AND EXPENSES

GROSS INCOME PER MONTH $19,167

Salary	19,167
Interest	
Dividends	
Other (_____)	
Other (_____)	

LESS:

1. **Tithe** $2,150

2. **Tax** (Est. - Incl. Fed., State, FICA) $7,301

    NET SPENDABLE INCOME $9,716

3. **Housing** $2,765

Mortgage (rent)	2,200
Insurance	(incl)
Taxes	(incl)
Electricity	225
Gas	65
Water	30
Sanitation	10
Telephone	120
Maintenance	50
Lawn Service	65
Other (_____)	

4. **Food** $490

5. **Automobile(s)** $1,940

Payments	1,310
Gas and Oil	190
Insurance	210
License/Taxes	30
Maint./Repair/Replace	200

6. **Insurance** $120

Life	120
Medical	
Other (_____)	

7. **Debts** $1,200

Credit Card	1,200
Loans and Notes	
Other (_____)	
Other (_____)	

8. **Enter./Recreation** $815

Eating Out	150
Baby Sitters	
Activities/Trips	150
Vacation	515
Other (_____)	
Other (_____)	

9. **Clothing** $350

10. **Savings** $400

11. **Medical Expenses** $50

Doctor	20
Dentist	20
Drugs	10
Other (_____)	

12. **Miscellaneous** $886

Toiletry, cosmetics	35
Beauty, barber	60
Laundry, cleaning	71
Allowances, lunches	50
Subscriptions	20
Gifts (incl. Christmas)	150
Cash	300
Cable/Internet	100
Cell Phones	100
Other (_____)	

13. **Investments** $700

14. **School/Child Care** $0

Tuition	
Materials	
Transportation	
Day Care	
Other (_____)	

    TOTAL EXPENSES $9,716

INCOME VERSUS EXPENSES

Net Spendable Income	$9,716
Less Expenses	$9,716

15. **Unallocated Surplus Income**[1]

---

[1] This category is used when surplus income is received. This would be kept in the checking account to be used within a few weeks; otherwise, it should be transferred to an allocated category.

CASE STUDY TWELVE
FINANCIAL STATEMENT

ASSETS

    Liquid Assets[1]

Checking Account	$5,000
Money Market	6,000
Savings	7,500

Total Liquid Assets $18,500

Invested Assets[2]

Stocks	$60,000
CD	10,000

Total Invested $70,000

Use Assets[3]

Residence	$300,000
Toyota	25,000
Ford SUV	35,000

Total Use Assets $360,000

TOTAL ASSETS $448,500

LIABILITIES[4]

Regions Bank (Residence)	$250,000
Bank of America (Toyota)	20,000
Bank of America (Ford)	28,000
American Express	1,200

TOTAL LIABILITIES $299,200

NET WORTH $149,300
(Assets-Liabilities)

TOTAL LIABILITIES AND NET WORTH $448,500

[1] Cash, Savings Accounts, Checking Accounts
[2] IRAs, TSAs, 401(k)s, Investment, Real Estate, CDs, Antiques presented at fair market value.
[3] Residence, Autos, Personal Belongings presented at fair market value.
[4] Outstanding Real Estate Loans, Credit Cards, Auto Loans, Personal Loans.

LIST OF DEBTS
CASE STUDY TWELVE

To Whom Owed	Contact Name Phone Number	Pay Off	Payments Left	Monthly Payment	Date Due	Interest Rate
Regions Bank		$250,000	352	$2,220	15th	9%
Bank of America		$20,000	57	$450	10th	10%
Bank of America		$28,000	36	$860	20th	6.6%
American Express		$1,200	1	$1,200	20th	N/A

CASE STUDY TWELVE—WORKSHEET
MONTHLY INCOME AND EXPENSES

GROSS INCOME PER MONTH _____

    Salary _____

    Interest _____

    Dividends _____

    Other (_____) _____

    Other (_____) _____

LESS:

  1. Tithe _____

  2. Tax (Est. - Incl. Fed., State, FICA) _____

     NET SPENDABLE INCOME _____

  3. Housing _____

    Mortgage (rent) _____

    Insurance _____

    Taxes _____

    Electricity _____

    Gas _____

    Water _____

    Sanitation _____

    Telephone _____

    Maintenance _____

    Other (_____) _____

    Other (_____) _____

  4. Food _____

  5. Automobile(s) _____

    Payments _____

    Gas and Oil _____

    Insurance _____

    License/Taxes _____

    Maint./Repair/Replace _____

  6. Insurance _____

    Life _____

    Medical _____

    Other (_____) _____

  7. Debts _____

    Credit Card _____

    Loans and Notes _____

    Other (_____) _____

    Other (_____) _____

8. Enter./Recreation _____

    Eating Out _____

    Baby Sitters _____

    Activities/Trips _____

    Vacation _____

    Other (_____) _____

    Other (_____) _____

9. Clothing _____

10. Savings _____

11. Medical Expenses _____

    Doctor _____

    Dentist _____

    Credit Card _____

    Other (_____) _____

12. Miscellaneous _____

    Toiletry, cosmetics _____

    Beauty, barber _____

    Laundry, cleaning _____

    Allowances, lunches _____

    Subscriptions _____

    Gifts (incl. Christmas) _____

    Cash _____

    Cable/Internet _____

    Other (_____) _____

    Other (_____) _____

13. Investments _____

14. School/Child Care _____

    Tuition _____

    Materials _____

    Transportation _____

    Day Care _____

    Other (_____) _____

TOTAL EXPENSES _____

INCOME VERSUS EXPENSES

    Net Spendable Income _____

    Less Expenses _____

15. Unallocated Surplus Income[1]

---

[1] This category is used when surplus income is received. This would be kept in the checking account to be used within a few weeks; otherwise, it should be transferred to an allocated category.

CASE STUDY TWELVE
COMMENTS

Case Study Ten Answers

The Curreys truly desire to do what is best for their family. More day care is not an option for them. They believe that each child is a gift from God and is given to them to love and to teach the ways of God. After discussing their options, they decided to create a budget based only on Mark's salary.

They decided that if at all possible they wanted to continue to give the $150 toward missions.

After reviewing the entire budget with you, they decided to sell the BMW, pay it off, and buy a van.

Bonnie should be able to complete the school term before the twins arrive. They decided to use her salary to pay off the school loan and the credit cards. Because Bonnie has not used her sick days, she will also get a check to pay her for the sick days she did not use. This check, along with the pay she receives, should be enough to pay off the entire school loan and credit card debts.

Other decisions were to reduce their cash allowance, reduce their clothing allowance—especially since Bonnie will not need clothes for work—reduce the amount they spend on eating out, and reduce their vacation spending.

They also reduced their long distance telephone bill by going to a slightly higher plan on their cell phone and using it for some of the long distance calls. They decided to temporarily lower their investment allocation.

You had the opportunity to remind them of what the Bible says about God's ownership and how He has entrusted them with material possessions to manage. You encouraged them to continue to remain faithful.

CASE STUDY TEN—ANSWER
MONTHLY INCOME AND EXPENSES

GROSS INCOME PER MONTH $6,250

Salary	6,250
Interest	
Dividends	
Other (_____)	
Other (_____)	

LESS:

1. Tithe $780

2. Tax (Est. - Incl. Fed., State, FICA) $1,402

NET SPENDABLE INCOME $4,068

3. Housing $1,963

Mortgage (rent)	1,575
Insurance	(incl.)
Taxes	(incl.)
Electricity	175
Gas	53
Water	30
Sanitation	10
Telephone	70
Maintenance	50
Other (_____)	
Other (_____)	

4. Food $400

5. Automobile(s) $375

Payments	
Gas and Oil	100
Insurance	150
License/Taxes	25
Maint./Repair/Replace	100

6. Insurance $25

Life (Bonnie 100,000 Term)	25
Medical	
Other (_____)	

7. Debts $0

Credit Card	
Loans and Notes	
Other (_____)	
Other (_____)	

8. Enter./Recreation $350

Eating Out	100
Baby Sitters	50
Activities/Trips	100
Vacation	100
Other (_____)	
Other (_____)	

9. Clothing $100

10. Savings $175

11. Medical Expenses $70

Doctor	30
Dentist	20
Drugs	20
Other (_____)	

12. Miscellaneous $510

Toiletry, cosmetics	30
Beauty, barber	50
Laundry, cleaning	50
Allowances, lunches	25
Subscriptions	25
Gifts (incl. Christmas)	100
Cash	120
Cable/Internet	50
Cell Phone	60
Other (_____)	

13. Investments $100

14. School/Child Care $0

Tuition	
Materials	
Transportation	
Day Care	
Other (_____)	

TOTAL EXPENSES $4,068

INCOME VERSUS EXPENSES

Net Spendable Income	$4,068
Less Expenses	$4,068

15. Unallocated Surplus Income[1]   _____

---

[1] This category is used when surplus income is received. This would be kept in the checking account to be used within a few weeks; otherwise, it should be transferred to an allocated category.

CASE STUDY ELEVEN ANSWERS

The Williamses were a blessing to you because you were able to lead them to a saving knowledge of the Lord. Mike and Carrie thought they were Christians, because they had always attended church and tried to do what was right. When you described your personal relationship with Christ, Mike and Carrie realized that they did not know Christ as Savior and Lord. You shared how Christ has changed your life and given you peace and this deeply impacted them.

You turned to pages 60-62 in their *Journey to Financial Freedom* manual and reviewed.

YOU CAN KNOW THE LORD

You may coach people who do not yet know Christ as their personal Savior and Lord. The following five steps describe how a person can enter into this relationship with the Lord.

1. God loves you and wants you to experience a meaningful life.

God created people in His own image, and He desires an intimate relationship with each of us. *"God so loved the world, that He gave His only begotten Son, that whoever believes in Him shall not perish, but have eternal life"* (John 3:16). *"I [Jesus] came that they may have life, and have it abundantly"* (John 10:10). God the Father loved us so much that He gave His only Son, Jesus Christ, to die for us so that we could enjoy eternal life with Him.

2. Unfortunately, we are separated from God.

God is holy—which means God is perfect, and He cannot have a relationship with anyone who is not perfect. Every person has sinned, and the consequence of sin was separation from God. *"All have sinned and fall short of the glory of God"* (Romans 3:23). *"Your sins have cut you off from God"* (Isaiah 59:2, TLB).

The diagram below illustrates an enormous gap that separates people from God. Individuals try without success to bridge this gap through their own efforts, such as philosophy, religion, material goods, charitable activity, or living a good moral life.

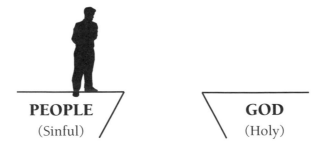

PEOPLE
(Sinful)

GOD
(Holy)

3. God's only provision to bridge this gap is Jesus Christ.

Jesus Christ died on the cross to pay the penalty for our sins. He bridged the gap between us and God. *"Jesus said to him, 'I am the way, and the truth, and the life; no one comes to the Father but through Me' "* (John 14:6). *"God demonstrates His own love toward us, in that while we were yet sinners, Christ died for us"* (Romans 5:8).

This diagram illustrates our union with God through Jesus Christ.

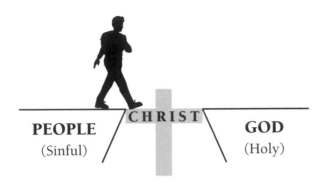

PEOPLE   **CHRIST**   **GOD**
(Sinful)   (Holy)

4. This relationship is a gift from God.

By an act of faith we can receive the free gift of a relationship with God. *"By grace you have been saved through faith; and that not of yourselves, it is the gift of God; not as a result of works, so that no one may boast"* (Ephesians 2:8-9).

5. We must each receive Jesus Christ individually.

We need to ask Jesus Christ to forgive us of our sins and to come into our lives to be Savior and Lord.

If you are helping coaching participants who are not certain whether they have this relationship, they may receive Christ by praying a prayer similar to this one: "Father God, I need You. I invite Jesus to come into my life as my Savior and Lord and make me the person You want me to be. Thank You for forgiving my sins and giving me the gift of eternal life."

If you are not certain you have a relationship with the Lord, we encourage you to pray that prayer right now. Nothing in life compares to knowing Christ. If you asked Him into your life, please tell someone from your church or let us know at Crown so that we can assist you in your spiritual growth.

. . . .

Then you focused on the Williams's budget. They realized that they were overspending $100 a month. On the second visit, they asked if you would help them design a budget based solely on Mike's income, to see if they could afford to allow Carrie to stay at home.

Adjustments were made in the Food, Miscellaneous, Clothing, and Entertainment/ Recreation categories.

Mike found that he could provide adequate health coverage for his children and save money if he raised their very low deductible. They also were able to refinance the mortgage and save a significant amount each month.

They sold enough stock to pay off the VISA and MasterCard, and they pledged to accumulate no more credit. Their use of heating and air conditioning was not regulated, and they chose to reduce their energy spending. They also decided to use basic cable, rather than the full service.

Even with these reductions, they were not able to balance their budget. Mike and Carrie prayed about what they should do. Mike was beginning to get discouraged. So he talked to his pastor. He told his pastor that he and Carrie knew what God wanted them to do but did not know how they could accomplish it without more income. After listening, his pastor asked if Mike was willing to work on a project that no one else was willing to do.

Mike responded that he was willing to do whatever it took to provide for his family. There were two elderly widows and an elderly couple who needed help with lawn maintenance, general home repair, and minor car maintenance. Each was able to pay for the work. Mike and Carrie prayed about this option, evaluated the time it would take Mike away from the family, and decided that Mike would do it. Each widow and the couple paid $75 a month to Mike. Carrie's 9-year-old son helped Mike with some of the chores on the weekends and after school.

This experience reminded you of the importance of prayer.

CASE STUDY ELEVEN—ANSWER
MONTHLY INCOME AND EXPENSES

GROSS INCOME PER MONTH $4,392

Salary	4,167	
Interest		
Dividends		
Other (_____)	225	
Other (_____)		

LESS:

1. **Tithe** $439

2. **Tax** (Est. - Incl. Fed., State, FICA) $430

NET SPENDABLE INCOME $3,523

3. **Housing** $1,180

Mortgage (rent)	900	
Insurance	(incl)	
Taxes	(incl)	
Electricity	130	
Gas	30	
Water	25	
Sanitation	10	
Telephone	45	
Maintenance	40	
Other (_____)		
Other (_____)		

4. **Food** $350

5. **Automobile(s)** $805

Payments	585	
Gas and Oil	80	
Insurance	80	
License/Taxes	20	
Maint./Repair/Replace	40	

6. **Insurance** $177

Life	50	
Medical	127	
Other (_____)		

7. **Debts** $0

Credit Card		
Loans and Notes		
Other (_____)		
Other (_____)		

8. **Enter./Recreation** $140

Eating Out	30	
Baby Sitters	10	
Activities/Trips	50	
Vacation	50	
Other (_____)		
Other (_____)		

9. **Clothing** $60

10. **Savings** $50

11. **Medical Expenses** $55

Doctor	30	
Dentist	15	
Drugs	10	
Other (_____)		

12. **Miscellaneous** $706

Toiletry, cosmetics	10	
Beauty, barber	10	
Laundry, cleaning	10	
Allowances, lunches	10	
Subscriptions	5	
Gifts (incl. Christmas)	30	
Cash	80	
Cable/Internet	26	
Child Support	525	
Other (_____)		

13. **Investments** $0

14. **School/Child Care** $0

Tuition		
Materials		
Transportation		
Day Care		
Other (_____)		

TOTAL EXPENSES $3,523

INCOME VERSUS EXPENSES

Net Spendable Income	$3,523
Less Expenses	$3,523

15. **Unallocated Surplus Income**[1]

---

[1] This category is used when surplus income is received. This would be kept in the checking account to be used within a few weeks; otherwise, it should be transferred to an allocated category.

CASE STUDY TWELVE ANSWERS

You were not prepared for what you would have to face with the Hollingers. To date, most of your coaching participants were challenged by not having enough funds. The Hollingers had too much, it seemed. They didn't even fit on your percentage guideline charts!

During your first session together they shared that they never realized what true stewardship meant and wanted to learn more about living God's way. As you listened to them, you understood that they both had a heart for giving. As the topic of children surfaced, Ron and Stacie got quiet and you sensed that something was wrong. Ron revealed that Stacie was not able to have children and that they did not feel comfortable with adoption. After about an hour, you decided to ask them what their goals were financially and how you could assist them in realizing their goals. The first session ended in prayer, and you assigned the first two homework sections to be done by your next meeting.

During the second session, you evaluated their spending habits and helped them determine where they were spending frivolously. Vacations were the first to be reduced, along with Clothing, the amount they charged on their American Express card, and their Food bill. You assigned the next two homework sections for them to complete before they met with you again.

During the third session, the Hollingers said that since they would not be having children of their own they would like to help the children of single parents get a college education. Their church had a benevolence fund that helped single parents, and they wanted to do what they could to help. They believed God entrusted them with that much money to give it to God's work, not to spend on themselves. So with the help of professionals a college fund was established, and an additional $200 was given to the benevolence committee to help single parents.

You met with the Hollingers one more time and gave them the rest of the homework assignments. You also suggested that they participate in a *Crown Special Edition* small group study. This study is for those who have been entrusted with a measure of wealth. They expressed their gratitude for your willingness to help and told you that when they talked about you at home they referred to you as "God's blessing!" To honor the sacrifice of time you gave to them, they decided to name the college scholarship fund after you: "God's blessing."

CASE STUDY TWELVE—ANSWER
MONTHLY INCOME AND EXPENSES

GROSS INCOME PER MONTH		$19,167	
Salary	19,167		
Interest			
Dividends			
Other (_____)			
Other (_____)			

LESS:

1. **Tithe**		$3,000	
2. **Tax** (Est. - Incl. Fed., State, FICA)		$7,301	
NET SPENDABLE INCOME		$8,866	

3. **Housing**		$2,765	
Mortgage (rent)	2,200		
Insurance	(incl)		
Taxes	(incl)		
Electricity	225		
Gas	65		
Water	30		
Sanitation	10		
Telephone	120		
Maintenance	50		
Lawn Service	65		
Other (_____)			
4. **Food**		$400	
5. **Automobile(s)**		$1,940	
Payments	1,310		
Gas and Oil	190		
Insurance	210		
License/Taxes	30		
Maint./Repair/Replace	200		
6. **Insurance**		$120	
Life	120		
Medical			
Other (_____)			
7. **Debts**		$0	
Credit Card			
Loans and Notes			
Other (_____)			
Other (_____)			

8. **Enter./Recreation**		$700	
Eating Out	250		
Baby Sitters			
Activities/Trips	100		
Vacation	350		
Other (_____)			
Other (_____)			
9. **Clothing**		$250	
10. **Savings**		$755	
11. **Medical Expenses**		$50	
Doctor	20		
Dentist	20		
Drugs	10		
Other (_____)			
12. **Miscellaneous**		$886	
Toiletry, cosmetics	35		
Beauty, barber	60		
Laundry, cleaning	71		
Allowances, lunches	50		
Subscriptions	20		
Gifts (incl. Christmas)	150		
Cash	300		
Cable/Internet	100		
Cell Phones	100		
Other (_____)			
13. **Investments**		$1,000	
14. **School/Child Care**		$0	
Tuition			
Materials			
Transportation			
Day Care			
Other (_____)			
TOTAL EXPENSES		$8,866	

INCOME VERSUS EXPENSES

Net Spendable Income		$8,866
Less Expenses		$8,866
15. **Unallocated Surplus Income**[1]		

[1] This category is used when surplus income is received. This would be kept in the checking account to be used within a few weeks; otherwise, it should be transferred to an allocated category.

[Intentionally blank]

REVIEW QUESTIONS

T F 1. The ideal location to meet for your coaching appointment is the coaching participant's home. This way you can get a good idea of his or her home life.

T F 2. It works best to keep the coaching session to one and one-half hours or less.

T F 3. The first step at the initial coaching visit is to define the problem.

T F 4. Coaches should always ask "what" questions versus "why" questions.

T F 5. A daily diary is recommended for coaching participants to record questions they might have for the next coaching visit.

T F 6. If the coaching participants do not complete their homework assignment, you should postpone future visits until the assignments are complete.

T F 7. All coaching participants need to agree to no more borrowing, except in emergencies.

T F 8. You may handle the checkbook for the coaching participants and pay their bills.

T F 9. Based on Proverbs 3:27-28, all assets of a coaching participant should be considered for possible liquidation.

T F 10. In order for you to coach successfully, you must be totally debt free.

T F 11. Most states will allow creditors to file suit against debtors and request garnishment of wages.

T F 12. Chapter 7 bankruptcy will not eradicate most IRS taxes owed.

T F 13. You can claim Chapter 7 bankruptcy against student loans backed by the U.S. government.

T F 14. The word *bankruptcy* is found in Scripture five times.

T F 15. It is not a sin to file for bankruptcy.

T F 16. It is not necessary to include the Financial Statement in the payment plan package because all debts are listed on the Debt Payment form.

REVIEW ANSWERS

1.   **False**   The ideal location is a neutral place, such as a church.

2.   **True**   If you coach for longer than one and one-half hours, you tire and don't accomplish much more.

3.   **False**   The first step is to open with prayer.

4.   **True**   "Why" questions might put the coaching participant on the defensive.

5.   **False**   A daily diary is recommended for coaching participants to record all of their spending, even down to 25 cents.

6.   **True**   This is a small requirement to ask of them. They need to develop discipline, and this is one of the first steps.

7.   **False**   They need to agree to no more borrowing. Period.

8.   **False**   Never handle a coaching participant's checkbook or pay bills for him or her.

9.   **True**   These verses are clear. Nothing should be held back if the coaching participant is serious about getting financially free.

10.   **False**   Coaches must be totally familiar with God's principles of finances and have their own budget under control.

11.   **True**   Not every state allows this but most do.

12.   **True**   You can file Chapter 7 bankruptcy against the IRS only on certain taxes under a very specific set of circumstances.

13.   **False**   These loans are also exempt from Chapter 7 bankruptcy.

14.   **False**   The word "bankruptcy" is not found anywhere in Scripture. Psalm 37:21 and Ecclesiastes 5:4-5 state that if you borrow you owe.

15.   **True**   It is a violation of Scripture not to pay back what you have borrowed. As a Christian, even after bankruptcy, you should make an effort to repay. Please seek the counsel of an attorney.

16.   **False**   The Financial Statement's purpose is to reveal all assets to the creditors.

APPENDIX

APPENDIX CONTENTS

RESOURCES AND HELPS

Coaching will uncover many areas that will be beyond the scope of the lay Money Map Coach's abilities. When that occurs, be prepared to seek qualified help for those you are coaching. *Remember, you are a Money Map Coach, not a marriage counselor, a tax advisor, an investment advisor, or an attorney.*

Know your areas of expertise and don't exceed them. In Steve Levicoff's book, *Christian Counseling and the Law,* he points out, "In the realm of counseling . . . two types of charlatans are practicing today: those who intend to defraud, and those who sincerely believe they're ordained to do something they're not qualified to do. Legally, then, there is one central point that may determine the liability of a counselor: Is the counselor purporting to be something that he or she is not?"

As you assist your church in the development of a financial ministry, you will need to pull together resources. With the assistance of your church leadership, it's wise to develop a list of professionals who may be willing to assist people in need free of charge or at reduced cost. Examples would be licensed coaches, attorneys, tax advisors, auto mechanics, dentists, doctors, and the like. The church leadership should know them well so that they can be recommended with confidence.

The following are other organizations that can provide specialized assistance.

PEACEMAKER MINISTRY
1537 Ave D Ste 352
Billings MT 59102
(406) 256-1583
www.HisPeace.org

This organization trains and directs a national network of Certified Christian Conciliators™ who provide biblically based conflict coaching, mediation, and arbitration to help Christians resolve personal and family conflicts, business disputes, congregational divisions, and lawsuits. It also provides educational resources and seminars on biblical conflict resolution to churches.

ALLIANCE DEFENSE FUND
8960 E Raintree Rd Ste 300
Scottsdale AZ 85260
(800) TELL-ADF (835-5233)
www.alliancedefensefund.org

This organization defends religious freedoms.

CHRISTIAN FINANCIAL PROFESSIONALS NETWORK

5605 Glenridge Dr Ste 845
Atlanta GA 30342
Phone: 404-497-7680
Fax: 404-497-7685
Web site: www.cfpn.org

This organization is a professional membership organization of experienced Christian financial professionals who are dedicated to utilizing biblical principles in their financial practices.

FINANCIAL HOPE

Crown Financial Ministries offers an Internet driven resource for finding answers to financial questions. It is clear that finances touch every life and no matter where someone is in his or her personal financial journey Crown Financial Ministries can assist in finding the guidance desired. Visit Financial Hope to see what all is offered on this Web site. The Web address is www.financialhope.com.

COACHING TERMINOLOGY

- **Crown Money Map Coach:** An individual who has completed the *Money Map Coach Training Course* and has approval of his or her pastor to minister in the church as a Money Map Coach.

- **Coaching participant:** The person who requests to meet with a Money Map Coach.

- **Client:** An individual who is a user of a service.

- **Partner Church:** A church that has joined Crown Financial Ministries in the effort of training people to manage money God's way. This church will have an active Money Map coaching ministry and is implementing the Crown program.

- **Crown Money Map Referral Coach:** An individual who has completed the *Money Map Coach Training Course* and has submitted the forms signed by his or her pastor to Crown Financial Ministries. These coaches receive coaching referrals directly from Crown, unless they are a part of a Partner Church Ministry.

- **Net Spendable Income:** Income available after the tithe and taxes have been paid.

- **Suggested Percentage Guidelines:** Percentage examples for each expense category. These are suggestions and should be viewed as being flexible.

- **Ministry:** A Bible-based, nonprofit organization that provides a service to the Christian community, such as Single Parent Ministry, Benevolence Ministry, or Car-Care Ministry.

- **Debt Management Plan:** The term used for an approved reduced debt payment plan arranged through credit counseling organizations, such as CCCS-Atlanta.

- **Crown Church Program:** A comprehensive program to teach God's financial principles to everyone in a church, using Crown's small group studies, Money Map coaching, Financial Seminar, and Video Series.

GLOSSARY

The purpose of the glossary is to define a broad spectrum of common financial and legal terms. Although the glossary is not exhaustive, it will provide you with a working foundation.

A-B Trust: A trust that is divided into two separate portions called Trust A and B.

Acceleration: The right of a creditor to demand full and immediate payment if a borrower defaults.

Accidental Death Benefits: Life insurance provision sometimes put in a policy that calls for payment of double benefits in the event of death by accidental means.

Accrued Interest: Interest that accumulates on a bond since the last payment.

Accumulation Plan: A plan designed to systematically accumulate mutual fund shares through periodic investments of income dividends.

Actual Cash Value Clause: Used in a home owner's policy that states the insurer pays the actual cash value of the loss of real property insured, if the loss does not exceed the policy's face value.

Actuary: A professional who is trained in the statistical aspects of life insurance.

Administration: The period of time after death when a decedent's affairs are handled under court supervision, often synonymous with *Probate*.

Administrator: The person appointed by a court to handle the administration when there is no will that names an executor. Called a personal representative in some states.

Alternate Valuation Date: The date six months after a decedent's death when all the assets of the estate may be valued.

American Stock Exchange (AMEX): A major stock exchange in the U.S.A.

Amortization: An accounting term for recording expenses, such as depreciation and taxes as they are applicable rather than as paid.

Annual Exclusion: A sum of money ($11,000 at this printing) that is free of federal gift taxes, which may be given every year by each donor to each donee.

Annual Percentage Rate (APR): The amount, expressed as a percentage that reflects all costs of a loan for a year.

Annual Report: A financial report issued by a corporation every year that expresses assets, liabilities, earnings, and other data of interest to shareholders.

Annuitant: A person who has a contractual agreement with a life insurance company to receive periodic payments over the course of a specific number of years or for life.

Appointee: A person who receives property when a power of appointment has been exercised in her or his favor.

Apportionment Clause: The clause in an insurance policy that prevents a homeowner from collecting more money than a house is worth.

Arbitrage: The practice of dealing in differences, such as buying on one stock exchange while simultaneously selling short on another at a higher price.

Asset: Items that are shown as owned or receivable on a balance sheet. An asset is anything of value.

Assigned Risk Plans: Plans that provide a method of showing financial responsibility for drivers who cannot obtain liability insurance because of poor driving records.

Assigning Wage Clause: Section in an agreement that allows a creditor to go directly to an employer and get a portion of the debtor's wages without first obtaining a court order.

Authorized Stocks: The total number of shares of stock that are authorized for issue by a company's shareholders.

Automated Teller Machines (ATMs): Electronic terminals located where customers can make deposits, withdrawals, or other transactions.

Automatic Funds Transfer (AFT): Funds transferred automatically from savings to checking accounts and vice versa.

Automatic Premium Loan (APL): The provision in an insurance policy that grants the insured an automatic loan, used to pay premiums after the grace period has expired.

Balanced Fund: An investment company that holds varying proportions of bonds and common and preferred stocks to maintain stability in both capital and income.

Balance Sheet: A financial statement that shows assets, liabilities, and capital for a given date. It shows what is owned, how much is owed, and the stockholders' ownership in the company.

Balloon Clause: A clause calling for a final payment of an installment loan.

Basis: Basis is usually the original cost of an asset, and capital gain is calculated on the excess of selling price over basis.

Bear Market: A stock market that is declining. A *bear* is considered to be one who believes the stock market will decline.

Bearer Bond: A bond that isn't registered with an owner's name on the books of the issuing company. It is payable to the holder.

Beneficiary: The recipient of benefit plans, gifts in a will, life insurance proceeds, or the person for whom a trust is managed.

Better Business Bureau: An organization established by the business community to provide fairness in the marketplace.

Bid and Asked: The *bid* is the highest price anyone is willing to pay for a security at a given time; the *asked* is the lowest price. Also called a quote.

Big Board: Term popularly used for the New York Stock Exchange, Inc. (NYSE).

Billing Cycle: A time interval between regular periodic billing dates—usually a month.

Block: A large stock transaction, generally considered to be 10,000 shares or more or with a value over $200,000.

Blue-Chip Stock: Common stock of financially strong, large corporations that have good records of earnings and dividend.

Blue Sky Laws: Regulatory state laws that govern the sale of securities and the activities of security dealers, brokers, and salespersons.

Bond:

- ❖ An agreement to make up for a loss negligently caused by an administrator, which is guaranteed by an insurance or similar company.

- ❖ Or a promissory note or IOU of a corporation issued in multiples of $1,000. A bond represents debt on which an issuing company promises to pay bondholders interest for a certain time and repay the entire loan on the expiration date.

Bond Fund: A mutual fund with all investments in bonds.

Book Value: The value of a stock that is determined by adding all assets, then deducting all liabilities, and that sum is divided by the number of outstanding common shares. The result is *book value* per share, but it may have no relationship to market value.

Broker: An agent who is licensed to handle orders to buy and sell securities, commodities, or other properties, such as real estate. Brokers charge commissions for their services.

Bull Market: An advancing stock market. A *bull* is considered to be one who believes the stock market will rise.

Business Cycle: The characteristic business cycle represented by long-term economic booms followed by economic downturns.

Business Days: Financial institutions are required to declare the days it counts as business days.

Buy-Sell Agreement: An agreement among owners of a business in which they promise to buy out an owner who dies or because of other occurrences.

By-Pass Trust: A trust designed to avoid estate taxes when a person that holds a lifetime interest in the trust dies.

Call: An option to buy a specific number of shares of a security, at a definite price, within a specified time period.

Call Price: The price at which a corporation can prematurely retire bonds.

Callable: All or part of a bond issue that may be redeemed by the issuing corporation before the bonds mature under definite conditions. Also refers to preferred shares that may be redeemed.

Capital: The total assets of a business.

Capital Gains: The market appreciation in the value of an asset above its basis.

Capital Gains Tax: A tax that must be paid by those receiving capital gains.

Capital Loss: The decline in the market value of an asset below its basis.

Capital Market: The securities market dealing in long-term issues of both debt and stocks.

Capital Stock: All shares, including both preferred and common, that represent the ownership of a business.

Capitalization: The total amount of securities issued by a corporation is called capitalization and may include bonds, common and preferred stocks. It also refers to the initial investment made to start a business.

Cash Discount: The discount a customer receives when paying cash for a purchase.

Cash Surrender Value: The amount of cash that may be obtained by a person when voluntarily surrendering a life insurance policy.

Cashier's Check: A check that may be

bought from a bank by a depositor or non-depositor to make payments to a designated payee. It is written by the bank on itself.

Certificate of Deposit (CD): An account into which deposited funds are not to be withdrawn until a specific time. CDs vary in terms of yields and maturity.

Certificate: The document that gives evidence of ownership in a corporation.

Certified Check: Method of assuring the *payee* that a check is good. The sum is deducted from the account before the check is issued.

Charitable Foundation: An organization designed to distribute its income among charities.

Charitable Remainder Annuity Trust: A trust that pays either annual fixed dollar amounts or a percentage of the initial trust value to an individual during his or her lifetime. A charity has been named as the ultimate beneficiary.

Charitable Remainder Unitrust: Similar to a Charitable Remainder Annuity Trust, except that the annual sums may be based on fixed percentages of the value of the trust as it is recalculated annually.

Clifford Trust: A temporary trust designed to give income annually to a beneficiary. The trust reverts to the creator at the end of ten years and one day. Tax law changes of 1986 make this trust less attractive.

Closed-End Investment Company: An investment company that issues a fixed number of shares and does not redeem them.

Closely Held Corporation: A corporation whose shares are not traded on the stock exchange.

Closing Costs: Costs incurred when settling a real estate sale between two parties. These costs include title insurance, fees for attorneys, and recording documents.

Codicil: Document created to amend a will.

Collateral: Property pledged to a creditor to assure loan repayment. The *collateral* is subject to seizure for default or failure to comply with any promises made by the borrower.

Commingling: Combining community property with separate property in one bank account.

Commission: A basic fee charged by a broker for purchasing or selling property or securities as an agent.

Common Law States: The 42 states in the United States that take their marital law from English common law.

Common Stock: A security that represents ownership interest in a corporation. If the corporation has also issued preferred stock, then both the common and preferred stocks represent ownership rights. Common stockholders generally exercise greater control and assume greater risk but also may gain greater reward in the form of dividends and capital appreciation.

Common Stock Fund: A mutual fund with the stated policy of making all asset investments in common stocks.

Community Property: All property acquired by persons during marriage that is not separate property in one of the eight community-property states of Arizona, California, Idaho, Louisiana, Nevada, New Mexico, Texas, or Washington.

Conditional Buy (Sell) Order: An order to buy (or sell) a certain number of shares

259

of a stock under specific conditions, such as at a certain future price. The order will be executed only if the market reaches or betters that price.

Confirmation: The written description of the terms of a securities transaction supplied by a broker or dealer to a customer or another broker or dealer.

Conglomerate: A corporation with diversified operations in widely varied industries.

Conservatorship: Resembles a guardianship of an incompetent but without having the stigma of incompetence. It is not available in all states.

Constructive Receipt: An IRS Department rule that requires income to be reported in the year that it could have been received if the taxpayer had wished. For example, when mutual fund dividends are automatically reinvested they are taxable in the year they were reinvested because they were available to the taxpayer to reinvest.

Consumer Credit: Credit extended to individuals for the purpose of buying consumer items.

Consumer Finance Company: A firm that specializes in consumer loans, usually at higher interest rates than other lenders.

Consumer Leasing Act: A federal law that requires disclosure of information to help consumers compare the cost and terms of one lease with another.

Consumer Price Index: A statistical measure of cost-of-living increases.

Contemplation of Death: Estate taxation because certain gifts are made by a decedent within three years of death.

Contribution Theory: The rule governing the estate taxation of property held in joint tenancy, based on the contribution of the decedent.

Conventional Mortgage: A mortgage solely between a buyer and a lending institution; they are not VA or FHA regulated and will be insured by private mortgage insurers.

Convertible: A bond, debenture, or preferred share whose issuance allow the owner to exchange it for common stock or another security.

Corporate Bond: Indebtedness issued by a corporation.

Corporation: An organization chartered by a state government. It generally refers to a for-profit business. However, there are nonprofit corporations and municipalities.

Corpus: The property that makes up a trust.

Cosigner: A person who signs the loan of another and assumes responsibility for the loan.

Coupon Bond: A bond with interest coupons attached. As interest on the bond becomes due, coupons are clipped and presented for payment of interest.

Credit: The right authorized by a creditor to pay in the future in order to borrow or buy in the present; also a sum of money due a person or business.

Credit Bureau: An agency that maintains your credit record.

Credit Life and Disability Insurance: Insurance that is purchased with a credit transaction. It usually pays the entire debt if the insured dies or makes payments while a borrower is disabled.

Credit Report: A report that provides the credit history of a consumer. Credit bureaus will submit this information to creditors, employers, or insurance companies on request.

Credit Scoring System: A statistical method for rating the credit worthiness of applicants.

Credit Standards: Standards that creditors establish and consumers must meet in order to borrow money or buy on credit.

Credit Unions: A cooperative depository institution designed to make loans to members for reasonable purposes.

Creditor: A person or firm to whom money is owed that has extended credit by loaning money, selling property or goods on credit, furnishing credit cards, and so forth.

Creditor's Claims: A document that must be filed by creditors in order to get paid from the assets of a decedent's estate.

Credits: Subtractions that are made directly from a tax owed—more beneficial than deductions.

Creditworthiness: A person's past and future ability to repay debts.

Crummy Trust: A life insurance trust that is irrevocable and designed to permit tax-free premiums to be paid with dollars given to the trust gift. The Crummy Power trust provides the donor with more flexibility in planning, but the trust provisions are very technical.

Cumulative Preferred Stock: On this preferred stock, corporations are required to pay all dividends missed in prior years before dividends on common stock can be paid.

Cumulative Voting: Shareholder voting in which the number of shares held is multiplied by the number of directors to be elected, which determines the number of votes a shareholder may cast.

Current Assets: Assets of a company that are reasonably expected to be realized in cash or sold or consumed during a normal business operating cycle.

Current Liabilities: Money that is owed and payable by a company, usually within one year.

Curtesy: A husband's rights upon the death of his wife in the real property of an estate that she either solely owned or inherited, provided they bore a child capable of inheriting the estate.

Custodian: A corporation, usually a bank, responsible for safekeeping securities. Anyone entrusted with keeping gifts, property, or records until the time when the person for whom these items are being held is of age.

Cyclical Stock: The stock of companies whose sales and earnings vary with swings in the business cycles.

Dealer: Individuals or firms engaged in the securities business who act as principals rather than agents. They buy for their own accounts and sell to customers from their inventory. They may function, at different times, as brokers or dealers.

Debenture: A variety of bonds that are secured by no specific assets but by the general credit and all assets of a corporation.

Debit Card: A card that consumers may use to make purchases, withdrawals, or other types of electronic fund transfers (EFTs) from their checking accounts.

Decedent: An individual who has died.

Decreasing Term Rider: Term insurance in which the contract payout by the insurance company, or face value of the insurance, decreases as time passes.

Deductions: Items allowed to be subtracted from taxable income, a taxable estate, or taxable gifts that will lower the amount on which tax is due.

Deed of Trust: A special mortgage that conveys the title of a property to a third party rather than to the lender.

Default: Failure to repay a loan or otherwise fail to meet the terms of an agreement.

Default Taker: The person who succeeds to property when the holder of Power of Appointment fails to exercise that power.

Defensive Stock: A stock that tends to decline less than other securities in a downward turn of the market because of the nature of its business.

Deficiency: Additional tax that the IRS may claim is due after it has audited a tax return.

Deflation: A continuous decrease in the overall price level that results in an appreciation in the value of the dollar.

Demand Deposits: Deposits payable to the depositor on demand, such as funds placed in a checking account.

Depletion: A noncash expense charged to allocate the cost of a natural resource asset, such as mines, oil and gas wells, or timber, over an estimated useful life.

Depreciation: A bookkeeping entry against earnings to write off the cost, less salvage value, of an asset over its estimated useful life. It represents no cash outlay.

Director: A person elected by shareholders to establish company policies. Directors then elect the president, vice president, and all other operating officers of the com-

pany; and they also determine other matters, such as when dividends will be paid.

Disability Insurance: Insurance that provides income if the policyholder is disabled due to an accident or illness.

Disclaimer: A document that, when filed on time, allows an heir to give up his or her right to inherit property without any adverse tax consequences.

Disclosure Statement: The information that lenders must give borrowers before a credit contract is signed. The statement must include the finance charge, annual percentage rate, loan fees, and insurance premiums. Similar disclosure information may be required for other transactions.

Discount: The amount a preferred stock or bond may sell below its par value.

Discretionary Account: In this type of account, the customer gives the broker or another person the discretion to buy or sell on his or her behalf. This may be either complete or within specific limits.

Discretionary Trust: A trust that allows the trustee to distribute the annual income of the trust among the persons that he or she specifies.

Diversification: Spreading the risk and lessening the likelihood of loss by investing in the securities of a variety of different firms and industries.

Diversified Investing Company: A company that invests 75 percent of its total assets so that no more than 5 percent of the total assets are invested in the securities of any one issuer.

Dividend: Payment designated by the board of directors to be distributed pro rata among the shares outstanding.

Dividend Reinvestment Plan: A program

in which dividends and any capital gains distributions are automatically reinvested in additional shares. These are often mutual fund share accounts.

Dollar-Cost-Averaging: Buying securities at regular intervals with a fixed dollar amount. In this way, payments buy more when the price is low and fewer when it rises.

Domicile: The state or country within which a decedent's estate will be probated. It is the location where that person intended his or her permanent home to be.

Donee: The person to whom property is given.

Donor: The person who gives property.

Double Indemnity: A clause in a life insurance policy that requires double payment in the case of accidental death.

Double Taxation: A term that refers to the federal government taxation of corporate profits and then the taxation of the remaining profits that have been distributed as dividends to stockholders.

Dow Theory: A value-oriented method of evaluating the market, and timing entrances or exits, according to market trends based on the performance of the Dow Jones indexes.

Dow Jones Average: An index that lists 30 stocks of large companies. There are four different averages: industrial stocks, transportation stocks, utility stocks, and a composite average of those three.

Drafts: Check written by one bank on its account in another bank, commonly used for long-distance payments.

Drawee: Usually a bank or other savings institution that is requested to pay the stated amount of a check.

Drawer: The person who writes a check against his or her checking account and orders that a payment be made.

Dual Fund: A closed-end investment organization that has two classes of shares: income and capital outstanding.

Earnest Money: A deposit made by a person purchasing real estate as evidence of good faith.

Earning Assets: Assets that yield a return in the form of interest, dividends, or rent from such things as bonds, real estate, savings accounts, and stocks.

Earnings: Income of a corporation after all expenses, including preferred dividend payments, are paid.

Elderly Applicant: The Equal Credit Opportunity Act defines someone as *elderly* when 62 or older.

Electronic Funds Transfer (EFT): Using electronic means to facilitate fund transfers among accounts.

Encumbrance: Anything that limits or affects the title of a property, such as a mortgage, lease, or other restriction.

Endowment Life Insurance Policy: An insurance policy that provides protection for a specified number of years. At the end of the time period, the insured will have cash value in the policy equal to the face value of the policy.

Equal Credit Opportunity Act: A federal consumer credit law that prohibits discrimination against an applicant for credit because of age, color, marital status, national origin, race, receipt of public assistance, religion, or sex.

Equity: Ownership interest in company stock, or monetary interest in real estate that is in excess of mortgage indebtedness.

Escheat: When a person dies *intestate* (without a will) and there are no heirs to take the decedent's property, it *escheats* and reverts to the state.

Escrow: An agreement under which executed documents, such as deeds, are delivered to a third party to be held until certain conditions are met. The documents then are returned to those who have executed the documents. Also identifies that portion of a mortgagor's monthly payment held by a lender to pay taxes, insurance, and other items as they come due.

Estate Tax: Imposed by the federal government and some states on the estate of a decedent.

Estate Trust: A trust that qualifies for the marital deduction so that a widow does not have to receive all the annual income of a trust but can leave the trust property to her estate at her death.

Ex-Dividend: A stock is called *ex-dividend* when buyers are no longer entitled to receive the last declared dividend. Typically, the price falls to reflect the value of the dividend and then rises again later, as shareholders look ahead to the next payout. A stock that is listed on stock tables as *ex-dividend* has an "x" following the name.

Executor: A man named in a will to handle a probate managed under court supervision.

Executrix: A woman named in a will to handle a probate managed under court supervision.

Exemption: A term describing an amount on which a tax will not apply.

Extended Term Insurance: An insurance policy with a clause, stating that if the holder fails to pay premiums during the grace period the policy will remain in force as term insurance for as long as the cash surrender value of the policy will permit.

Face Value: The value of a bond that appears on the face of the bond. Ordinarily the amount the issuing company promises to pay at maturity. Face value does not indicate market value.

Fair Credit Billing Act: The federal consumer credit law that establishes procedures for correcting errors on a consumer's credit account and prevents damage to a credit rating while under dispute.

Fair Credit Reporting Act: The federal consumer law that establishes procedures for promptly correcting mistakes on a consumer's credit record and requires that the record be kept confidential.

Fair Market Value: What a willing buyer would pay a willing seller. This is the standard at which property is valued for estate tax purposes.

Family Allowance: The amount a probate court allows for the monthly support of a surviving spouse and surviving children. This allowance takes precedence over the claims of most creditors

Federal Deposit Insurance Corporation (FDIC): The federal authority that provides insurance protection for persons that have deposits of $100,000 or less.

Federal Home Loan Bank Board (FHLBB): The federal agency that regulates savings and loan associations.

Federal Reserve: The central bank of the United States. The Federal Reserve is one of the federal agencies that oversees commercial banks.

Fee Simple: The ownership of property, unburdened by any future interest.

FHA Mortgage: A loan made by an

approved lending institution that is insured by the FHA (Federal Housing Administration). To qualify for an FHA insured mortgage loan, borrowers, lenders, and property must all meet the FHA's standards.

Fiduciary: A person who acts for another under the highest possible standard of care as an executor, trustee, or guardian.

Fiduciary Income Tax Return: The tax return that must be filed by an estate, trust, or other entity managed by a fiduciary.

Finance Charge: A cost the consumer pays for borrowing money or buying on credit, required by the *Truth in Lending Act*. Finance charges also may include various other charges in addition to interest.

Finance Company: A financial institution that specializes in making small loans to consumers.

Financial Assets: Assets such as bank accounts, bonds, cash, currency, or stocks.

Financial Risk: The risk related to the debt-versus-equity ratio of a company. A high risk indicates that a corporation has high fixed obligations due each year, which indicates the possibility that creditors could force bankruptcy.

Fiscal Year: A non-calendar, 12-month year often adopted by estates and trusts.

Fixed Annuity: A contract with a life insurance company that provides periodic payments of fixed amounts of dollars for a specific period of time or for life.

Fixed Income Security: A preferred stock or a bond that has a stated or fixed percentage of income return.

Flower Bonds: United States Treasury obligations that are redeemable at par in the payment of federal estate taxes even if they were purchased at a discount.

Fully Managed Fund: A mutual fund whose policy gives its management complete flexibility concerning the types of investments made.

Funded Trust: A living trust to which property has been transferred.

General Obligation Bonds: Municipal bonds that are secured by the credit and full faith of the entity issuing them.

General Power of Appointment: The power to appoint anyone, including the power holder and his or her creditors.

Generation Skipping Tax: A tax that costs the same as an estate tax if a trust has beneficiaries in two or more generations who are younger than the trustor.

Gift Taxes: Taxes that are imposed on the giver, which are essentially taxes on the privilege to give away what you own.

Gilt-Edged: A high-grade bond that is issued by a company that has demonstrated its ability to pay its bondholders their interest without interruption.

Good Til Cancelled Order (GTC): An order to buy or sell that remains in effect until it is executed or cancelled.

Government Bonds: Obligations of the U.S. government that are regarded as the highest grade issues.

Graduated Payment Mortgage (GPM): The payments of this type of mortgage begin below what they should be and then increase as time goes on. The GPM is often used by young people who expect their income to rise.

Grantee: A person to whom a conveyance is made by deed.

Grantor: The person who makes a conveyance or creates a trust.

Gross National Product (GPN): The total market value of all goods and services produced in the United States per year.

Group Life Insurance: Insurance sold to a business that provides each insured employee with insurance. The business usually withholds the premiums (or a partial premium payment) from the employees' wages. Employees are then provided with some term life insurance and some medical insurance that would be very expensive for an individual to obtain.

Growth Fund: A fund with a rate of growth over a period of time that is considerably greater than that of others.

Growth Stock: Stock that has shown better than average earnings growth and a better than average appreciation.

Guarantor: A person who agrees to pay someone else's debt if that person does not.

Guardianship: The court-supervised administration of the property and person of either a minor or an incompetent adult.

Health Maintenance Organization (HMO): A method of medical expense protection that provides medical care for HMO members for a fixed monthly fee. The HMOs own and operate clinics and hospitals and hire doctors and nurses.

Hedge Fund: A mutual fund or investment company that protects its market commitments by holding certain securities that it believes will increase in value. At the same time it sells others short because it believes they are likely to decline in value.

Heir: Anyone taking property provided in a will or without one.

Holding Company: A corporation that owns the securities of another and in most cases has voting control.

Holographic Will: A will written entirely in the handwriting of the testator.

Home Equity Line of Credit: A form of open-end credit in which the borrower's home serves as collateral.

Homeowner's Insurance Policy: Property insurance that provides protection for the owner's home, personal property loss, and liability and medical payment coverage.

Homestead: In probate law, generally considered the house and land where the head of the family lives. In most states, homestead passes to the widow after the death of her husband and is exempt from the claims of creditors of the estate.

Income Averaging: A method of saving money on tax liability if a taxpayer's income fluctuates sharply—either up or down—by averaging the income over several years.

Income Bonds: Bonds on which interest is paid only if it is earned.

Income Fund: A mutual fund that has the primary objective of current income.

Income Statement: An account that reports financial position over a period of time, such as a year. It measures both income and expenditure.

Income Stock: The stock of a corporation with a historical record of above average earnings and dividends.

Income: The annual earnings of a person, probate estate, property, or trust.

Indenture: A written agreement used when bonds and debentures are issued that sets the maturity date, interest rate, and other terms.

Individual Retirement Account (IRA): A qualified retirement plan in which an individual's contributions may be deductible in addition to being tax deferred. Deductibility limits are pegged to income levels and participation in other qualified plans.

Inflation: An overall general upward price movement of all goods and services.

Inheritance Tax: A tax levied when inheriting property.

Installment Credit: Any type of credit that is extended to individuals and is to be repaid in two or more installments.

Installment Sale: A sale that complies with certain rules that allows the capital gain resulting from that sale to be taxed over the time during which the payments are actually received.

Insurance Dividend: The payment made to owners of mutual life insurance policies, part of which may be considered return of premiums and part as earnings.

Inter Vivos: A Latin term meaning "during life" used to describe a trust or anything else that is established or done during a person's lifetime. See *Living Trust*.

Interest Rate Risk: The risk of loss that may occur from market changes in the price of bonds due to changes in prevailing interest rates. This type of risk is relevant only to fixed obligation investments, such as bonds and preferred stock.

Interest-Free Loan: A method of shifting income taxes to lower bracket taxpayers or providing funds for investments to others, usually relatives.

Intestacy: The state of a person who dies without a valid will. State law then determines what becomes of the decedent's property.

Intestate: A person who dies without leaving a valid will.

Inventory: The probate court document that lists, and often values, all the property contained in the probate estate.

Investment Bankers: The person who acts between a corporation issuing new securities and the public. Also known as an *underwriter.*

Investment Company: A company or a trust that uses its capital to invest in other companies.

Irrevocable Trust: A trust established when the grantor gives away property without any right to or control over the principal. The grantor may never reclaim the property and the trust may never be revoked or amended by its creator.

Issue: Any securities of a company or the distribution of such securities.

Itemized Deduction: Deductions that can be used when calculating federal income tax; deductions allowed include state and local taxes and charitable contributions.

Joint Account: A checking account held by two or more people; all have the use of the account and all assume legal responsibility for the account.

Joint and Mutual Will: A will that is signed by both husband and wife that disposes of their property at each death. This type of will should usually be avoided.

Joint and Survivor Annuity: A guaranteed sum that is paid (usually monthly) first to one person for his or her lifetime and then to the designated survivor.

Joint Tenancy: Co-ownership between two or more people with the right of survivorship, which allows a survivor automatically to become owners of a decedent's interest and thus avoids probate.

Keogh Plan: A qualified tax-deferred individual retirement plan for persons who are self-employed or who earn extra income aside from their regular employment. The interest and capital gains these investments earn are not taxed until they are withdrawn. Also known as a HR-10 plan.

Late Charge: The additional penalty a borrower is required to pay for failure to pay a regular installment when it is due.

Legacy: A gift of property in a will, usually cash.

Legatee: Person who receives a legacy or bequest.

Lessee: A person who holds a lease, a tenant.

Lessor: A person who grants a lease, a landlord.

Letters Testamentary: What many states call the document that gives evidence of the authority an executor has to act for a decedent's estate.

Level Premium Life Insurance: A life insurance policy with fixed premiums over the life of the policy. The premiums build up reserves in the early years of the policy to be used in later years. This amounts to averaging the premiums over the period of the insurance contract.

Leverage: The effect on the earnings of a company's stock when large amounts must be paid for bond or preferred stock interest before the common stock is entitled to share in earnings. *Leverage* also refers to funds used in financing real estate.

Lien: A claim against property that has been mortgaged or pledged to secure the performance of an obligation.

Lienholder: The person who holds legal claim to another person's property as security for a debt.

Life Estate: The right to use and enjoy property for a period of time measured by someone's life.

Life Insurance Trust: An irrevocable life insurance trust owns your policy, pays the premiums to keep the insurance in force, collects the death benefits when you die, and distributes the money according to the terms of the trust. The trust proceeds aren't included in your estate because you don't own the insurance.

Limit Order: An order given to a broker to buy a stock only if its price falls to a specified level or to sell stock only if the price rises to a specified level.

Limited Payments Life Insurance Policy: A type of whole life insurance that provides for the payment of premiums for a certain number of years.

Line of Credit: An agreement that a bank or other financial institution makes to extend a certain amount of credit, for a specified time, to a borrower.

Liquid: Anything that is easily converted to cash.

Liquidity: A term that refers to how quickly assets can be converted to cash.

Listed Stock: A company's stock that is traded on a securities exchange.

Living Trust: A trust created during life.

Load: Fees that must be paid when buying mutual funds. Fees vary and some funds have no *load*.

Loan Shark: Someone who makes loans illegally and charges excessively high interest rates.

Major Medical Insurance: An insurance policy that pays large medical bills. Medical bills are paid with a deductible amount the insured pays, and the insurance company pays expenses beyond that amount.

Malpractice Insurance: Designed to protect doctors and nurses against personal liability suits that arise from alleged negligence.

Management: The board of directors (who are elected by stockholders) and the officers of the company (who are appointed by the board of directors).

Management Fee: A fee paid to the investment manager of a mutual fund, usually based on a percentage of the average assets annually.

Margin Call: A demand made on a customer to put up money or securities with the broker. The call is made when a purchase is made or when the customer's equity in a margin account declines below an established minimum.

Margin Purchase: Buying securities with money that is partially borrowed.

Margin Requirement: The percentage of the price of a security that must be paid with the buyer's money. The balance may be borrowed.

Marital Deduction: For estate tax purposes, a deduction that allows you to transfer assets tax-free to your spouse.

Marital Property: Property that is acquired by married persons after their marriage but does not include property that either of them received by gift or inheritance.

Market Order: A buy or sell order for a specific number of shares of a security at the current market price.

Market Price: The price of a security usually considered to be the last reported price at which the stock or bond sold.

Market Risk: The risk that results from fluctuations in market prices of securities.

Maturity: The date on which a loan, bond, or debenture comes due for payment.

Member Firm: A securities brokerage firm organized as a corporation or partnership that owns a seat on an exchange.

Money Market Funds: Mutual funds that specialize in very short-term securities. These funds were designed to enable small investors to enter the money market.

Money Market Instruments: Short-term instrument (one year or less), such as commercial paper and Treasury bills that investors buy.

Monthly Investment Plan: An agreement that can be made with most firms to regularly purchase stock listed on the New York Stock Exchange.

Moody's: A bond rating service that assigns credit ratings to bonds so that investors may assess their degree of risk.

Mortality Tables: Indexes developed from past experience by insurance companies that indicate the number of deaths per thousand at various ages.

Mortgage: The instrument that is used to finance real estate purchases. It gives the lender the right to sell the property in order to repay the loan if the borrower defaults.

Mortgage Banker: A firm or individual with the primary function of originating real estate loans and then selling them to institutional lenders and other investors.

Mortgagee: The lender, one to whom a

mortgage is given as security for a loan and to whom payments are made.

Mortgagor: The borrower, one who gives a mortgage to secure a loan.

Municipal Bond: A bond issued by a political entity, such as a state, county, or city. Also bonds issued by state agencies. Interest paid on municipal bonds is generally exempt from federal taxes and state and local taxes within the issuing state.

Mutual Fund: An investment company that invests the money of its shareholders, usually in a diversified group of securities, and redeems the shares on demand.

Mutual Life Insurance Company: An insurance company owned by its policyholders.

Mutual Savings Banks: Financial institutions that primarily accept deposits and make mortgage loans, similar to savings and loan associations.

NASD: The National Association of Securities Dealers, an alliance of brokers and dealers that trade over-the-counter securities. Some objectives for NASD members are to enforce fair practice, prevent fraudulent and manipulative practices, and promote just principles of trade.

NASDAQ: The acronym for National Association of Securities Dealers Automated Quotations, the information network that provides brokers and dealers with price quotations on securities that are traded over the counter.

National Auto Dealers Association (NADA): The organization that publishes the *Blue Book,* a guide that contains information on the value of used cars.

Negotiable Security: The title to this security is transferable by delivery from one person to another. Examples include coupon bonds, bearer notes, and stock certificates—the opposite of registered securities.

Net Asset Value: A term that means a stock's net asset value per share. Investment companies usually compute this daily by totaling the market value of all the assets they own, deducting the liabilities, and then dividing the balance by the number of outstanding shares.

Net Worth: The best measure of financial worth is determined by computing the difference between assets and liabilities. The result is *net worth.*

New Issue: A stock or bond being sold for the first time.

New York Stock Exchange (NYSE): The largest organized stock exchange in the United States.

No Contest Clause: A clause in a will that attempts to disinherit any person who attacks the legal validity of the will.

No-Load Funds: Mutual funds that do not charge a commission on their sales and that must be purchased directly from a company.

Non-Court Trust: A trust that is not subject to the ongoing jurisdiction of a probate court.

Noncumulative: A preferred stock on which the unpaid dividends do not accrue and are, as a rule, gone forever.

Nonfinancial Assets: Personal assets such as automobiles, clothing, or jewelry.

Nonforfeiture Options: Options available to holders of life insurance policies if they discontinue premium payments. Usually the policy value is taken in cash, either as extended term insurance or as reduced paid-up insurance.

Notice to Creditors: Notifying a decedent's creditors that he or she has died and informing them that they should enter their claims against the estate.

NOW Account (Negotiated Order of Withdrawal): An account that bears interest and allows customers to write drafts against money held on deposit.

NYSE Common Stock Index: A composite index that is computed continuously. This index is based on the close of the market on December 31, 1965 as 50.00 and is weighted according to the number of shares listed for each issue.

Odd Lot: An amount of stock that is less than the established 100-share unit or 10-share unit of trading.

Offer: The price at which a person is willing to sell. The opposite is *bid*—the price at which a person is ready to buy.

Open Account: A type of mutual fund account in which the investor may add or withdraw shares at any time. In an *open account,* the account holder may receive dividends in cash or reinvest them.

Open Order: The type of order to buy or sell securities at a stipulated price that remains in effect until it is either executed or canceled.

Open-End Investment Company: A company that has outstanding, redeemable shares. Also applied to investment companies that continuously offer new shares to the public and stand ready at any time to redeem their outstanding shares.

Option: The right to buy or sell specific securities or properties within a specified time and at a specified price.

Orphan's Court: This what some states call their *Probate Court.*

Over-the-Counter: A securities market made up of securities dealers that may or may not be members of a securities exchange. The *Over-the-Counter* market is conducted mostly by telephone and computer. Dealers involved with this type of securities trading either act as principals or as brokers for customers.

Overbought: An opinion regarding price levels of a security or refers to the market after a period of vigorous buying, when it's argued that prices are too high.

Overdraft Checking: A line of credit that allows check writing for more than the account balance that involves interest charges on the overdraft.

Oversold: An opinion regarding price levels of a single security or market that, it is believed, has declined to an unreasonable level.

Paid-Up-Insurance: Premiums are no longer due but insurance is still in force.

Paper Profit: Unrealized profit on a security. Paper profits become realized profits only when the security is sold.

Par Value: The stated value of a bond or stock. In the case of common stock this is meaningless. However, for preferred stocks or bonds, the *Par Value* usually indicates the dollar value on which the dividends or annual interest are paid.

Participating Preferred: A type of preferred stock. If the corporation's profits are sufficient, the preferred stockholders are given their agreed dividends and also entitled to share equally in the dividends paid to common stockholders.

Partition: A court proceeding that allows any co-owner of property to force a separation of co-ownership interests. This is usually accomplished by a court-ordered auction sale, with proceeds being divided equally among the owners.

Partnership: A business organization comprised of two or more partners, each of whom have specified duties, rights, and liabilities.

Payee: A person to whom a check is made payable.

Penny Stocks: Stocks that sell at less than $1 a share and are highly speculative.

Pension and Profit-Sharing Plans: These are plans that can be established only by corporations.

Periodic Statement: A statement sent to consumers who have *open-end* accounts. Usually, these statements are sent monthly and show the current balance, charges, payments made since the last statement, the interest rate, and the amount of interest that was charged for the period.

Personal Property: All property that is not real estate.

Personal Representative: The term used for a person who handles an estate during the period of administration.

Plain English Policies: Insurance policies that have had the legal phraseology replaced with language anyone can understand.

Point: When used in reference to shares of a stock, a point means $1. In bonds, a point means $10, and if, for example, the Dow-Jones industrial average rises from 890.75 to 891.75, it has risen a point.

Points and Origination Fees: One point equals one percent of a loan amount, and points are finance charges paid at the initiation of a mortgage in addition to the monthly interest. Origination fees cover the lender's cost to prepare a loan.

Policy Loan: A loan that an insurance company makes to a policyholder on the cash surrender value of the policy.

Portfolio: Securities that are held by an individual or institution. A portfolio may contain bonds, preferred stocks, and common stocks of a variety of enterprises.

Pour-Over Will or Trust: The *Pour-Over Will* leaves property to an existing trust, called a *Pour-Over Trust.*

Power of Appointment: Authority to grant ownership of property when it is necessary to transfer after a person's death.

Power of Appointment Trust: A trust that qualifies for the marital deduction.

Preemptive Rights: Rights held by existing stockholders to buy a prorated share of a new issue of common stock that a corporation may issue.

Preferred Stock: Stock that has a claim on the earnings of a company before payment may be made on common stock. Also, when the board of directors declares a dividend, *Preferred Stock* is usually entitled to dividends before dividends are paid on common stock.

Preliminary Distribution: The interim distribution of some of the property in a probate estate before the estate is actually ready to be closed.

Premium: This is the amount by which a preferred stock or bond may sell above its par value. For new issues of bonds or stocks, the *premium* is the amount the market price rises over the original selling price. In regard to insurance policies, the *premium* is the payment due.

Price-Earnings Ratio: The price of a share of stock divided by earnings per share for a 12-month period. If a stock sells for $100 a share and earns $5 a share, it is said to sell at a *price-earning ratio* of 20 to 1.

Principal: The person for whom a broker executes a securities order; or a dealer buying or selling for his or her own account. The term also refers to a person's capital or the face amount of a bond.

Prior Taxed Property, Credit For: Credit that is allowed against estate tax owed if the estate includes property that was taxed in the estate of a prior decedent within 10 years.

Private Annuity: A contract that is non-commercial in which one person sells property to another in exchange for the promise of lifetime income.

Probate: The period of time after death when a decedent's affairs are handled under the supervision of a court.

Probate Court: The branch of a state's court system where probate matters are handled.

Profit-Taking: Selling stock that has appreciated in value since its purchase in order to realize profit. The term is also used to explain a market downturn following a period of rising prices.

Prohibited Bases: The Consumer Credit Protection Act prevent creditors from denying credit to a consumer based on age (if of legal age), color, marital status, national origin, or race.

Prospectus: The document that offers a new issue of securities to the public.

Proxy: Written authorization that a share-holder gives to someone else to vote his or her shares at a shareholder's meeting.

Proxy Statement: Information that the SEC requires to be given to stockholders before solicitation of proxies.

Prudent Man's Rule: An investment standard where a fiduciary, such as a trustee, may invest a fund's money only in a list of securities designated by the state—the so-called *Legal List.* In other states the trustee may invest in a security if it is one that a prudent person would buy if she or he were seeking a reasonable income and preservation of capital.

Punitive Damages: Damages that a court awards above the actual damages as punishment for the violation of a law.

Purchase Money Mortgage: A mortgage taken by a seller to help finance the purchase.

Put: An option to sell a number of shares at a definite price within a specified period of time.

Q-Tip Trust: A type of trust that qualifies for the *marital deduction.*

Qualified Plans: Pension and profit sharing plans that have been qualified by the IRS and provide many tax advantages.

Quotation: The highest bid to buy and the lowest offer to sell a security at a given time. Often shortened to *quote.* When you ask for a quotation on a stock, a broker will say something like "The highest price buyers want to pay is $25.25. And $25.00 was the lowest price sellers would take."

Rally: A brisk rise that follows a decline in the general price level of the market or an individual stock.

Real Property: Land or real estate, together with whatever is growing on it, erected on it, or affixed to it.

Real Yield: The yield that is derived by adjusting for inflation.

Record Date: The date on which a shareholder must be registered on the stock book of a company in order to receive a dividend or vote on company affairs.

Recourse: The responsibility a dealer has, when involved in a consumer loan, to repay a lender if the purchaser fails to make the required payments.

Redemption Price: The price at which a bond may be redeemed before it matures. The term also applies to the price an open-end investment company must pay to call in certain types of preferred stock.

Registered Bond: A bond registered in the owner's name on the books of the issuing company. It can be transferred only by the registered owner.

Registered Representative: A person who has met the requirements of an exchange concerning the knowledge of the securities business. For purposes of NASD membership admission, the broker/dealer and its principals must be registered in the state in which the firm's home office is located.

Registrar: Usually a bank or trust company that is charged with the responsibility of preventing the issuance of more stock than a company has authorized.

Registration: Before a public offering of new securities may be made by controlling stockholders, the securities must be registered. The issuing company must file a registration application with the SEC and the exchange and disclose all pertinent information related to the company's operations and the purpose of the offering.

Regulation T: The federal regulation that governs the amount of credit that brokers and dealers may advance to customers for the purchase of listed stocks.

Regulation U: The federal regulation that governs the amount of credit that banks may advance to its customers for the purchase of listed stocks.

REIT: A Real Estate Investment Trust concentrates its funds in real estate investments. The yield from REITs is generally liberal, because they distribute 90 percent of their income.

Remainder: The property interest that is passed to a new owner after a life estate or other interim interest has terminated.

Reorganization: A change that is made in the stock structure or stock ownership rights of a corporation.

Repossession: The creditor's reclaiming of property when the buyer fails to make payments as agreed or otherwise defaults.

Recission: The right that a consumer has to cancel, within a certain number of days, certain transactions.

Residence: The place where one currently lives.

Residue: All the property that is left to be disposed of by the will after specific items have been bequeathed.

Return: Synonymous with *Yield.*

Revenue Bonds: Municipal bonds that are repaid by revenue generated by what the bonds have financed, such as toll roads.

Reverse Mortgages: Used when one sells a debt-free home to a lending institution and the person living in the home receives monthly payment and the equity declines with time.

Reversion: The possibility that after a donor has given property away it will come back to the donor.

Revive: To reinstate a will that has previously been revoked.

Revocable Trust: A trust that may be amended or revoked at any time by its creator.

Revolving Credit: It is synonymous with *Open-End Credit.*

Right of Representation: What an heir is said to have when he or she represents a deceased relative and shares the inheritance that the relative would have received.

Right of Survivorship: In joint tenancy ownership it means that the surviving tenant will automatically become the owner of the property when the other tenant dies.

Rights: When companies want to raise funds by issuing additional securities, they may give stockholders the opportunity to buy the new securities, often below current market price and in proportion to what they already own, before others. The document that gives evidence of this privilege is known as a *right.*

Rule Against Perpetuities: A rule that determines how long a trust may exist or that prescribes the maximum amount of time an owner may determine who shall own or use her or his property.

Sales Finance Companies: Companies that primarily engage in purchasing merchants' sales contracts that arise from the sale of goods to consumers.

SEC (Securities and Exchange Commission): The SEC was established by Congress to help protect investors.

Second Mortgage: A second mortgage is recorded after the first mortgage, and both mortgages are for the same property. In the event of foreclosure of the property on which the mortgagor has defaulted, the second mortgage is not paid off until the first mortgage has been completely repaid.

Secondary Distribution: The redistribution of a block of stock, which is usually quite large, after the initial sale by the issuing company.

Security: Property that is pledged to a creditor in case a borrower defaults on a loan.

Security Agreement: An agreement between a lender and a debtor that gives the lender a *security interest.*

Security Interest: Any interest in property that secures the payment of a debt.

Senior Securities: Bonds and preferred stocks that have a higher claim than common stocks on earnings, as well as on assets when liquidation occurs.

Separate Property: In community property and common law states, this refers to property that is owned by a spouse before marriage or acquired during marriage by gift or inheritance.

Serial Bonds: Bonds that are numbered according to their issue and retired at various times in accordance with their numbers.

Service Charge: A portion of finance charges: such as the fee for the use of an overdraft checking account.

Settlor: The person who has created a trust.

Severance: The action of breaking up a *joint tenancy* when one of the joint tenants acts in such a way to make it inequitable to continue as a joint tenancy, which then becomes a *Tenancy in Common.*

Short Sales: Securities that are borrowed from a broker, then sold in the hope of buying them back when the price falls, in order to repay the broker.

Sinking Fund: Money that is regularly set aside for the purpose of redeeming its bonds or preferred stock.

Small Claims Court: Courts that are able to handle claims quickly and at lower cost than by regular legal action. The amount of damages for which a person may sue is usually limited from $1,000 to about $7,500.

Social Security: The basic method in the United States of providing income when earnings are reduced or stopped due to death, disability, or retirement.

Sole Proprietorship: The simplest form of business organization. It has no charter and is owned by one person.

Speculative Stocks: Untried securities that are often the stocks of small, new firms. The probability of gain may be small; however, if there is gain it could be large.

Speculators: Those who assume relatively large risk in the hope of large gain. Their principal goal is to increase capital rather than dividend income.

Spendthrift Clause: A protective trust clause that states the beneficiary's interest may not be attacked by his or her creditors or taken in bankruptcy.

Spread: The difference between a price bid and the offering price. The *spread* also refers to the combination of a *put* and *call* known as "points away" from the market.

Sprinkling Trust: A trust in which the trustee can "sprinkle" income among the various beneficiaries.

Stepped-Up Basis: The provision whereby an heir's basis in inherited property is equal to its value at the date of the death.

Stock: Ownership of the shares of a corporation.

Stock Certificate: A certificate that provides physical evidence of a person's ownership in a stock.

Stock Dividend: A dividend that is paid in securities rather than cash. The dividend may be either additional shares of the issuing company or shares of another company held by the issuing company.

Stock Exchange: A registered organization that has facilities for the buying and selling of securities in a two-way auction.

Stock Split: Dividing the existing shares of a corporation in order to increase the number of shares. For example, a two-for-one split results in two new shares for each old share.

Stock Warrant: A certificate that authorizes an owner to buy a company's stock at a specific price for a specified period of time.

Stockholder of Record: A stockholder whose name is registered on the books of the corporation that has issued the stock.

Stop Order: An order to either buy at a price that is above or sell at a price that is below the current market. These orders are used to limit loss on a holding. Also refers to stopping payment on a check.

Street Name: When securities are held in the name of a broker, rather than the customer, they are carried in a *street name*. This occurs when securities have been bought on margin or when a customer wants securities held by a broker.

Suitability Rule: The rule that requires a member to have reasonable grounds to believe that a recommendation being made to a customer is suitably based on financial objectives and abilities.

Surrogate Court: What is called, in some states, a *Probate Court.*

Tax Credit: A credit that reduces the actual tax. Common tax credits are for religious contributions, investment tax credits, and child- or dependent-care credit.

Tax Shelter: Certain investments that permit tax write-offs by generating deductible expenses, such as depreciation.

Ten-Year Trust: Synonymous with *Clifford Trust.*

Tenancy by the Entirety: The same as a *joint tenancy* between husband and wife, with the right of survivorship.

Tenancy in Common: When two or more people hold co-ownership, with each tenant owning a defined percentage of the whole.

Tenant: A person who rents an apartment or house from an owner.

Term Insurance: Life insurance that provides protection only for a contracted period of time and has no savings feature.

Testamentary Trust: A trust that is created in a will but that does not come into existence until the testator's death.

Testate: A person who has left a will, as opposed to dying without a will, *intestate.*

Testator: The man, or woman *testatrix,* who makes a will.

Thin Market: A market that has few offers to either buy or sell. The term can refer to a single security or to the entire market.

Thrift Institutions: Financial institutions whose principal source of funds is the savings of the public. Some examples are credit unions, mutual savings banks, and savings and loan associations.

Throwback Rule: When accumulated trust income is distributed in a tax year after the one in which it was earned, generally it is taxed in the income bracket of the beneficiary for the year in which it was actually earned.

Trader: A person who buys and sells for a personal account for short-term profit.

Transfer Agent: The person who keeps the record of each registered shareholder's name, address, and number of shares owned.

Treasury Bill: Short-term U.S. government debt that has no stated interest rate. It is sold at discount in competitive bidding and reaches maturity in 95 days or less.

Treasury Bond: A U.S. government bond that is issued in $1,000 units with maturity dates of five years or longer and traded on the market like other bonds.

Treasury Note: United States government note with maturity dates from one to five years.

Treasury Stock: These stocks are issued by a company but later reacquired. They may be held in the company indefinitely, then reissued to the public or retired. Treasury stock receives no dividends and has no vote while being held by the company.

Trust: The arrangement whereby title to property is transferred by the creator or settlor to another person, the trustee, for the benefit of a third party, the beneficiary.

Trustee: The person who holds property in trust for the benefit of another.

Trustor: The person who has created a trust.

Truth-in-Lending Act: The federal consumer credit law that requires disclosure of the finance charge and annual percentage rate of interest charged.

U.S. Government Bonds (Treasury Bonds): Marketable obligations of five years or more issued by the U.S. government. These bonds have coupons, and interest is paid every six months.

Undivided Interest: The percentage of interest that is held by a *Tenant in Common.*

Unfunded Trust: A living trust that has had no property actually transferred to it.

Uniform Gifts to Minors Act: A law that enables a gift of property to a custodian to be held for a minor until the minor comes of age.

Uniform Probate Court: An act adopted in several states that attempts to reduce a court's involvement in the probate process, thus speeding up the probate for the purpose of making it less costly.

United States Savings Bonds: Bonds of the federal government that are designed for the smaller investor.

Unlimited Marital Deduction: A law that allows one spouse to transfer any amount of property to the other spouse, completely free of any transfer tax, either during life or at death.

Unlisted: A security that is not listed on any stock exchange.

V.A.-Guaranteed Mortgage: A mortgage that the Department of Veteran's Affairs guarantees payment to the lending institution in the event of default by the buyer.

Variable Annuity: An annuity contract with a life insurance company under which the dollar payments received are not fixed but vary, usually with the price of common stock.

Variable Rate Mortgage (VRM): A mortgage with an interest rate that may move up or down, depending on the market conditions.

Vesting of Interests: Referring to the legal ownership of certain benefits of such things as a pension fund. This is a very important consideration if a person leaves an employer prior to retirement.

Voting Right: The right of a stockholder to vote his or her stock owned in the affairs of that company. Most commons shares have one vote each. Preferred stock ordinarily has the right to vote if the preferred dividends have been in default for a specified period. Voting rights may be delegated to another person, called a *Proxy.*

Warranty: A guarantee of the integrity of a product or service and of the maker's responsibility to repair or replace any defective product or part.

Widow's Election: A device used mostly in community property states when one spouse purports to dispose of the property belonging to the other spouse, giving the survivor an option for whether to agree with that attempt.

Will: The legal document that directs the disposition of one's property after death.

Withdrawal Plan: A mutual fund plan that allows monthly or quarterly withdrawal of specified dollar amounts, usually involving the invasion of principal.

Working Control: Theoretically this refers to ownership of 51 percent of a company's voting stock being necessary to exercise control. In practice, particularly in large corporations, effective control sometimes can be exerted through ownership (by an individual or by a group acting in concert) of less than 50 percent.

Wrap-Around Mortgage: A form of financing in which the face amount of the second loan *(wrap-around)* is equal to the balance of the first loan plus the amount of the new financing.

Yield: Dividends or interest paid by a company, expressed as a percentage of the current price of a stock. A stock with a current market value of $20 a share that has paid a dividend of $1 in the preceding 12 months has returned 5 percent.

Younger Generation Beneficiary: A person who is in a younger generation than the creator of a trust, whose presence may cause the *Generation Skipping Tax* to apply.

Resources

This section is provided for general information only. Crown Financial Ministries does not endorse or recommend any of these services. Contact information may change from time to time. If you cannot find what you need, search the Internet or visit your local library for contact information.

AUTOMOTIVE

Automotive Problem Resolution

NADA (National Automobile Dealers Association) Automated Response Line is 703-821-7144.

Better Business Bureau Autoline 1-800-955-5100
   Will mediate with some manufacturers: Acura, Alfa Romeo, AM, GM, Audi, Honda, Hummer, Hyundai, Infiniti, Isuzu, Kia, Land Rover, Lexus, Nissan, Porsche, Saab, Saturn, Sterling, Toyota, and VW.

Safety and Recalls
   www.hwysafety.org
   Center for auto safety 202-328-7700
   National Highway Traffic Safety Adm
      1-800-424-9393 (for seatbelts and auto recalls)

Recalls
   www.nhtsa.cot.gov
      Must have type of engine, make, model and year

Auto safety bulletins
   www.nhtsa.dot.gov
   www.autosafety.org

Car Insurance
   Consumer Reports 1-800-807-8050
   www.insweb.com
      Information on insurance comparisons

Federal Trade Commission
   1-877-438-4338
   Will enforce the consumers right to sue a car manufacturer for a lemon (Lemon Law)

Buying a Car

The Center for Study of Services 1-800-475-7283

www.carbargains.com

For information on rebates on new cars.

Cost: $7 each or $80 for one year.

Consumer Reports New Car Price Service 1-800-933-5555

www.consumerreports.org

Buying Cars on the Web

www.carsdirect.com

www.intellichoice.com

www.carorder.com

www.openauto.com

Car Buying Guides

www.edmunds.com

This will include new car pricing.

Moroney Sticker

Prices of new cars 202-307-0066.

Web Information on Used Cars

www.nada.com

www.carfax.com or 1-800-4CARFAX

Call if you want to know if the car had been in a wreck. You will need the VIN#.

www.autotrader.com

COLLEGE INFORMATION SITES

College Information Sites

www.collegeboard.org

www.collegequest.com

Distance Learning

www.degree.net

Financial Aid

National Association of Student Financial Aid 1-800-4FED-AID

US Department of Education

Student Loan Problem Hotline 1-800-647-8733 press #1

Refinancing Student Loans

Contact your lender or the Federal Aid Student Information Center at 1-800-433-3243.

Nellie Mae

> Financing for student loans 1-800-9TUITION
>
> They have a pamphlet called "Be a Wise Borrower."

Financial Aid Sites

www.finaid.com

www.collegeispossible.org

www.savingforcollege.com

www.scholarships.com

ELDER CARE

Information about senior citizens care

www.careguide.com

> Supplies or resources, including day care, senior centers, and nursing homes.

www.hahc.org

> National Association for Home Care

www.medicare.gov

> Medicare nursing home comparison

www.aoa.dhhs.gov

> Administration on Aging, Long Term Care Ombudsman

FEDERAL GOVERNMENT

Banks

If a consumer has a complaint against a bank or federal credit union, he or she can contact the following agencies.

> State Chartered FDIC 1-800-934-3342
>
> Federally Chartered 1-800-613-6743
>
> Credit Union National Association, Inc 1-800-356-9655

Business

Federal Trade Commission 1-877-382-4357 or 877-438-4338

Government Auctions

> EGG Dynatrend, Pension Dept FS 2300, Clarendon Blvd Ste 205, Arlington VA 22201

Credit card rankings and rates

Cardtrak 1-800-344-7714 – best deals on credit cards

Ram Research – CardWeb 1-800-874-8999

Immigration and Naturalization Service

1-800-375-5283

Safety

US Consumer Product Safety Commission 1-800-638-CPSC

National Highway Traffic Safety Administration 1-800-424-9393
 (Auto Safety hotline.)

Center for Auto Safety 202-328-7700
 (Handles recalls, complaint statistics on auto defects, defective auto paint.)

Savings and Loan Regulation

1-800-842-6929

Savings bonds

Savings Bond Inquiry Center 1-304-480-6112

Social Security

1-800-772-1213

Telephone

Federal Communications Commissions FCC 1-888-225-5322
 Regulates problems with telephones, TV, long distance carriers, and telephone
 slamming

For telemarketing information
 www.fraud.org
 www.usdoj.gov
 www.ftc.gov
 or call the Fraud Hot Line 1-800-876-7060

To get out of credit card offers

For all three bureaus, call 1-888-567-8688 (This will establish a two-year opt out.
For permanent opt-out status, you must request in writing).

Veterans Affairs

1-800-827-1000

Web sites

www.usajobs.com
 Government jobs

www.ezgov.com
 General government information

www.missingmoney.com

HOME BUILDING

Plumbing

Consumer Plumbing Recovery Center 1-800-876-4698

(Conditions under which a homeowner could qualify for reimbursement for the blue polybutylene pipe leaks.)

Repair and Improvements

American Homeowner's Foundation 1-703-536-7776

American Society of Home Inspectors (ASHI) 1-800-743-ASHI

LEGAL ACTION INFORMATION

www.cybersettle.com

Online mediation for legal issues

MEDICAL

Affordable prescription drugs

The Medicine Program 1-573-996-7300

PHRMA Public Affairs Division 1-202-835-3400

General Information

Medical Information Bureau (MIB) 1-617-426-3660

(Provides a copy of your medical records, claims, insurance applications for a $9 charge) www.mib.com

Government/governing bodies

American Board of Medical Specialties 1-866-ask-abms

(Provides information about individual doctor's board certification)

Medicaid/Medicare

Medicare Information Hotline 1-800-MEDICARE (633-4227)

Medicare/Medicaid Fraud or Abuse 1-800-447-8477

Replacement of Medicare or Social Security Cards 1-800-772-1213

Web sites

www.healthmarket.com

Use this site to evaluate doctors and pricing structure

www.goldenrule.com

Information on health plans and MSAs

www.personalmd.co

Basic medical information

www.nih.gov National Institutes for Health

REGULATORY SERVICES FOR TELEMARKETERS/TELEPHONES/ INTERNET INFORMATION/SCAMS

The Federal Trade Commission can help you stop unwanted calls. The FTC gives the state the right to prosecute fraudulent telemarketers who operate across state lines. If you are a victim, contact the FTC at 1-877-438-4338.

The Federal Communications Commission 1-888-225-5322

Regulates the Telephone Consumer Protection Act which deals with audio-dialing, unauthorized faxes, and telephone solicitation.

SCAMS

General guidelines

The FTC (Federal Trade Commission) 1-877-382-4357 (Call this number if you are a victim.)

Internet hoaxes

www.hoaxbusters.org
www.ifccfbi.gov

Fraud complaint Center

To Avoid Pyramid and/or Multilevel Marketing Schemes

1. Be suspicious of anything that asks for you to spend money up front, especially if it is high priced.

2. Research, research, research. Check the Better Business Bureau or your state's attorney general's office about any organization you may be considering.

3. If it sounds too good to be true, it is.

If you believe you are a victim of telemarketing fraud, contact the appropriate authorities:

Your state's attorney general's office
The Better Business Bureau
Your state's Securities Commission
U.S. Postal Inspectors—for scams through the mail
The FBI
The Commodity Futures Trading Commission
The Federal Trade Commission

RELOCATION PROBLEM RESOLUTION

American Movers Dispute Settlement Program 1-703-683-7410

TAXES

Electronic filing

Turbotax
HD Vest Financial Services
Taxcut

General Record Keeping

Cancelled checks = 7 years

Bank deposit slips = 7 years

Bank statements = 7 years

Contracts = FOREVER

Employment tax returns = 7 years

Expense reports = 7 years

Entertainment records = 7 years

Financial statements = FOREVER

Investment records = Ownership plus 7 years

Tax returns = FOREVER

IRS

Internal Revenue Service 1-800-829-1040

Tax coaching

AARP Tax Coaching for the Elderly (Each state is a different number; contact your local chapter for information.)

VOICEMAIL

Free services

www.onebox.com

www.ureach.com

WIRELESS RATES

Comparing long distance to wireless

www.consumer-action.org

www.point.com

PRIVACY PROTECTION

There has been escalation of identity theft in recent years. If this has happened to you or someone you are working with, steps need to be taken quickly to reduce the damage. First, contact the credit reporting agencies and request that a fraud alert be indicated on your file. Then contact the Social Security Administration's Fraud Hotline at 800-269-0271 and report the fraudulent use of your identity.

	To report fraud call	*To obtain a credit report call*
Equifax	800-525-6285	800-685-1111
Experian	888-524-3666	888-397-3742
Trans Union	800-680-7289	800-916-8800

You should also consider getting a copy of your credit report from one of the agencies listed above. Check for any accounts that have been opened without your approval. Also check for unauthorized charges that appear on your report.

You may want to contact your local Department of Motor Vehicles to check on any unauthorized license number with your name. Be sure to notify them that your identity has been stolen.

If you want more information, you can contact the Federal Trade Commission. They provide a brochure, *ID Theft: When Bad Things Happen to Your Good Name.* Their contact information is Identity Theft Clearinghouse, Federal Trade Commisssion, 600 Pennsylvania Ave NW, Washington DC 20580-0001 or online, www.consumer.gov/idtheft.

MARKETING LISTS

Your coaching participant may benefit from not receiving marketing information in the mail. The amount of material received through the mail, by telephone or by e-mail, can be limited. A letter should be written to the Direct Marketing Association; choose the applicable address listed below. Be sure to include your name, address, telephone number, and e-mail address with your letter.

E-Mail Preference Service
www.e-mps.org

Mail Preference Service
c/o Direct Marketing Association
PO Box 9008
Farmingdale NY 11735

Telephone Preference Service
c/o Direct Marketing Association
PO Box 9014
Farmingdale NY 11735

FORMS

TELEPHONE CONTACT CHECKLIST

Name of church _____

Name of coach _____

Contact date _____

Name _____

Address _____

City_____State _____Zip Code_____

Telephone: Home (____) _____ Office (____) _____

E-mail Address _____

1. Is this the first time you have contacted us?

2. Are you seeking coaching on ❑ budget ❑ business ❑ debt ❑ other _____?

3. How urgent is the need for coaching? _____

4. Will a telephone conference be enough? _____

5. If married, will both husband and wife attend? _____

6. Who referred you to us? _____

7. Are you a member of a church? _____Which one? _____

8. Has your church ever provided financial assistance to you? _____

PERSONAL DATA

Name(s) (Mr.) (Mrs.) (Miss) (Ms) _____

Address _____

City_____State _____Zip Code_____

Telephone: Office (____) _____ Home (____) _____

E-mail Address _____

Children _____

_____

FINANCIAL SUMMARY

To provide good coaching, it is important that as much financial data as possible be available. The following is a list of sources that will be helpful.

Money Map Coaching

1. Bring your checkbook register, income tax forms, paycheck stubs, bank statements, current bills, or other related information.

2. Fill out the accompanying forms to the best of your ability:
   a. Monthly Income and Expenses
   b. List of Debts
   c. Financial Statement.

COACHING AGREEMENT

Coaching is provided without cost. To be the best stewards of your time and ours, it is important that you understand and agree with the following conditions.

1. All coaching is based on biblical financial principles.

2. If married, under most situations both husband and wife must agree to attend coaching sessions.

3. All required preparation should be completed prior to each coaching session, if possible.

FOLLOW-UP NOTICE

Coaching participant(s) _____

Address _____

City_____State _____Zip Code_____

Telephone: Office (____) _____ Home (____) _____

E-mail Address _____

Next visit _____

Call by_____

FOLLOW-UP NOTICE

Coaching participant(s) _____

Address _____

City_____State _____Zip Code_____

Telephone: Office (____) _____ Home (____) _____

E-mail Address _____

Next visit _____

Call by_____

FOLLOW-UP NOTICE

Coaching participant(s) _____

Address _____

City_____State _____Zip Code_____

Telephone: Office (____) _____ Home (____) _____

E-mail Address _____

Next visit _____

Call by_____

COACHING FILE LOG

Notice: Only the undersigned individuals are authorized to access the coaching files without written permission from _____.

Authorized names:

1. _____

2. _____

3. _____

4. _____

5. _____

Sign Out	Purpose	Sign In

COACH'S REVIEW

Coach _____

Session # _____

Date _____

Coaching participant(s) name(s) _____

Address _____

City_____State _____Zip Code_____

Telephone: Office (____) _____ Home (____) _____

E-mail Address _____ Cell Phone (____) _____

Category of problems
❏ Budget   ❏ Debt   ❏ Business   ❏ Other _____

Analysis of problems
❏ Critical   ❏ Bad   ❏ Nominal   ❏ None

Status of debts
❏ Legal action filed   ❏ Delinquent   ❏ Month current   ❏ None

Budget analysis
❏ Overspending   ❏ Month break even   ❏ Balanced   ❏ Surplus

Spiritual analysis
❏ Unsaved   ❏ Unsure   ❏ Saved   ❏ Mature

Marital analysis
❏ Divorced   ❏ Separated   ❏ Single/widow   ❏ Married
❏ Poor communication   ❏ Average communication
❏ Good communication

Recommendations
❏ Thirty-day diary   ❏ Homework assigned
❏ Contact creditors   ❏ Balance checkbook   ❏ Develop budget
❏ Other _____

Coach's comments and summary

_____

_____

_____

_____

_____

_____

_____

DEBT PAYMENT COMPUTATION

Total amount available for debts $_____   Date _____

To Whom Owed	Pay Off	Monthly Payment Required	Payments Left	Date Amount Due	Percent of Total Debts	Monthly Payment Available
Name _____ Address _____ City _____State _____ Zip _____Acct. # _____ Contact name _____ Telephone # _____						
Name _____ Address _____ City _____State _____ Zip _____Acct. # _____ Contact name _____ Telephone # _____						
Name _____ Address _____ City _____State _____ Zip _____Acct. # _____ Contact name _____ Telephone # _____						
Name _____ Address _____ City _____State _____ Zip _____Acct. # _____ Contact name _____ Telephone # _____						
Name _____ Address _____ City _____State _____ Zip _____Acct. # _____ Contact name _____ Telephone # _____						

Crown Financial Ministries 2/03

CREDITOR CONTACT LETTER

Address _____

Date _____

Re: Account # _____

Dear _____,

Please accept my/our apology for not contacting you earlier about my account. During the past few months, my financial situation has deteriorated considerably. I realize that the timely payment of debts is a firm obligation on my part; nevertheless, there have been insufficient funds to accomplish such payment on a regular basis. I would like to arrange a payment schedule that will be acceptable to your company and feasible within my budget.

In an effort to alleviate the situation, I am currently working with _____, a Money Map Coach from _____ (church), whose phone number is (____)_____. Together, a spending plan has been developed that should provide a long-term means of satisfying all obligations on a scheduled basis, even though it reduces the originally stated rates of debt payment.

Attached are a Financial Statement and a Monthly Income and Expenses form. The amount I am able to pay you on a monthly basis is $_____.

The proposed schedule of payments is predicated on income at my present job. No increase in income is assumed; however, if this does occur, payments will be increased proportionately. It is my intention to pay every creditor in full. However, this plan requires the cooperation of every creditor. To assure no further indebtedness I have made a commitment to using no credit in the future.

I would appreciate your written acceptance of this plan, as well as any indication of smaller payments, interest, and late charge waivers or any principal reductions that would be acceptable to you. If you cannot approve this plan, please direct this letter to someone who has that authority. You may contact me at _____ between _____ and _____. Thank you for your patience.

Sincerely,

ACCEPTANCE _____

Date: _____

Organization: _____

By: _____

Comments: _____

P.S. Please return this signed acceptance to me.

[This is given as a simple letter and should be personalized for each coaching participant's situation.]

CREDITOR CONTACT LETTER

Address _____

Date _____

Re: Account #_____

Dear   _____,

I am working, as a volunteer from my church, with one of your customers, _____ regarding an outstanding indebtedness. Attached you will find copies of an earlier letter and forms regarding this subject.

Mr. and Mrs. _____ related that all creditors except your organization have agreed to the attached payment plan. I want to confirm that I am working with the _____ on a monthly basis, and I assisted them in developing this payment plan. I will continue to supervise this payment plan and will notify all creditors if the agreed conditions are not being met.

I have had training in the area of budget and debt coaching through Crown Financial Ministries, a nonprofit teaching and educational ministry. If you would like information about this organization, please visit www.crown.org.

The success of this plan depends on the concurrence of all creditors. Without this approval, the only recourse remaining will be through the courts. It is to the advantage of all parties concerned to avoid this if possible. If you have any questions for me, I can be reached at _____ between _____ and _____.

I trust your organization will agree to the submitted plan and will sign and return the acceptance.

Sincerely,

[This is given as a sample letter that a Crown registered volunteer Money Map Coach might use. If you are not a registered volunteer Money Map Coach, this format should not be used.]

FINANCIAL STATEMENT

as of _____

ASSETS
Liquid Assets[1]

_____ $ _____

_____

_____

_____

_____

Total Liquid Assets $ _____

Invested Assets[2]

_____ $ _____

_____

_____

_____

_____

Total Invested $ _____

Use Assets[3]

_____ $ _____

_____

_____

_____

_____

Total Use Assets $ _____

TOTAL ASSETS $ _____

LIABILITIES[4]

_____ $ _____

_____

_____

_____

_____

TOTAL LIABILITIES $ _____

NET WORTH $ _____
(Assets-Liabilities)

**TOTAL LIABILITIES
AND NET WORTH** $ _____

[1] Cash, Savings Accounts, Checking Accounts
[2] IRAs, TSAs, 401(k)s, Investment, Real Estate, CDs, Antiques presented at fair market value.
[3] Residence, Autos, Personal Belongings presented at fair market value.
[4] Outstanding Real Estate Loans, Credit Cards, Auto Loans, Personal Loans.

Crown Financial Ministries 2/03

298

Financial goals for the _____ family.

Category	Specific Goal	Time Frame	Goal Successfully Met
Savings	We will save $5 a week toward a lamp replacement.	6 weeks	1-Jun-01
Debt Retirement	We will reduce our consumer debt by $100 per month until it is gone.	Monthly	1/31, 2/29, 3/31, 4/31
Offering	We will give an additional $25 per month to the church for missionary work.	Ongoing as God provides	1/31, 2/29,

Personal and spiritual goals for the _____ family.

Category	Specific Goal	Time Frame	Goal Successfully Met
Personal Goals			
Spiritual Goals			

Crown Financial Ministries 2/03

CROWN FINANCIAL MINISTRIES
True Financial Freedom

Money Map Coach Training Course
Small Group Format
Facilitator's Guide

Introduction

Special Note

Crown Financial Ministries recently changed "Budget Counselors" to "Budget Coaches" and then to "Money Map Coaches." This document will refer to Money Map Coaches. The term is synonymous with all references to "Budget Counselor" used throughout the former *Budget Counselor Training Course.*

Reason for This Guide

The *Money Map Coach Training Course* (MMCTC) Small Group Format provides the opportunity for student coaches to interact with an experienced facilitator and peers as they complete the MMCTC kit. The student coach's learning experience is enhanced through small group relationship dynamics as well as through daily prayer, Scripture memory, discussion of biblical principles, and role playing case studies. MMCTC small groups may be formed within one local church or in a community of several churches.

Qualifications of a MMCTC Small Group Facilitator

- Validated by church leadership; and
- Experienced *Crown Biblical Financial Study* small group facilitator; and
- Experienced Crown Money Map Coach

Purpose of the MMCTC Small Group

- Learn biblical and practical Money Map coaching principles
- Facilitate peer-to-peer learning
- Establish relationships among student Money Map coaches
- Share experiences and insights

Format of the MMCTC Small Group

10-week course, 2 hours per session with homework.

Use of Bible study in Lessons 1-7/How Would You Respond?

Some student coaches who are *Crown Biblical Financial Study* small group graduates mistakenly view the Bible study contained in lessons 1-7 as a repeat of the Biblical Financial Study small group. However, as the facilitator, you will encourage them to review the Scriptures in light of their application to specific Money Map coaching scenarios.

The most effective way to accomplish this is to use the Biblical Principle class discussion time each week to focus on the vignettes in the section titled "How Would You Respond to the Coaching Participant?" (located after the Notes section of each week's Bible study). Challenge the student coaches to find specific Scriptures in response to each scenario.

The 2,350 Bible verses located on the Textbook Resources CD-ROM are a helpful guide.

Role playing

Role playing is the primary method used to learn specific Money Map coaching techniques. The student coaches should progress from observing to emulating what they have observed to coaching on their own.

Materials

The syllabus and assignment sheet accompanying this Facilitator's Guide lead the facilitator and student coaches through the entire MMCTC kit following the order of topics in the coaching participant's manual, *Journey to Financial Freedom Manual*. When participating in a MMCTC small group, the student coaches should disregard the Weekly Assignment sheet found on page 4 of the MMCTC Textbook. They will follow the assignments as outlined in the MMCTC small group syllabus.

Acknowledgments

The following pioneers walked alongside me the past five years as this format was inaugurated with over 150 student coaches in the Dallas/Fort Worth area: Charlie Sizemore, Skip Bryan, Marvin Benson & Brad Jack.

Dwight & Kathy Youngberg and Dave Kosanke took the initiative with a very skeleton outline to implement additional beta groups in Kansas City, KS and Tulsa, OK.

Christy Speer developed the Role Play Observations.

Tom Wells and Connie Parks contributed much wisdom and insight from their years of Money Map coaching experience.

Most importantly, the Lord gave Howard Dayton a small group model of discipling that is effective not only for students of the *Biblical Financial Study* but also for training Money Map coaches.

All glory to God,
Sharon B. Epps

Guide for Training Money Map Coaches

You have undertaken a great work—training new Money Map coaches. Without knowing it, many of God's people worship money while giving lip service to worshiping God. When they get in trouble, they seek help from Money Map coaches. You are preparing these student coaches to do God's work by drawing coaching participants away from a fixation on money and back to a fixation on God.

A successful facilitator's method is to motivate learning by the student coach. There's a difference between teaching and learning. Teaching focuses on what the facilitator knows, expecting the student coach to adopt it and behave accordingly. Unfortunately, this doesn't work too often. In fact, the student coach may seemingly agree with everything then go out and do it his/her own way.

The facilitator is most effective when helping the student coaches learn. The responsibility for learning falls on the student coach's shoulders, not yours. You can guide and encourage the student coaches, but in the end they will decide what they learn.

This guide is designed to lead you through a process of helping student coaches learn to provide a ministry of Money Map coaching. This process extends over a period of ten weeks. Tools such as case studies and role playing will be utilized during the training to assist the student coach in his or her practice.

Your main task is to point the student coaches in the right direction, encourage them, help them focus on key ideas, and lead them to the point where they have the confidence to try it themselves.

Weekly homework

The student coaches will have several hours of homework each week. It must be made clear to them that it must be done ahead of time. The class time will be devoted to discussions of that homework.

Here's a good chance to build a habit. Encourage the student coaches to set aside time each day to do the homework. Same time, same place each time. Hold the student coaches accountable. ("Who has a regular time of study? Tell us about it.")

Ten sessions of training

Each session lasts two hours. It combines Bible study, prayer, case studies and role-playing. During the first hour pray, recite the memory verse, and review biblical principles from the *MMCTC Textbook*. During the second hour, introduce new material and role-play.

Crown's Biblical Financial Small Group Bible Study

As a general rule, it is most helpful for each student coach to complete Crown's Biblical Financial Small Group Study prior to joining the *Money Map Coach Training Course* Small Group. The Bible is the foundation for budget coaching. With more than 2,350 verses devoted to money, property and related matters, the student coach needs a foundation in the Biblical principles.

If this isn't possible, then encourage the student coaches to complete all of the Scripture homework in the *Money Map Coach Training Course Textbook*. Hold them accountable for doing it. You may have to do this with a short Q&A session before or after the MMCTC small group meeting.

Role Plays

The purpose of role-playing is to see Money Map coaching in action and practice it in a safe environment. It's a good idea to have a trained Money Map coach first play the role of the coach to model for the student coaches. You can use student coaches as coaching participants.

After several sessions where the student coaches have had the opportunity to observe, divide the student coaches into clusters of three. One will serve as the Money Map coach, the second as the coaching participant and the third as the observer/note taker. Whoever plays the budget coach first will then become the coaching participant. Rotate until all three student coaches have filled all three roles.

In each role-playing session, the observer/note taker should highlight the positive things they observed and the areas that needed improvement. Peer learning is a very effective way to develop good habits for coaching.

Finally

Your student coaches are preparing for a great work for the Lord. It won't always appear to be successful. If the Money Map coach encourages the coaching participants to begin to think seriously about the choices they are making, that will be a big first step. Remember what Paul wrote to the Corinthians: *"I planted, Apollos watered, but God gave the increase."*[1] You do your part, and God will do His. That will bring glory to Him.

---

[1] 1 Corinthians 3:7

WEEKLY SMALL GROUP AGENDA

5 minutes	Prayer
5 minutes	Memory Verse
30 minute	Biblical Principles
10 minutes	Break
50 minutes	Practical Subjects/Role Play
5 minutes	Next Week's Assignment/Review
15 minutes	Prayer Requests/Prayer

Session 1 – Introduction & Course Overview

Goals for the session

Give student coaches an overview of the next nine weeks. Introduce them to the facilitator(s) and material.
- Welcome and introductions
- Outline of rest of course
- Review of homework
- Introduction to procedures and tools for Money Map coaching

Handouts for the session

- Syllabus
- Homework Assignment sheet
- Class roster
- "Some Principles of Money Map Coaching"

Schedule – 1st Hour: Introduction to course

Open with prayer.

Make sure students have name tags, ask them to introduce themselves (Week 1 style from the *Biblical Financial Study*) and state why they would like to become a Money Map coach.

Overview

Money Map coaching is not just about money and budgeting. Its true purpose is to develop a more intimate relationship with Christ. *"Therefore if you have not been faithful in the use of worldly* wealth, who will entrust the true riches to you?"* (Jesus in Luke 16:11 NASB, *NIV).

During coaching we'll continually refer to the Bible as our manual and source of guidance.

Money Map coaching is a relational activity. While it is easy to focus on forms and numbers, most coaching participants want personal attention and someone to listen.

Each case is unique. One size doesn't fit all. It's important that you be alert to this fact.

The reading materials provide you with principles and tools to use in coaching. We will spend time learning these principles and becoming familiar with the tools.

Two most important items each week: (1) the memory verse and (2) "How would you respond?" Both point to Scripture as the wisdom for coaching.

Generally, you will want to answer coaching participants with a verse from Scripture or a restatement of a scriptural principle (For example, "Actually it's likely that we can develop a plan to pay off your debt. Then you want to avoid debt in the future [Romans 13:8]. Being in debt cripples your ability to serve Christ.")

The case studies and role playing will introduce you to some realities of the human experience.

The facilitator and/or another trained Money Map coach will model a Money Map coaching session first.

Student coaches will be given opportunities to practice and evaluate each other.

Successful Money Map coaching occurs in an environment of trust led by the Holy Spirit. Prayer is essential. The budget forms and numbers are merely communication and planning tools, not the focus of Money Map coaching.

Procedures and forms are guides to helping people change habits. They keep you on track, but are not a substitute for learning delayed gratification and financial discipline.

The key is to build trust as a foundation for communication between the Money Map coach and the coaching participant.

Materials

There is a variety of materials in the box called the *Money Map Coach Training Course*. The *Money Map Coach Training Course Textbook* ("Textbook") contains readings, exercises and cases.

A Textbook Resource CD-ROM contains a number of useful reference materials. Especially important are the bible verses about money and possessions. These will be especially important in answering questions from the coaching participants as well as providing guidance. You should become familiar with the subjects and some of the verses.

The *Family Financial Workbook* ("FFW") contains a step-by-step process for creating and using a budget.

You and your coaching participants will use the *Journey to Financial Freedom Manual* ("JFFM"). You should become thoroughly familiar with it. It is one of the important tools.

A page of Bible verses may be found in the Appendix. Most of these you have memorized from the *Biblical Financial Study*. Occasionally go back over them to refresh your memorization of them. Like many of the other things in this course, they are tools to help your coaching participants reach their goals.

- The rest of the materials are useful for ideas and references. You will read portions of them throughout the small group and will also refer to them from time to time as continuing education.

Schedule – 2nd Hour: Coaching Basics/Introduction to Role of Personality

Hand out "Some Principles of Money Map Coaching." Go over key points.

Purpose of coaching is to help coaching participants change for the better, particularly moving toward the fullness of Christ.

Coaching participants respond to situations and to other people in different ways. You need to understand how they think about things, and how you think about things.

Use the DISC profile to identify four basic personality types. Describe these with examples.

Encourage questions as you go along.

If the students don't ask questions, ask some yourself: "What kind of a person is a 'D'?" "Any questions about filling out the profile?"

Homework for next session

Review materials in kit. Show the student coaches what they will use in the course. Walk them through pages of the assignment for next week.

Helpful resource information may be found at www.crown.org.

Listen to Welcome C.

Read chapter one of the *Money Map Coach Training Course Textbook*. If you have already taken the Crown *Biblical Financial Study*, review your notes. Otherwise do all of the daily studies and read the material on pages 9 through 18.

Answer "How Would You Respond?" with specific Scriptures. If you don't know a specific Scripture for a given question, leave it blank.

Memorize 1 Chronicles 29:11.

Take the *Personality I.D.*® Only after taking I.D., read pages 93 to 96 in *Money Map Coach Training Course Textbook*.

Read the "Family Budgeting" article on the Textbook Resource CD-ROM located in the back of the *Money Map Coach Training Course Textbook*.

Student coaches will need to attend at least 8 of the 10 sessions in order to successfully complete the course.

Some Principles of Money Map Coaching

It's easy to get mired in details of Money Map coaching. There are so many things that come up that it's tempting to try to provide rules for everything. This quickly proves frustrating and fruitless.

It's useful to focus on a few ideas. When things start getting bogged down, you should go back to the biblical principles and stop to pray.

You can't change people. Allow God to change them.

They have to see what they can do that will work for them. The most you can do is guide them in the right direction.

It's about habits.

Most people get in trouble because they drift into destructive behaviors. Why do we carry credit cards? Habit. Except on trips, you can generally leave them at home without causing any problems.

The Money Map coach wants to help the coaching participants see their behaviors in context of biblical principles, then encourage them to come up with some solutions.

"All the extra spending shows up on the Visa card." "Well then, what do you think you can do about it? What will work for you?"

It will be important to hold the coaching participant accountable for coming up with a working solution at each session: "What did you decide about the Visa card? How has it worked?"

It's about emotions.

Frequently, coaching participants will come to a session frightened, upset, or at odds with one another. The first task is to create and maintain a calm environment. As sailors say, "Keep an even strain on things."

Some spending changes, no matter how logical, are not going to be made. A wife may have her children in preschool. Eliminating that cost would go a long way toward bringing spending in line with income. The preschool is wrapped up with her identity, and it's going to be hard to get her to drop it. She would prefer to do without essentials rather than take the blow to self-esteem. Be on the lookout for these situations and tread carefully.

It's not hard to start making improvements.

In many cases, only two or three things need to change to start turning things around. (1) Leave the credit cards at home, (2) Use cash for daily expenses, and (3) Create a special account for irregular expenses, such as doctors' visits or car repairs. This is important for eliminating debt.

Paper is a means to an end, not an end in itself.

It's very easy to focus on filling out all sorts of forms or filling them out completely when it isn't necessary. The coaching participants then lose sight of what they are trying to accomplish: finding the two or three things that will work for them.

The purpose of a form is insight, not numbers. Only two forms are absolutely essential: a financial statement and the monthly income and expenses form.

The financial statement can be filled out once every six months. It's like a checkup to see how they are doing.

Other forms are available to the coach, but their use isn't indicated in all situations.

We're Money Map and debt coaches, not lawyers, tax accountants, or marriage coaches.

If other expertise is indicated, send the coaching participants to an expert. Keep on track.

Moving forward is better than perfection.

Managing money is a journey. Your job, as a coach, is to help the coaching participants move toward their destination. As long as they are making progress, encourage them, answer their questions, and pat them on the back.

Session 2 - Personality

Goals for the session

Recognize that coaching participants must first understand God's Part and Our Part before lives will change.

Understand the role of personality in coaching. Identify different personality groups using DISC. Develop strategies for coaching each personality group.

Schedule – 1st Hour: Biblical Principles

Housekeeping matters, circulate Prayer Request Log (may use copies from the *Crown Biblical Financial Study*).

Memory verse

Class discussion, "How would you respond?"

Schedule – 2nd Hour: Practical Application/Role Play

Overview of role of personality

Personality Exercise

Divide into four groups by DISC classification, e.g., all Cs in one group.

Each group should write two questions they would ask a coaching participant, and one sentence of guidance for the coaching participant.

Upon reconvening, ask the spokesman for each group to share answers.

Discuss difference in responses based on personality type and application to the student coach as a counselor and to the coaching participant.

Homework for next session

Next week's assignment

Close with prayer

PERSONALITY EXERCISES

INSTRUCTIONS: As a group, write two questions you would want ask these coaching participants. Then write one sentence of guidance or direction to the coaching participant.

Situation #1

A divorced single mom comes for coaching because she's considering filing bankruptcy. As part of her divorce settlement, her ex-husband is supposed to pay off a credit card and a personal loan, which were both made in her name but were used for his expenses. He is not making the payments as agreed and the creditors are calling her for payment. She tells you that she lives on what she makes but can't afford to make the payments on these debts.

Question #1:

Question #2:

Guidance or direction:

Situation #2

A man asks for coaching to help him payoff his escalating credit card debt. After you visit with him for a while you learn that he is working at his fourth job in four years. He's been laid off of the last three jobs and has been without work for 6-9 months each time. Each successive new job has involved a cut in pay. He tells you that he is living on a bare bones budget and has had to use the credit cards for basic living expenses. He states, "I've done everything right, it just seems like the whole world is against me."

Question #1:

Question #2:

Guidance or direction:

Sessions 3–10 Planning Guide

Goals for the session

Handouts for the session

Schedule – 1st Hour:

Schedule – 2nd Hour:

Homework for next session

Notes for building the outlines for each session:

After opening with prayer & memory verse, discuss homework.

Use Bible verses for "How would you respond?" Look to Scripture for guidance.

Review the assigned case(s).

Role play.

Close in small groups of four or five praying for one another.

Listening[2]

Listening is a very important way to show respect for others. Being a good listener makes others want to be around you. This is because being a good listener makes the person speaking feel:

- Important
- That his or her thoughts are worth the attention of others
- You are interested
- Respected

Listening is a difficult skill. It requires more than just being quiet. A good listener needs to think actively about what is said. To do this, a good listener needs to clear his or her mind of other distractions and focus on what is said, how it is said, and what is not being said. It requires concentration and can take a lot of energy. Being a good listener takes practice.

Listening Suggestions

Clear distractions

- Turn off noisy equipment in the background (e.g., TV, cell phone).
- Reducing noise helps the speaker to think and speak clearly, and it makes it easier for the listener to understand what is being said.

Be quiet with both mouth and mind.

- Do your best not to interrupt: the speaker has a flow.
- Keep your focus on the speaker's topic, not on what you are getting ready to say.
- Avoid thinking about your own mental "errand list" of things you need to get done once the conversation is over.

Use good attending behaviors.

- Face the person talking to you.
- Lean forward slightly.
- Be interested in what is being said. That way you will look and act interested.
- Use eye contact.
- Nod your head; say "Umm" or "Uh-huh" occasionally.
- Use a moderate verbal tone and speech rate.
- Stay on point; don't change the subject.
- Silence can be awkward, but useful at appropriate times. This allows the person to think through what he or she wants to say. Silence can say more than words in important moments.

---

[2] Based on a paper of the same name by Dr. Jan Hall, Richland Hills Counseling Center, N. Richland Hills, TX

Listen for feelings.

- Reflecting a feeling back to the speaker helps to increase understanding of the speaker and the speaker's conversation.
- Examples: "Sounds like you are frustrated." Or, "I'm sure you are excited."

Clarify a statement

- Helps increase understanding.
- Examples: "Let me see if I understand this; you said…" or "It sounds like you said…" or "I hear you saying…"

Be an encourager.

- This helps the speaker to elaborate and continue talking; it often encourages talk toward deeper meanings.
- One example is to pick out a key word or phrase and restate it. Then the speaker may elaborate the meaning. For example, "I had a great time last night." "A great time?" "Yeah, I went to a …"
- Examples: "I'm wondering about…", I'm curious about…", "Tell me about…"

Avoid making judgmental statements.

- Examples: "That was dumb!", "What a stupid move!" or "You should have known better!"

Ask only necessary questions.

- Questions should clarify or increase your understanding.
- Too many questions tend to put people on the defensive or cause confusion.
- Person asking questions is often in control of the conversation.
- Open-ended questions encourage others to talk and provide maximum information.
- Examples: "What happened?", "Expand on that a little bit. How did it come about?" or "What are you going to do?"

Summarize from time to time.

- "Correct me if I'm wrong, but here is what I heard…"
- "Let me summarize. It sounds like…"

Script for First Budget Coaching Session and Suggested Statements for Building Trust

- Welcome coaching participants
- Make them comfortable; offer coffee or water if appropriate.
- Begin with prayer.
- Review information and help set them at ease as you go along ("How old are your children? Where do they go to school?")
- "I'd like to start by learning a little more about you, what brought you here and what you would like to see happen. Stacy, tell me a little about yourself, your family, how you met Mark."
  - Repeat with Mark.
- "Tell me a little about how you decided to meet with me. What led you here? When we're done, what would you like to see as a result?"
  - Record goals. Achieving these goals will tell you when the coaching is done. You may need to add to these as time goes on and you become more familiar with the coaching participants.
- "Let me tell you a little bit about myself and how I like to work."
  - Describe what led you to become a coach including any formal credentials (e.g., Certified Financial Planner licensee). Two minutes maximum.
  - "The Bible has more than 2,350 verses dealing with money, property and related matters. We look to these verses for guidance about principles and values."
  - "I'm not going to judge what you are doing. I may point out some biblical principles that will lead you in another direction, but it will be up to you to decide. Does this make sense so far? Any concerns or questions?"
  - "This is your money, and it's your job to decide what to do with it. My job is to help you collect some data and point out things that might help you reach your goals."
  - "There will be some work on your part, but I'm going to try to keep the paperwork to a minimum."
  - Refer to the confidentiality of the Money Map coaching sessions.
- "I'm willing to work with you as we make progress toward your goals. This is going to take work on both our parts. It's important that you do the assignments."
  - "If you feel that you are well on your way to reaching your goals or if you feel we aren't going to make any progress, we can stop at any time. The only thing I ask is that you call me and let me know. That way, I will have more time to devote to other people."
  - "Is this OK with you? If so, I'd like for you to look over this commitment statement and sign it." (The Commitment to Counseling is located on p. 7 of the *Journey to Financial Freedom Manual*.)

- ○ "Well, let's get started. First we need to collect some data about income and spending. "
  - ○ As you go along ask if there are any questions.
- "Now, let me make an assignment. I'd like you to start recording income and spending for 30 days." (Use the 30-Day Diary located in the *Journey to Financial Freedom Manual* p. 14, 15.)
  - ○ "Whenever you receive some income or spend some money, record the amount in the proper column."
  - ○ "You'll need to keep all the receipts and statements for 30 days. I suggest you put them in a manila folder."
  - ○ "If you pay with cash, put the receipt in your billfold or purse until you can transfer it to the folder or record it."
  - ○ "This is going to be the foundation for reaching your goals. Until you see where your money comes from and where it goes, you are going to have trouble making good decisions to reach your goals."
  - ○ "Any questions? Will you do this for at least 30 days?"
- "What do you think so far? Any concerns? Will this work for you?" [Given them a chance to answer even if it means being quiet until they do.]
- "OK, let's review."
  - ○ "If I understand correctly, here are the things you'd like to see happen." Review their goals you have written down.
  - ○ "You're going to start recording your spending and income for the next 30 days. Now, if you have any questions about how to do this, please call me immediately. I'll walk you through it, or we can meet to discuss it."
- "Let's set a time for our next meeting. I'd like to make it in two weeks to see how things are going. Would the same time and place in two week work for you?" [Write the date on your calendar.] "If something unexpected causes you to change, please call me immediately."
  - ○ "Please bring your manila folder with receipts and statements along with the partially completed 30-Day Diary."
- "How do you feel so far? What do you think?"
- "Let's close in prayer."

PREPARATION WORKSHEET FOR MONEY MAP COACHING SESSION ONE

Step 1: Greet your coaching participants

Step 2: Pray

Step 3: Explain your ministry and budgeting background

    My background:

    This ministry:

Step 4: Get to know your coaching participant and complete the Personal Information Sheet (located on p. 6 of the *Journey to Financial Freedom Manual*).

Step 5: Review the financial information provided by the coaching participant

Step 6: Identify Goals

Step 7: Explain the 30-Day Diary

    • Keep in convenient place

    • Record daily

    • Round to nearest dollar

Step 8: Assign Additional Action Items

- Bible study

- Daily Record

- Monthly Income & Expense Form

- *Your Money Counts*

- Other information

Step 9: Sign the Commitment to Coaching

Step 10: Set up the next meeting

Step 11: Pray

Step 12: Complete a Client Progress Report

MONEY MAP COACHING ROLE PLAY
OBSERVATION SHEET

INSTRUCTIONS: In groups of three, role play the case study. Whoever plays the Money Map coach first will then become the coaching participant. Rotate until all three participants have filled all three roles.

Roles –   Money Map Coach
                 Coaching participant
                 Observer–You are to watch for Money Map coaching skills discussed and
                 note specifics of good/excellent interactions. Note areas for improvement.

Observers: *Circle the number to indicate your rating 5 = Outstanding, 1 = Needs Development;*
Note specifics to review during feedback session.

ENTRY	
1	Greeting & introductions
2	Confirm purpose of meeting
3	_____
4	_____
5	_____
	_____
	_____

ENGAGE		
1	Prayer	Confidence
2	Eye Contact	Get to know coaching participant
3	_____	
4	_____	
5	_____	
	_____	
	_____	

RAPPORT	
1	Money Map Coach explains his/her background
2	_____
3	_____
4	_____
5	_____
	_____
	_____

CREDIBILITY	
1	Complete Personal Information Sheet
2	Review financial information provided
3	_____
4	_____
5	_____
	_____
	_____

PROFILE	
1	Gain Agreement to Proceed to Identify Goals
2	Effective Questioning
3	Active Listening
4	_____
5	_____
	_____
	_____
	_____
	_____

ANALYZE/ SOLVE	Suggested Action Steps including 30-Day Diary
1	_____
2	_____
3	_____
4	_____
5	_____
	_____

RECOMMEN- DATION	Explained Benefits of Coaching Participants Completing Homework Assignment
1	_____
2	_____
3	_____
4	_____
5	_____

CLOSE	
1	Gained Agreement on Next Steps
2	Instructions for Next Steps
3	Signed Commitment to Coaching
4	Ended in prayer
5	_____
	_____
	_____
	_____
	_____

OTHER OBSERVATIONS/NOTES: _____

_____

_____

_____

_____

_____

_____

_____

_____

_____

_____

_____

_____

_____

_____

Crown Money Map Coach Training Course Small Group Syllabus

Date	Week	Memory Verse	Biblical Principle/Textbook Material	Practical Subject	Case Studies for Role Play
	1			Introduction/Course Overview	
	2	I Chronicles 29:11	God Owns Everything/ We Are Stewards - Discuss Ch. 1	What Makes a Good Coach - Role of Personality	Personality I.D.
	3	Proverbs 22:7	Becoming Debt Free - Discuss Ch. 3	Session One - Building Trust/Identifying Goals	1
	4	Philippians 4:11-13	Peace and Contentment - Discuss Ch. 7	Session Two - Gathering Accurate Information	2, 3
	5	Acts 20:35	Give Generously - Discuss Ch. 2	Session Three - Balancing the Budget & Creating Debt Repayment Plan	4
	6	Proverbs 21:20	Saving & Other Practical Principles - Discuss Ch. 4	Session Four - Saving for an Emergency Fund	5
	7	Proverbs 22:6	Serve Your Family - Discuss Ch. 5	Session Five - Implementation/Freedom Account	6
	8	Colossians 3:23, 24	Work As Unto The Lord - Discuss Ch. 6	Major Purchases: Housing & Cars	7
	9	Proverbs 3:27, 28	Discuss Scriptures from CD related to Case Studies	Dealing with Crisis: Widows & Bankruptcy	8, 9, 10
	10	Luke 14:28; Psalm 50:15	Discuss Scriptures from CD related to Case Studies	Establishing A Counseling Ministry*	11, 12

* Use Section 4 "Money Map Coaching" of the Church Manual (may be downloaded from www.crown.org/FinancialWisdom/church/ChurchManual.asp)

5-24-2005

Crown Money Map Coach Training Course Small Group Homework Assignments

Date	For Week	Memorize	MMCTC Textbook (Focus on "How Would You Respond?")	Practical Applications	Additional Readings (Textbook Resources CD & *Family Financial Wrkbk*)
	1			Introduction/Course Overview	
	2	1 Chronicles 29:11	Chapter 1	Welcome CD; Personality I.D. (take test & read pp. 93-96 in textbook)	Family Budgeting
	3	Proverbs 22:7	Chapter 3	Listening Handout: Case Study 1 Building Trust/Identifying Goals	FFW** Chapter 1-3; Debt & Credit; SnapShot Gold
	4	Philippians 4:11-13	Chapter 7	Pp. 116-135 of textbook; Case Studies 2, 3	FFW Chapters 4-9
	5	Acts 20:35	Chapter 2	Case Study 4	Giving & Tithing
	6	Proverbs 21:20	Chapter 4	Case Study 5	Gambling & Lotteries
	7	Proverbs 22:6	Chapter 5	Case Study 6 Implementation/Freedom Account	Insurance
	8	Colossians 3:23, 24	Chapter 6	Case Study 7	Major Purchases
	9	Proverbs 3:27, 28	Scriptures from CD applied to Case Study	Case Studies 8, 9, 10	Widow's Guide; Bankruptcy
	10	Luke 14:28; Psalm 50:15	Scriptures from CD applies to Case Study	Read Money Map Coaching Section of Church Manual; Case Studies 11, 12	Investing

** FFW = *Family Financial Workbook*

*** NOTE: This schedule replaces p. 4 in the *Money Map Coach Training Course Textbook*.

Additional Learning Opportunities: It is beneficial to provide an opportunity for student coaches to observe live coaching sessions as early as possible in the training process. The coaching participant's consent should be obtained prior to the session.

5-24-2005

PASTOR AUTHORIZATION FORM

Crown's Money Map Coaching Program

[This form must be completed by all new Money Map Coaches.]

Purpose of Crown's Money Map Coaching Program

1. To equip godly men and women to teach and coach, using biblical principles of handling money, under the authority of their local churches and utilizing the materials available through Crown.
2. To channel requests for personal budget coaching to the local church or to a Money Map Coach in that community.

Requirements of Crown's Money Map Coaching Program

1. All individuals must have completed Crown's Money Map Coach Training Course.
2. All individuals are required to live on a written budget.
3. Money Map Coaches are to be under the direct authority of their local church leadership when utilizing Crown materials in teaching and/or coaching.

Goals of Crown's Money Map Coaching Program

1. To develop a network of Crown-trained Money Map Coaches.
2. To train laypersons to work with their pastor's and/or church's coaching/counseling ministries to become a part of (or help develop) the ongoing financial ministries in their churches and local communities and minister to those who need instruction in the area of personal budgeting.
3. To provide Crown Money Map Coaches with ongoing training—through newsletters, bulletins, and conferences—and to encourage regular communication between coaches for fellowship, support, and the exchange of information.

Special Note: The Crown Money Map Coach named below may choose to minister in the local church/community only **OR** he/she may also choose to accept coaching referrals from Crown Financial Ministries.

As pastor of my church, I agree to support Crown's Money Map Coaching Program. I will encourage the individual named below to help us minister to our local church and community as needs arise.

Name (Mr.) (Mrs.) (Miss.) _____

Pastor's name _____

Church name _____

Church address _____

City _____ State _____ Zip_____

Church phone (_____) _____ Pastor's phone (_____) _____

Pastor's Signature _____ Date _____

Please send/fax to Crown Financial Ministries
Attention: Coaching Department, 601 Broad St, Gainesville GA 30501
Fax: 770-536-7226

STATEMENT OF COMPLETION
of the
Money Map Coach Training Course
[This form must be completed by all new Money Map Coaches.]

I certify that I have fully completed the *Money Map Coach Training Course* (formerly called the *Budget Counselor Training Course*). I also certify that my pastor has seen this course material and has signed the Pastor's Authorization Form on the reverse side of this page, acknowledging and verifying my completion of this course.

Name (Mr.) (Mrs.) (Miss.) _____

Address _____

City _____ State _____ Zip _____

E-mail Address _____

Home phone (_____) _____ Business phone (_____) _____

Signature _____ Date _____

Please send/fax to Crown Financial Ministries
Attention: Coaching Department, 601 Broad St, Gainesville GA 30501 • Fax: 770-536-7226

CROWN MONEY MAP REFERRAL COACH APPLICATION

[Crown Money Map Referral Coaches are coaches who agree to allow Crown to refer coaching participants to them. This form is required **ONLY** for coaches applying to become Money Map Referral Coaches.]

Important Note: In order to apply to become a Crown Money Map Referral Coach, you MUST have:

1. Completed the *Money Map Coach Training Course* individually AND attended a Money Map Training Workshop (formerly called the Budget Counselor Training Workshop).

Signature of Workshop Instructor _____ **Date** _____

- OR -

2. Completed Crown's Money Map Coach Training Course as a member of a small group training program.

Signature of Small Group Facilitator _____ **Date** _____

Phone and/or e-mail address to be used for referrals, IF DIFFERENT from those on Statement of Completion:

Phone for referrals (_____) _____ E-mail for referrals_____

Other languages: I am fluent in _____

As a Crown Money Map Referral Coach, I agree to abide by the following requirements:

1. I will provide Money Map coaching under the authority of my church, and I will not charge fees for my coaching.
2. I will not use my coaching ministry for any kind of personal gain, nor will I solicit clients for my profession.
3. I will not use the name of Crown Financial Ministries, Larry Burkett, or Howard Dayton in any form of public-accessed media.

Signature _____ Date _____

Please send/fax to Crown Financial Ministries
Attention: Coaching Department, 601 Broad St, Gainesville GA 30501 • Fax: 770-536-7226